The Politics of the Welfare State in Turkey

T0385467

The Politics of the
Welfare State in Turkey

*How Social Movements and Elite
Competition Created a Welfare State*

Erdem Yörük

University of Michigan Press
Ann Arbor

Published in the United States of America by the
University of Michigan Press
Manufactured in the United States of America
Printed on acid-free paper
First published May 2022

A CIP catalog record for this book is available from the British Library.

Library of Congress Cataloging-in-Publication data has been applied for.

Library of Congress Control Number: 2022931227
LC record available at https://lccn.loc.gov/2022931227

ISBN 978-0-472-13304-8 (hardcover : alk. paper)
ISBN 978-0-472-03902-9 (paper : alk. paper)
ISBN 978-0-472-90282-8 (open access ebook)

https://doi.org/10.3998/mpub.11429032

An electronic version of this book is freely available, thanks in part to the
support of libraries working with Knowledge Unlatched (KU). KU is a
collaborative initiative designed to make high quality books Open Access for
the public good. More information about the initiative and links to the Open
Access version can be found at www.knowledgeunlatched.org.

The University of Michigan Press's open access publishing program is made
possible thanks to additional funding from the University of Michigan Office
of the Provost and the generous support of contributing libraries.

Cover design by Circle Graphic Communication Design Studio, Department
of Media and Visual Arts, Koç University, Istanbul. Photograph: Shutterstock /
umut rosa.

To Özgen and Ali

Contents

Digital materials related to the title can be found on
the Fulcrum platform via the following citable URL:
https://doi.org/10.3998/mpub.11429032

Acknowledgments

This book is about the relations between state and society. I began my PhD studies in sociology at Johns Hopkins University with the central question in mind about the proletarianization dynamics in contemporary Turkey, focusing on the Kurdish ethnic conflict. Then I became interested in the political sociology of the state, especially from a historical and comparative perspective as part of the tradition of the Hopkins Sociology Department. Nevertheless, the question of grassroots dynamics always remained intact in my mind, eventually leading me to formulate a dissertation research question that explored the grassroots political causes of welfare system change.

After receiving my PhD degree in 2012, I continued to explore this topic further. I received two research grants from the European Commission (a Marie Curie Actions grant and a European Research Council grant), which allowed me to theoretically and empirically broaden my dissertation into this book that you are about to read. In particular, the ERC grant has enabled me to update my protest events dataset and extend it to other countries. The result of this larger project is the Global Contentious Politics dataset, which is available at glocon.ku.edu.tr. The part of the GLOCON data that is about Turkey constituted the empirical basis of my analysis.

I would like to present my deepest thanks to my PhD advisor, Joel Andreas. His intellectually rich and analytically powerful guidance not only led to a successful dissertation but eventually culminated in a larger research program, which I have spent my last decade pursuing since receiving my PhD.

I am deeply indebted to my previous advisor, Giovanni Arrighi, much beloved and respected scholar of historical sociology, who passed away in 2009. His comparative and historical insights have always enlightened my perspective. He will be deeply missed.

Also, I have to sincerely thank Frances Fox Piven, whose help has been invaluable at various critical junctures of this journey and who has acted as a mentor since we met in 2009.

I would like to thank my dear friends and colleagues who helped me during the entire period since I began this project: Burak Gürel, Çağrı Yoltar, Başak Can, Nazan Üstündağ, Caitlin G. Pearce, Mustafa Avcı, Ali Sipahi, Mehmet Fatih Uslu, Murat Koyuncu, Ergin Bulut, Gizem Erdem, Cihan Tuğal, Resul Cesur, Haydar Darıcı, Dan Pasciuti, Eske van Gils, Savaş Şahan Karataşlı, Şefika Kumral, İlhan Can Özen, Barış Çetin Eren, Bilgin Ayata, Emek Karaca, Gizem Koşar, the other Erdem Yörük (2), Savaş İnanç Dedebaş, Murat Eroğlu, Yusuf Berber, Norah Andrews, Çetin Çelik, Can Nacar, Ali Hürriyetoğlu, Mark Baker, and Linda Burkhardt (my "US mom").

I would like to thank everyone who contributed to the coding of the protest events, including Aslı Can, Hüsniye Koç, Meryem İnce, Bağlan Deniz, Balacan Fatıma Ayar, Tuğçe Bidav. While I thank every member of the Emerging Welfare ERC project for their tremendous contributions, my special thanks go to Enes Sarı and Ali Bargu for finalizing the protest dataset and to Aysel Öztürk, Erdem Kayserilioğlu, and Deniz Sert for data collection and detailed readings of the manuscript.

Research for this book was possible with financial support from the National Science Foundation, the Ford Foundation Middle East Research Competition, the European Commission Marie Curie Action Grants, and the European Research Council. I would like to thank these institutions for their generous support. I also want to thank KONDA for sharing their survey data.

I would like to thank the two anonymous reviewers for their extensive reports that guided my revisions of the manuscript and the entire editorial team of the University of Michigan Press for their excellent work.

Finally, much of my gratitude goes to my family for being a great support at every point of my life. My dear wife, Özgen, has always been an incredible support. I am really very lucky to have such a great family.

Figures

Tables

Abbreviations

AKP	Justice and Development Party (Adalet ve Kalkınma Partisi)
ANAP	Motherland Party (Anavatan Partisi)
AP	Justice Party (Adalet Partisi)
CHP	Republican People's Party (Cumhuriyet Halk Partisi)
DISK	Confederation of Revolutionary Labor Unions (Devrimci İşçi Sendikaları Konfederasyonu)
DP	Democrat Party (Demokrat Parti)
DSP	Democratic Left Party (Demokratik Sol Parti)
DYP	True Path Party (Doğru Yol Partisi)
FP	Virtue Party (Fazilet Partisi)
HDP	Free Democrat Party (Hür Demokrat Parti)
HDP	People's Democracy Party (Halkların Demokrasi Partisi)
IDP	internally displaced people
MHP	Nationalist Movement Party (Milliyetçi Hareket Partisi)
PKK	Kurdistan Workers' Party (Partiya Karkeren Kurdistan)
RP	Welfare Party (Refah Partisi)
SHP	Social Democratic Populist Party (Sosyal Demokrat Halkçı Parti)
SSK	Social Insurance Institution
SYDV	Social Assistance and Solidarity Foundations
THKO	People's Liberation Army of Turkey
THKP	People's Liberation Party
TKP	Communist Party of Turkey
TKP-ML	Communist Party of Turkey–Marxist-Leninist
TL	Turkish lira

Introduction

If today there is no social explosion in Ankara, social assistance
programs and social projects have a large effect on this.
—Melih Gökçek, the former mayor of Ankara, 2010

Turkey is a difficult country to live in, but perhaps more difficult to rule.
This book attempts to answer difficult questions about how Turkish state
elites rule a land of unruly populations. At the same time, it explains how
this political intercourse between the state and the population has shaped
the transformation of the Turkish welfare system during the last half century. It is intriguing, for example, to see how the Turkish state has survived
the four-decade-old Kurdish uprising led by one of the largest guerrilla
organizations in the world. Keeping in mind that Kurds constitute around
one-sixth of the population of Turkey and are more than forty million
strong in Turkey, Syria, Iraq, and Iran, how has the Turkish state managed
to survive an uprising that comprises armed and unarmed components
spanning massive mobilizations in Turkey and neighboring countries,
in addition to a large diasporic community in Europe? Can the military
strength of the Turkish state alone explain it? To what extent have other
less coercive measures played a role, and how has the positive targeting of
Kurds in social assistance programs helped the containment of a Kurdish
insurgency in which the Kurdish poor is the central actor? This strategy
may explain why the Turkish state clearly privileges the Kurdish poor when
delivering social assistance benefits.

In a similar vein, one can ask how President Recep Tayyip Erdoğan has
survived all the serious challenges he has faced since the early 2000s. How

did he cope with the threat of a military coup led by a Kemalist army in the 2000s and Fethullah Gülen–led army officials in the late 2010s? How did he overcome massive popular unrest during the Gezi protests, which mobilized around 15% of the population in Istanbul alone (Yörük and Yüksel 2014)? How did he survive the difficult period when news about the largest corruption scandal in Turkish history erupted? Wide popular support from the poor has built a strong wall of protection for Erdoğan, and the expansion of social assistance programs for the poor has been a key factor in mobilizing this support.

A more general question concerns how the neoliberal transition in Turkey occurred so smoothly, a question Cihan Tuğal (2009) aptly asked. On the one hand, how did the powerful and militant working class of the 1970s lose its power so quickly as to prevent it from resisting neoliberal policies that dramatically undermined living and working conditions following the 1980s? Does the state violence accompanying the 1980 coup d'état explain this loss of power? Considering that the more intense state violence exercised in similar military interventions in Argentina or Chile failed to render the working class tranquil, it seems unlikely. Surely extra-repressive elements, such as the effect of Islamist mobilization, must be at play, as Tuğal has emphasized. An analysis of the material domain in which the working classes have been co-opted and contained requires a detailed look at welfare provision. For example, the expansion of the social security system in the early 1990s that "coincided" with the massive labor resistance (the so-called Spring Actions) of the declining formal working class in Turkey—or, alternatively, the expansion of generous and extensive social assistance programs targeting the informal proletarians—provide clues about how welfare provision has smoothed out the rough path to neoliberalism.

These events signal that, in different times and places, similar politicized logics of welfare provision have been applied in order to rule, regulate, or contain population groups in Turkey. These are not particular cases, but they do indicate a particular raison d'état of the Turkish state, one that systematically instrumentalized welfare provision in order to rule the population, contain social unrest, and mobilize popular support. This logic explains why the Turkish welfare system expanded dramatically during neoliberalism (this goes against most studies that emphasize neoliberal retrenchment) and how new welfare provisions are unevenly distributed (e.g., favoring the Kurds).

But this is not a development unique to Turkey. In India, Mexico, Brazil, and South Africa, we see similar patterns that define the relationship between welfare and politics. Many developing countries—especially the so-called emerging markets—are now characterized by a new global political economy in which the poor have gained political predominance as the main grassroots source of political threat to or political support for governments, or both. This change has pushed these countries into providing extensive and decommodifying social assistance as the central element of a new welfare regime—a common strategy for the political containment and mobilization of the political power of the poor. Emerging markets have expanded significantly new types of social assistance programs (e.g., conditional cash transfers) over the last decade, which have spread to other higher and lower income countries. During the 2000s, the Bolsa Familia program in Brazil has grown exponentially, expanding to cover 26.6 million people by 2005 and 44 million people by 2006, which represents one quarter of the Brazilian population. Brazil has introduced four other social assistance programs since the 1990s, which have also expanded dramatically (Lindert 2005). In China, a means-tested cash transfer program, called the Minimum Living Standard Program (Dibao), was introduced in 1994. It covered 2.6 million people in 1999, and by 2002 20.6 million people were receiving benefits. The adjusted level of social assistance per capita increased from one yuan to 43 yuan between 1988 and 2002 (Chen and Barrientos 2006). In 2011, the official poverty line was increased from US$180.7 to US$226, which sharply increased the number of eligible recipients/individuals from 36 million to 100 million (Xinzhen 2011). In India, five different social assistance programs have covered more than one quarter of the population since the 1990s (Barrientos and Holmes 2007). South Africa has implemented five different means-tested social assistance programs since the 2000s. In 2009, 18.2% of the population was covered by the Children Support Grant, which was introduced in 1998, and 5% of citizens received an old age pension (Case, Hosegood, and Lund 2005; Djebbari and Mayrand 2011).

This new welfare state regime, designated as the "populist welfare state regime" (Yörük, Öker, and Tafoya 2020), is characterized by (1) the earlier (postwar) limited development of fragmented and corporatist social security systems benefiting the privileged segments of formal sector workers and civil servants at the expense of the informal urban and rural poor, and (2) the neoliberal period's rapid development of social assistance and health care programs that target the previously excluded urban and rural poor. This welfare regime is populist because it is a historical outcome of two waves of populist politics that dominated the political economy of the developmentalist and neoliberal periods.

The first such wave of populist politics is the traditional populism of the second and third quarters of the twentieth century, which came to be characterized by the political machines of the leaders of developing countries such as Getúlio Vargas in Brazil, Juan Peron in Argentina, Bülent Ecevit in Turkey, Salvador Allende in Chile, and António de Oliveira Salazar in Portugal. This developmentalist-style populism expanded the welfare state by extending social security benefits to the privileged minority of formal sector workers in private and public sectors—a dual effort to contain working class radicalism and to mobilize massive popular support from the working class. The second populist wave materialized in the 2000s with an explicit emphasis on people versus elites and has been led by leaders such as Luiz Inácio Lula da Silva (Lula) in Brazil, Néstor Kirchner and Cristina Fernández de Kirchner in Argentina, Recep Tayyip Erdoğan in Turkey, Thaksin Shinawatra in Thailand, Viktor Orbán in Hungary, Narendra Modi in India, or Vladimir Putin in Russia. This time, the poor, or informal working classes, have risen as the main source of either political threat to or support for leaders who extended large social assistance and health care policies to the poor as a way to contain and mobilize them. The poor have emerged as the central grassroots political power in these emerging markets because during the neoliberal period, the rapid rural to urban migration, dispossession of rural producers, commodification of labor, low wages, and unemployment created huge poor populations (Davis 2004; Harvey 2005; Portes and Hoffman 2003). On the one hand, rising poverty has interacted with existing racial, ethnic, and religious grievances, as well as with radical ideological trends, making the poor the main source of political unrest (Wacquant 2009; Barron et al. 2009; Göbel and Ong 2012; Burgoon 2006; Stewart 2002). In Turkey, the poor have been radicalized mostly by Islamist or Kurdish groups. In Brazil, however, they have been mobilized by drug traffic, in India by Maoists and (Hindu and Muslim) fundamentalists, in Mexico by indigenous and criminal groups, in China by ethnic/religious movements and extralegal labor organizations, and in South Africa by left-wing neighborhood organizations, landless movements, and criminal groups (Yörük 2012; Nepal, Bohara, and Gawande 2011; Chenoweth 2007; Taydas and Peksen 2012). On the other hand, as part of the third wave of democratization (Huntington 2012), electoral politics and escalated intraelite competition in emerging markets have resulted in large electoral power for the poor and have transformed them into the main source of popular support due to their numerical majority. Electoral politics have also been accompanied by social and cultural polarizations, resulting in extraparliamentary forms of conflict and struggles ranging from waves of protests to failed coups d'état, as well as judicial interventions supported by the middle and upper classes, all of which have painted governments into a corner (Ashman and Vignon 2014; Sridharan 2014; Onuch 2014; Singer 2014; Yörük and Yüksël 2014; Moura 2007; Souza 2006). Most governments have failed to build multiclass bases and have thus had to rely on the poor, who appear to be their easiest source of popular support. In the West, "the poor were once again disadvantaged because their cooperation was less important to major institutions than the cooperation of other groups" (Piven and Minnite 2016). In emerging markets, however, the poor are now more important to major institutions than the cooperation of more structured sectors of society because they are able to participate in politics not only through protest but also by supporting governments.

Political exigencies have led the governments of the emerging economies to develop these social assistance policies, and these exigencies are a response to the growing social and political weight of the informal proletariat. The growing economic success of the emerging market economies has depended heavily on an abundance of cheap labor from the growing informal proletariat of the slums. Yet these slums have also become the new spatial and social epicenters of sociopolitical conflict and popular support for the governments in these countries (Davis 2006). This is because the rising poverty of the informal proletariat has interacted with existing racial and ethnic grievances to generate domestic political disorder. The political reaction of the slums worldwide against rising poverty and ethnic or racial inequality has increased government efforts to contain this threat. Moreover, the numerical strength of the informal proletariat and its tendency to respond to populist policies has increased the will to mobilize the popular support of the informal proletariat (Davis 2006). These political efforts have been further intensified by democratic electoral politics and party competition that exist in most of the emerging economies. As a result, the growing political weight of the informal proletariat in these emerging economies has become the enduring source of political threat as well as popular support for governments. New social assistance programs have been driven by this political change (Moura 2007; Hunter and Power 2007; Zucco 2008; Soares and Terron 2010; Gao 2006; Yörük and Şarlak 2019).

It seems very likely that there is a common raison d'état concerning welfare politics and population rule (particularly rule of the poor) in non-Western emerging markets. This book examines this logic by providing a detailed account of the Turkish case, where class, ethnicity, and religion fuse in delicate ways so as to radically shape contentious and electoral politics that might translate into radical reforms in the welfare state. This case, while illustrating how Turkish governments use welfare provision to rule the population, may help explain why emerging countries become new welfare state regimes.

Welfare System Reform in Turkey

Over the last four decades, the Turkish welfare system has undergone a major transformation. This transformation involves, in addition to an overall welfare state expansion, a shift from employment-based social security policies to income-based social assistance policies. Between the 1950s and the 1990s, the Turkish welfare system provided employment-based benefits, that is, social security programs, including (most importantly) pensions, job security, and free health care—primarily for formally employed workers and their families. These benefits, including diverse benefits for state sector employees, private-sector employees, self-employed people, and farmers, were distributed through different institutions according to the beneficiaries' employment status. Since the 1990s, the income level of citizens has increasingly supplanted employment status as the main criterion in welfare provision, and as such, Turkish welfare provision has become a system based on both employment status and income level. Accordingly, eligibility conditions for pensions have tightened, while job security and health care benefits have declined alongside real wages for workers. In the meantime, various income-based welfare programs, which benefited citizens according to their income level, that is, whether or not they are in poverty, have rapidly expanded to cover larger segments of the population, including means-tested social assistance programs and free health care services for the poor. A means test is a determination of whether an individual or family is eligible for social assistance, on the basis of the observation that the individual or family is in poverty. Hence, the last decade has witnessed a social assistance boom in Turkey.

Scholarly debates concerning Turkish welfare reform have largely been dominated by structural arguments emphasizing demographic and economic changes including an aging population, labor informalization, unemployment, globalization, deindustrialization, the rise of poverty, and the rise of the service sector. According to this dominant scholarship, structural changes have made it difficult to finance employment-based social security policies and to cover large segments of the population. Population aging has led to financial problems in employment-based social security systems because of the rising ratio of pension recipients to working citizens. Mass unemployment, deindustrialization, the rise of services, falling wages, the informalization of work, and precarious work conditions have also contributed to the problem of financial difficulties and an increasing dependence ratio. On the other hand, the increase in structural unemployment and rising poverty have been shown to be the main factors driving the expansion of social assistance programs.

These explanations have essentially disregarded political factors. Scholars tend to describe both global and local welfare system shifts as an almost automatic response to these aforementioned economic and demographic changes that transformed social needs. As such, the ways in which contemporary welfare system changes have been affected by governments' political concerns about contentious and electoral politics have been insufficiently explored. This book brings political factors to the fore and shows that government responses to changes in political exigencies have been *the* critical force driving the policy shift in Turkey, by focusing on two major concepts: welfare provision as political containment and the political mobilization of grassroots politics. Specifically, the book argues that (1) welfare institutions serve the political task of containing and mobilizing grassroots groups, and that (2) the center of grassroots politics in Turkey has moved from the formal proletariat to the informal proletariat, as well as from non-Kurds to Kurds. This indicates a shift of activities from city centers to slum and rural areas. Finally, (3) governments have increasingly prioritized income-based policies that prove to be more efficient for politically containing and mobilizing both Kurds and the informal proletariat.

In short, as the center of grassroots politics has moved from the formal proletariat to the informal proletariat, from Turks to Kurds, and from city centers to slum and rural areas, the focus of welfare provision has shifted accordingly from social security programs to social assistance. In other words, ethnic identity and political activism have become the determining factors in welfare provision. Employment-based benefits correlate with the political activism of the formal proletariat and income-based benefits with that of the informal proletariat—particularly Kurdish informal proletarians. Social assistance is therefore directed to Kurds, as well as to politically active poor areas, illustrating that social assistance is not simply expanded when and where people become poor, but when and where the poor become politicized. In Turkish policy-making, governments consider tendencies in grassroots politics and seek to contain and mobilize grassroots groups with maximum political effect and minimum economic cost.

This book considers the structural factors that underlie political processes, including an aging population, globalization, the decline in formal employment, deindustrialization, and informalization. These structural variables have either gained pace or stayed constant after the 1980s. However, despite such consistent long-term structural trends, changes in Turkish welfare policy have undergone spatial and temporal fluctuations, which have occurred because of politics. In other words, there has been no significant economic or demographic fluctuations in any other period since the 1980s, but welfare change has followed a tortuous path with twists and turns over certain periods since then. Four specific examples suggest that welfare policies do not simply follow structural exigencies.

The first is the significant expansion of social security benefits for formal sector workers during the 1990s. This occurred despite the neoliberal trend toward the type of welfare retrenchment highly recommended by the International Monetary Fund and the World Bank. Second, income-based social assistance programs in Turkey underwent a boom during the 2000s, while the rate of poverty either stayed constant or declined. Figures show that the decline in the poverty rate was not a result of social assistance programs. A report by the State Planning Organization in Turkey also indicates that social assistance programs in all forms were not responsible for the decline in the poverty rate during the 2000s (State Planning Organization 2009). If social assistance did not reduce poverty, one might question the government's motivation for dramatically expanding such assistance, especially during a period of declining poverty.

Another example is that the welfare system saw different geographical regions of Turkey with similar poverty rates receiving extremely different levels of social assistance. In other words, social assistance does not correspond to regional poverty rates. Namely, although poverty rates in the eastern and southeastern regions of Turkey, where Kurds constitute the majority, are very close to those found in the Central Anatolian region, where Turks are in the majority, the former regions receive much higher amounts of social assistance. Lastly, the strong statistical association between Kurdish ethnic identity and free health care card-holding status shows that Kurds are much more likely to receive this benefit, even when controlling for poverty and official socioeconomic determinants of social assistance. Structural explanations emphasizing that social assistance programs are responses to poverty cannot explain why Kurds receive much higher levels of social assistance.

These initial observations of current welfare system transformations reveal several spatial and temporal fluctuations and anomalies that structural perspectives cannot explain. These observations question the validity of existing structural arguments on contemporary welfare transformations and call for revisiting the previous literature on the concepts of political containment and mobilization about the earlier transformation of welfare provisions and for applying these concepts to understand the recent welfare system change. As such, they rule out the possibility that structural factors are exclusively responsible for welfare system changes in Turkey. Rather, while structural changes might establish a certain context for changes in welfare policy, they do not dictate such changes.

Understanding long-term policy outcomes and temporary welfare policy fluctuations requires a focus on state responses to grassroots politics and to intra-elite competition and struggle. Spatial and temporal fluctuations in the welfare system are symptoms of political concerns to contain and mobilize new grassroots groups—a motivation that has driven the change from employment-based to income-based policies. In order to analyze how politics have shaped welfare policies, the book presents temporal and spatial comparisons within the case of Turkey, examining how historical and spatial trajectories of political contentions and struggle have affected welfare policies. Structural changes generate grassroots groups and shape their material conditions, although this does not automatically drive state authorities to expand or contract welfare provision for these groups. The extent to which state authorities expand or contract welfare provision depends on the extent to which grassroots groups become politicized.

Methodology and Overview

This book is based on a multimethod strategy that encompasses a combination of historical, quantitative, and qualitative data collection methods. It will analyze the interaction between structural and political factors with a research design that allows for the methodological isolation of political factors from structural factors. This is because structural factors do not directly translate into welfare policies, as is often assumed in the literature, but are transmitted by political interests and competition, which determine the specific shape and trajectory of the changes. To establish this argument, I have created a dataset of grassroots political activism, run multivariate regression analyses, analyzed parliamentary discussions and policy documents, and conducted interviews and field observations.

The first method is an examination of newspaper archives from which a dataset of contentious political events that occurred in Turkey between 1970 and 2016 has been compiled (glocon.ku.edu.tr). The dataset provides trajectories of contentious politics over the last four decades, including the activities of the formal proletariat, the informal proletariat, the left, the Islamists, and the Kurds. Then descriptive and inferential statistical analyses using large sample surveys follow. The regression analysis shows that there is a strong association between social assistance provision and Kurdish ethnic identity. To explain this correlation, I conducted fieldwork at welfare institutions and poor neighborhoods in Istanbul and Ankara in 2011. This fieldwork research included interviews with high-level welfare officials and local caseworkers, grassroots observations on social assistance mechanisms, and interviews with Kurdish activists. I interviewed high-ranking officials in Ankara, who were responsible for the design and implementation of the Turkish social assistance system to understand their perspective on why social assistance is distributed disproportionately to Kurds.[1] In 2011, I conducted field research in two social assistance offices

---

1. I interviewed the general director of the General Directorate of Social Assistance at the Ministry of Family and Social Policy. This is the former Social Assistance and Solidarity Fund, which has recently been made part of this newly established ministry. I also interviewed the head of research and development at this directorate as well as a number of experts of social assistance, who were responsible for restructuring of the social assistance system in Turkey. I also interviewed the head of the Income Distribution and Social Inclusion Department at the Ministry of Development. The Ministry of Development is the former State Planning Organization, and it is responsible for coordinating and overseeing social policy projects and projections in Turkey.

in Istanbul that includes observations and interviews about the social assistance application, evaluation, and implementation processes. One of these offices was the local Social Assistance and Solidarity Fund office and the other one was the free health care card (Green Card) office. These offices were responsible for an area that covered a diverse range of working-class neighborhoods, including areas where Kurdish and Roma constituted the majority, as well as those where the socialist left or the Islamists were strong.

In order to establish the relationship between welfare policy changes and grassroots politics, I carried out an extensive document analysis. First, I analyzed parliamentary discussions on all welfare legislation since 1980, investigating whether members of parliament considered issues related to grassroots politics during welfare policy-making processes. My aim was to understand how economic, demographic, and fiscal concerns dominated the welfare reform agenda and to what extent political factors (such as the Kurdish insurgency and labor unrest) were driving changes in welfare policy. Finally, I also investigated publications by state institutions in charge of social welfare and social policy.

Chapter 1 presents an overview and discussion of the literature on welfare system transformations and grassroots politics, beginning with the observation that current Turkish welfare system transformation is part of the second systemic shift in global welfare systems. The literature on the first shift is a synthesis of structural and political explanations, while the literature on the current shift is largely limited to structural explanations. Underutilization of political explanations in the current literature is an important gap. The chapter borrows the concepts of political containment and political mobilization from the literature on the first welfare transformation in order to understand the current second shift in welfare systems, particularly in the Turkish welfare system. It locates the Turkish welfare system within a family of similar welfare systems in emerging economies, such as in Brazil, Indonesia, Mexico, South Africa, China, and India. This is not only because of similarities between their systems but also because of similarities between their grassroots politics. Global changes in grassroots politics have been shaped by grand transformations in class and ethnic structures. Finally, the chapter presents an overview of the emerging literature that establishes the link between counterterrorism and welfare provision. This literature identifies grassroots politics as the dependent variable and welfare provision as the independent variable. The book switches this causal direction.

Chapter 2 depicts the transformation of the Turkish welfare system over the last four decades, showing that alongside the general expansion in terms of coverage and expenditure, the Turkish welfare system has expanded from employment-based social security policies to income-based social assistance policies. The chapters first explains the emergence of the pre-1980s employment-based system by defining its institutional mechanisms and policy preferences. It then demonstrates the declining trend in social security services since the 1980s relative to social assistance. This is followed by an analysis of the income-based social assistance policies that have rapidly expanded since the 1990s. The declining trend in social security programs and expansion in social assistance programs indicate that a macro-level welfare policy change has indeed taken place in Turkey.

Based on a grassroots politics dataset generated from the archives of a Turkish daily newspaper, *Cumhuriyet*, chapter 3 is a detailed historical overview of grassroots politics (social movements and protest waves) in Turkey. This chapter is a major empirical contribution to social movement studies, as it presents the results of the first ever protest events database on Turkey and analyzes this dataset in order to locate patterns of social movements during the period between 1970 and 2017. This database contains more than 40,000 protest events coded from *Cumhuriyet*, and identifies the protestors, organizers, ideologies, ethnic and religious identities, and several other characteristics of these events. The dataset demonstrates that, over the last four decades, the center of grassroots politics in Turkey has shifted from the formal working class to the informal working class, as well as from non-Kurds to Kurds. To explain this pattern, the chapter analyzes structural as well as political factors, which cannot be reduced to a mere consequence of demographic and economic trends; political organizations, struggles, and interests have transformed structural processes into grassroots political actions in ways that structural forces would not necessarily have dictated. The chapter presents a history of the ways in which governing and opposition parties (as well as radical political groups) try to mobilize or contain grassroots groups. While the socialist left radicalized formal workers in the 1970s, the informal working class was radicalized first by the Islamist movement in the 1990s and subsequently by the Kurdish movement in the 2000s, pointing out how the political power of the formal working class vanished after the 1990s.

The following chapters continue to show how and why trends in welfare policies and grassroots politics are correlated. Chapter 4 presents an analysis of welfare policy-making processes in Turkey. This chapter is based on an in-depth qualitative investigation of 150 laws enacted since 1980, as well as on an investigation of parliamentary debates about this legislation. A quantified index of welfare legislation was created by coding these laws in order to show that the patterns of expansion and retrenchment in social security and social assistance have responded to the patterns of political contention and competition. Most importantly, this chapter shows that when enacting welfare laws, parliamentarians have focused on the grassroots political power of the lower classes, either as a threat of social unrest or as a source of popular support. Political struggles and interests have clearly determined which laws were approved and which policies were pursued.

By using a mixed method approach that combines quantitative analysis, interviews, and field observations, chapter 5 shows that the Turkish government uses social assistance to contain Kurdish unrest in Turkey. The quantitative analysis illustrates that social assistance programs in Turkey are disproportionately directed at the Kurdish minority, especially at the internally displaced Kurds in urban and metropolitan areas. The chapter analyzes a cross-sectional dataset generated by a 10,386-informant stratified random-sample survey conducted in 2010 by the KONDA research company and controls for possibly intervening socioeconomic factors and neighborhood-level fixed effects. The high ethnic disparity in social assistance is not due to higher poverty among Kurds; rather, the results identify Kurdish ethnic identity as the main determinant of access to social assistance, demonstrating that the Turkish government uses social assistance to contain Kurdish unrest in Turkey. The chapter then discusses how and why this occurs. In order to support this claim that social assistance is used as a counterinsurgency strategy, the chapter presents evidence from intense political competition over the informal workers of slums. Occurring among the governing Justice and Development Party (AKP), the main opposition Republican People's Party (CHP), and the Kurdish parties, this competition for power has been translated into party competition over social assistance provision, an issue that has been especially critical in the Kurdish region. The chapter then discusses the findings of a qualitative study that was conducted at national welfare institutions and analyzes the use of social assistance as a political instrument. The study includes interviews with high-ranking social assistance officials in Ankara and grassroots fieldwork data gathered through interviews and observations conducted in a welfare office in a poor slum in Istanbul. The chapter concludes that pressures generated from ethnic grassroots politics are responsible for the ethnically uneven distribution of social assistance programs in Turkey. The Turkish government seems to give social assistance not simply to places where people become poor, but to places where the poor become politicized, an observation that supports Fox Piven and Cloward's (1971) thesis that poor relief is driven by social unrest, rather than social need.

The concluding chapter presents the general results of the analysis of the Turkish welfare system's transformation and points out the ways in which grassroots politics have shaped the transition from employment-based to income-based welfare policies. While this transition in welfare policies is a global change affecting all countries, Turkey has experienced it in ways similar to other "emerging economies." The chapter ends with implications of the findings for other emerging economies.

CHAPTER 1

Theoretical Explanations for Changes in Welfare Systems

Welfare state studies is a huge area of scholarship. Yet, when it comes to contemporary welfare system changes, there is a significant gap in this literature. In contrast to the previous scholarship on the mid-20th-century welfare systems expansion, this current literature is largely limited to structural arguments. This means that this literature explains the shifts in welfare policy as a nearly automatic response to economic and demographic transformations, leaving behind a need for further political explanations. This book helps fill in this theoretical gap. The examination of the conditions of grassroots politics from a broad perspective will show that, in place of the formal working class of the developmentalist era, an informal working class has become the major source of grassroots political threat as well as a source of popular support for consecutive Turkish governments in the neoliberal era. Containment and mobilization of these informal proletarians are driving forces behind the rapid expansion of income-based social assistance programs, leading to the establishment of an entirely new welfare state regime. In this chapter, I will critically analyze the scholarship that examined the historical development of the welfare state and point out a large gap that characterizes the contemporary literature. This gap emanates from the scholarly underexamination of political, and particularly contentious political, factors that drive contemporary welfare policy changes. Let us begin by putting these arguments in the broader context of the history of welfare systems.

In the history of welfare systems, many scholars have observed two pendulum-like systemic shifts. First, from the late 18th century to the mid-20th century, welfare systems in many European countries shifted from an early limited phase of income-based poor relief systems to extensive employment-based social security systems, which provided formally employed people with social rights, including pensions, unemployment insurance, health care, unionization, and collective bargaining. Since the 1980s, the second shift has involved reducing guarantees of formal employment, adopting more restrictive unemployment insurance policies, tightening work requirements, privatizing services, and providing fewer benefits for workers, while increasing means-tested social assistance schemes, free health care services, and cash transfers for the poor (Pierson 1994; Barrientos and Hulme 2008; Goldberg and Rosenthal 2002; Lodemel and Trickey 2001; Heclo 1974; Brooks and Manza 2006; Goldberg and Rosenthal 2002; Iversen 2001; Saraceno 2002; Gao 2006; Haggard and Kaufman 2008). By social assistance programs, we refer to cash transfers and near cash (means tested or not), conditional cash transfers, social pensions, in-kind transfers, school supplies, public works, food for work programs, and fee waivers or targeted subsidies for health care, schooling, utilities, or transport (World Bank 2015). The second shift has occurred in the Global South, and, to a lesser degree, in the Global North as part of a new trend occasioned by emerging market economies.

In the first phase, most welfare systems in the Western world were based on traditional poor relief systems targeting the very poor (Heclo 1974; Perrin 1969; Quadagno 1982). In the second phase, between the 1930s and the 1980s, comprehensive employment-based welfare systems guaranteed workers a basic standard of living in many advanced capitalist countries. These welfare systems emerged as part of the developmentalist era, eventually spreading to many developing countries (Flora and Heidenheimer 1981; Myles 1984; Trattner 1984; Quadagno 1984). These welfare systems mainly provided workers with pensions, health insurance, unemployment benefits, and job security (Flora and Alber 1981; Shonfield 1965; Quadagno 1987). In the third phase, beginning in the 1980s, welfare systems in many countries increasingly moved away from employment-based social security policies for formal sector employees toward income-based social assistance policies for the poor. In that system, the income level of citizens again became the central criterion in welfare provision in addition to the employment status. There has been an increasing effort and capacity to provide certain welfare benefits for citizens with incomes under a certain threshold. The new welfare policy orientation emerged as part of the neo-liberal turn (Iversen 2001; Kitschelt 2001; Margarita, Torben, and David 1999). It must be noted that employment-based welfare provisions continued to exist in this third phase, just as income-based provisions existed in the second phase. However, rapid increases in demographic coverage and expenditures of these income-based programs for the poor and a parallel relative decline in employment-based social security benefits for workers indicate that there has been a systemic transition in welfare regimes toward income-based welfare provision rather than simple policy changes (Eatwell 1995; Ginsburg 2001).

The First Transition from Poor Relief to Social Security

Following World War II, the welfare state in Western countries displayed a tremendous expansion, which was mainly based on providing workers with social security. These systems sought the redistribution of income and wealth and complied with the objective of attaining full employment (Shonfield 1965). These employment-based welfare systems dramatically expanded health care insurance, old age pensions, unemployment insurance, job security, and high wages for workers, and developing countries soon adopted similar policies albeit with more limited capacity (Esping-Andersen 1990; Myles 1984; Quadagno 1987; Flora and Alber 1981). The welfare state materialized the institutionalization of social rights as the third stage of citizenship rights, following the civil and political rights established in the 18th and 19th century, respectively (Marshall 1973).

There is extensive literature that attempts to explain the causes of the first transition from the initially very limited phase of income-based poor relief policies to the second and much grander phase of employment-based social security policies. Dominant explanations for welfare development can be classified into two main clusters: political and structural explanations. Political explanations emphasize political interests, conflicts, motivations, ideologies, processes, strategies, and tactics that mediate and translate structural trends and forces into welfare policy-making. Structural explanations emphasize social, demographic, and economic transformations, needs, and constraints that determine the course of welfare policies independently of the political factors and interests involved. While the literature on the first welfare shift is a mature fusion of political and structural explanations, we see that the literature on the second has been dominated by structural explanations, underestimating the effect of political factors (particularly at the grassroots level).

For the first systemic shift in welfare systems, the *structuralist* "logic of industrialism" thesis suggested that the welfare state expanded as a "natural" response to industrialization and urbanization (Cowgill 1974; Goldthorpe et al. 1969; Form 1979; Pampel and Weiss 1983; Cutright 1965; Jackman 1974, 1975; Wilensky 1975). The first welfare system shift is described as a response to economic and demographic developments, which forced governments to expand welfare. The "logic of industrialism" thesis suggests that industrialization and urbanization processes created a need for public spending, because they reduced the social protection capacity of the traditional family and communal structures. As a result, the theory continues, states almost automatically expanded the provision of social security for the working classes (Cowgill 1974; Form 1979; Pampel and Weiss 1983; Cutright 1965; Jackman 1974, 1975; Wilensky 1975). By that logic, industry-based economic growth and the concomitant demographic changes were presented as the main causes of welfare state expansion. In addition to producing the need and rationale, industrialization also created the wealth, surplus, and extensive bureaucratic structure necessary to deliver social benefits (Goldthorpe 1969).

Some scholars have argued that states increased welfare expenditures in order to resolve the crisis of underconsumption following the Keynesian logic that public welfare expenditures could stimulate aggregate demand by increasing the purchasing power of workers as well as regulate fluctuations and instabilities in the business cycle (Janowitz 1977; Garraty 1978; Offe 1984; O'Connor 1973). States followed a strategy to boost consumer demand that included unionization, which led to higher wages and mass consumption. Governments followed the advice of John Maynard Keynes in pursuing unbalanced budgets, heavy public investments, and low interest rates to eliminate unemployment and to increase consumption, ensuring the sustainability of a healthy and productive working class, as well as capitalist profitability by lowering the reproduction cost of labor (Garraty 1978; Offe 1984). Quadagno (1984, 111) concludes that to attain high levels of welfare provision, "the high level of economic development between 1945 and 1973 provided the economic means, Keynesian economics provided the rationale, while the centralization of the federal government during national wartime mobilization expanded national bureaucratic capacity."

Scholars oriented toward *political* explanations of the first welfare shift argued that demographic and economic exigencies did not automatically lead to changes in welfare policies. Rather, socio-structural factors were translated into policies through political conflict and struggles, interests, and the balance of power. These scholars have considered the first welfare systems as part of a strategy to *contain* political disorder and *mobilize* popular support (Katznelson 1981; Goldberg and Rosenthal 2002). For them, structuralist theories have had limited explanatory capacity, because they did not account for class struggles and political conflicts that largely shaped welfare policy-making as well. Indeed, demographic and economic exigencies did not necessarily lead to changes in welfare policies. Rather, they were translated into policy through some mechanisms based on political struggles and the balance of power. Therefore, socialist party power and labor union strength appeared to be the main determinants of welfare state developments in many countries (Williamson and Weiss 1979). As Jill Quadagno put it, "The addition of class and political system variables undermined the argument that economic development alone can explain welfare state formation" (Quadagno 1984, 113). In order to address this gap, an alternative set of political arguments has been put forward mostly by neo-Marxist scholars, who have considered the first welfare system transition from poor relief structures to employment-based policies as part of a strategy of *containing* political disorder and *mobilizing* popular support (Katznelson 1981; Goldberg and Rosenthal 2002).

States expanded employment-based social security programs during the postwar era in order to contain political dissent originating from a "militant" working class and to impede communist expansion by buying off potentially insurgent workers, providing political-ideological legitimacy for capitalism (O'Connor 1973; Olson 1982; Phillipson 1983; Trempe 1983; Katznelson 1981; Arrighi 1990; Mead 1989; Mishra 1996; Silver 2004; Habermas 1975; Offe 1984). Ira Katznelson (1981) argued that "it is impossible to imagine that any capitalist society may achieve stability and continuity without adopting welfare state policies." Over time, social security came to be seen in the Western world as a permanent feature of capitalism for its contribution to political stability. The welfare state provided the means for political legitimacy necessary to contain the threat from grassroots groups, most importantly working-class movements (Goldberg 2002). Put simply, the welfare state functioned to contain social unrest (O'Connor 1973; Olson 1982; Phillipson 1983; Trempe 1983).

Marxist state theory provided the argument that the welfare state served to legitimize the capitalist system. The welfare state emerged as an "instrument" of the capitalist class, as a strategic action of a "relatively autonomous" state to oversee the sustainability of the broader capitalist order or as an outcome of a political consensus among capitalists, the state, and labor (Jessop 1994; Miliband 1969; Poulantzas 1978; O'Connor 1973; Offe 1982). Hence, the welfare state was regarded as an instrument of the capitalist class to ensure the stability of the class structure. The state in general and the welfare state in particular serve the interests of the capitalist class, mainly because governments are dominated by the members of the capitalist class (Miliband 1969). Some others, most importantly Nicos Poulantzas, put forward a more structuralist perspective, claiming that contradictions within the capitalist class necessitate the performance of the state as an organizing body that synthesizes competing and contradictory measures into state policies (Poulantzas 1978). The common ground for these theories is that welfare policies have functioned in the interests of the capitalist class and have worked to contain working-class militancy.

Class-based welfare theories emphasize the political consensus among capitalists, the state, and labor. This consensus underlay the employment-based welfare regimes that would maintain profitability and social harmony at the same time (Offe 1982). The welfare state created legitimacy for the capitalist system insofar as workers were convinced that economic growth and capitalist profits would increasingly generate an economic surplus used to sustain welfare benefits and increase income for workers. Capitalists, in turn, accepted the need for a welfare state in order to ensure a complacent working class. Competition with the USSR's model, which combined full employment and comprehensive benefit systems, has also been presented as a factor driving Western governments to expand social security policies in the postwar period (Mishra 1996; Arrighi 1990). Under the Soviet threat, the United States rebuilt European economies through the Marshall Plan and financed their welfare systems in order to buy off potentially insurgent workers and halt communist expansion by helping the decommodification of labor (Arrighi 1990; Mead 1989; Silver 2004). Pflanze (1990) noted that social insurance programs developed in the Bismarck period were deliberately designed as a safety valve mechanism against the socialist threat even in the 19th century. Thus, containment of the threat of socialism and working-class struggles was a major inducement for the creation of the Western welfare state.

States often used welfare provisions to politically *mobilize* the lower classes. Thus, one could conclude that increasing government need for popular support also caused the expansion of employment-based social security policies. Political mobilization became a significant cause due to two conditions of state formation: (1) war and (2) political competition. First, during wartime, states need to mobilize their citizens for mass patriotic support. Rising dependency on conscription and the industrialization of warfare entailed the cooperation of working classes in the war effort (Tilly 1988; McNeill 1982). This was because the bargaining power of the working class grew with capitalist accumulation and centralization and mere coercion did not suffice to lead workers toward support for the war effort. Beverly Silver (2004) analyzed the relationship between labor unrest and war and argued these dynamics pushed states to expand welfare and democratic rights for citizen through so-called socialization of the state, for example, the Great Society program during the Vietnam War. This increasing government reliance on the masses for a war effort made interstate rivalries and social conflict "far more intertwined," rendering states domestically much more vulnerable during war. For this reason, Silver argues, states have recently tended to increase the weight of capital-intensive (as opposed to labor-intensive) warfare as in the case of the wars in Kosovo and Iraq. It is likely that the reversal of welfare rights after the 1980s is related to this emancipation from dependence on worker-citizens for success in war (Silver 2004).

Second, political scientists investigated the effects of intra-elite and interparty competition on welfare state expansion in the postwar period (Kitschelt 2001). They argue that conflict and competition between elites and parties, especially in electoral politics, often lead to sharp increases in welfare provision. Although populism, clientelism, and patronage relations are often identified as exceptional and corruptive, the mechanisms of political mobilization are indeed the main and permanent features of welfare development. As such, the generosity of a state's social welfare policy depends on the mobilization of the lower classes in the electoral process (Jennings 1979). Moreover, parties' reputations and capacity to mobilize activists often rest on long-established commitments to social welfare provision (Kitschelt 2001). This is because success in intra-elite and interparty competition requires mass support, and competing actors attempt to utilize welfare provisions as a means of garnering popular support (Cnudde and McCrone 1969). Richard Dawson and James Robinson, therefore, argue that greater interparty competition leads to more extensive social welfare policies to obtain support from the electorate (Barrilleaux, Holbrook, and Langer 2002; Dawson and Robinson 1963). These policies often target the working class, which makes up a large proportion of the population (Hicks and Swank 1992; Jennings 1979). Nevertheless, there is no unique way of sustaining popular support in a given political context, and the prevalent form of welfare provision tends to be the one that maximizes the interests of the more powerful faction in elite competition (Fenton 1969).

The Second Transition from Social Security Policies to Social Assistance Policies

Since the 1980s, welfare systems have changed substantively. One central feature of this change is the expansion of social assistance policies and the retrenchment of social security programs. As I will illustrate, the literature on this change is dominated by structuralist approaches, while political analyses remain limited. In 1980, Albert Hirschman enunciated "the crisis of the welfare state," which has since then remained a popular depiction of the change taking place (Etxezarreta 1995). However, it is still debated whether this change comprises the withdrawal of states from welfare functions or whether it is a restructuring into new forms of welfare provision. On the one hand, the welfare state is regarded as a structure belonging to the developmentalist era, implying that welfare state retrenchment is inevitable. On the other hand, most countries have increased their social expenditures within the last three decades and this casts serious doubt on the view that the welfare state is withering away. Thus, the welfare state literature has come to suggest that there is actually an ongoing restructuring rather than an overall retrenchment (see the debate between Pierson 2001 and Scruggs and Allan 2014).

In an edited cross-national analysis of nine advanced capitalist states, Gertrude Goldberg and Marguerite Rosenthal supported the view that despite some retrenchment of welfare expenditures in certain provisions, the essential change is not a quantitative contraction, but rather a qualitative shift (Goldberg and Rosenthal 2002). Welfare systems are undergoing restructuring from employment-based welfare provision to income-based social assistance policies—or what Goldberg and Rosenthal (2002) call the poor-law states. On the one hand, this transformation has involved reducing guarantees of formal employment, adopting more restrictive unemployment insurance policies, tightening work requirements, the privatization of services, and fewer benefits for workers (Iversen 2001). On the other hand, it has increased means-tested social assistance schemes, free health care services, and cash transfers for the poor (Kitschelt 2001; Margarita, Torben, and David 1999). There is a systemic shift from employment-based social security policies for workers to income-based social assistance policies for the poor (Goldberg and Rosenthal 2002), which is part of what Paul Pierson called the programmatic retrenchment of the welfare state (Pierson 2001). According to Pierson, programmatic retrenchment occurs regardless of increases in social expenditure when means-tested benefits increase in share instead of universal benefits, the privatization of welfare provision rises, and benefit and eligibility rules change toward greater restrictions.

Thus, as opposed to the common belief, many scholars have shown that welfare systems are not being dissolved but are actually undergoing restructuring from employment-based to income-based policies (Brooks and Manza 2006; Goldberg and Rosenthal 2002; Saraceno 2002). While employment status used to be the main criterion in the postwar period, this has been replaced by the income level for increasing sections of the population. Thus, the main change is in the selection criteria for welfare provision. In many European countries, including the United Kingdom, Spain, France, and Italy, social assistance programs, premium-based health care services, cash transfers, and basic income schemes have dominated social policy debates since the 1990s (Ferrera, Matsaganis, and Sacchi 2002; Lewis and Surender 2004). There is a similar trend of welfare system changes in most emerging economies as well, including Turkey, Brazil, Mexico, Argentina, South Africa, India, South Korea, China, and Indonesia, where social assistance policies have gained prominence since the mid-1990s (Gao 2006; Haggard and Kaufman 2008; Jawad 2009). Low-income sub-Saharan African and Latin American countries that ceased to develop previously established extensive employment-based welfare systems now also have rapidly growing social assistance schemes with the financial support of the World Bank (Barrientos and Holmes 2007).

Since the publication of Gøsta Esping-Andersen's *The Three Worlds of Welfare Capitalism* in 1990, the comparative literature on the welfare state has focused on the notion of welfare state regimes. Although some scholars have questioned Esping-Andersen's categorization of liberal, conservative, and social democratic welfare state regimes, it has become the conventional approach to the study of social security systems in advanced capitalistic democracies (Esping-Andersen 1990). Yet in recent years there has been an ongoing debate about adding a fourth type, namely the Southern European welfare model. Scholars have claimed that welfare systems in Italy, Greece, Portugal, and Spain should be considered as a unique category that is characterized by fragmented welfare provision based on a segmented labor market and the centrality of the family in welfare provision (Alvarez and Guillen 2001). Many scholars have considered the employment-based welfare system in Turkey to fit within this group of Southern European welfare systems (Buğra and Keyder 2006; Gough 1996; Grütjen 2008; Saraceno 2002; see Powell and Yörük 2017). The reason is that Turkey has an elaborate, centrally organized, but highly fragmented and hierarchical system of welfare provision. This system operates within a labor market where self-employment, unpaid family labor, and informal employment are dominant. Moreover, the family has a central role in providing welfare along with the state.

The changing political economy in the global era of neoliberalism can lead us to envision new families of welfare states other than those of welfare regimes in advanced capitalist countries. Turkey is considered to be such an emerging economy, and welfare policy changes occurring in Turkey are part of a broader trend taking place in other emerging economies, including Brazil, China, India, South Africa, Argentina, Russia, and others. Social welfare programs in Turkey follow broader trends characterizing welfare programs in these emerging economies, where income-based social assistance programs are largely expanding relative to employment-based programs. This new welfare regime has been termed the populist welfare state regime (Yörük, Öker, and Tafoya 2020).

Since the 1990s, emerging economies have significantly expanded new types of social assistance programs (e.g., conditional cash transfers), which have also spread to other higher and lower income countries. In Brazil, for example, during the 2000s the Bolsa Familia program grew exponentially, eventually covering one quarter of the Brazilian population (Lindert 2005). Brazil also has four other centrally coordinated social assistance programs. They include a conditional cash program for poor families with laboring children (started in 1999, with 866,000 beneficiaries per year), another one demanding school attendance of children (started in 2001, with five million households), one means-tested but unconditional program providing approximately $50 per month for individuals aged over 65 (started in 1993, with 700,000 beneficiaries), and a cash transfer program that gives $55 per month to informal rural workers over 55 years old (started in 1991, with 4.6 million beneficiaries) (Barrientos and Holmes 2007).

In China, two new social assistance schemes, unemployment insurance and Minimum Living Standard Assistance (Dibao), were introduced in the mid-1990s. Housing benefits decreased, while cash transfers and health benefits increased. The Minimum Living Standard Assistance program, introduced in 1994, covered 2.6 million people in 1999, and by 2016, 60 million people were receiving benefits. In India, the Mahatma Gandhi National Rural Employment Guarantee Act began with 21 million households in the 200 most backward districts in 2006, and it has become the largest workfare program in the world by covering 50 million rural households (more than a quarter of rural households) in all 615 districts of India in 2018 (Pankaj 2015; Government of India 2008, 200; Ministry of Rural Development 2012). Other Indian social assistance programs currently target the poor. Since 1989, the Jawahar Rojgar Yohana program has provided food and cash to stave off poverty, mainly in rural areas. The National Old-Age Pension Scheme, founded in 1995, provides cash payments to destitute elderly households covering 25% of India's elderly. Since 1995, unconditional cash transfers in the form of child and family allowance provide benefits to pregnant women in households living below the poverty line, thus covering 1.2 million beneficiaries. Since that year, the National Family Benefit Scheme has provided support for 1.9 million households below the poverty line in the case of the death of a primary earner (Barrientos and Holmes 2007). In South Africa, since the 1990s the Social Pension Program has distributed unconditional old-age pensions to the poor elderly, mostly black. In 2002, 1.9 million beneficiaries were given $75 per month. The Child Support Grant Program, which was introduced in 1998, has experienced a considerable increase in its coverage, benefiting more than 12 million poor children in 2018 (Yörük and Gençer 2020).

Similar to the developments in these other emerging economies, over the last four decades the Turkish welfare system has undergone a transformation from employment-based to income-based policies (Agartan et al. 2007; Buğra and Keyder 2003). Between the 1950s and the 1990s, the logic of welfare provision in Turkey was primarily based on providing formally employed workers and their families with social insurance for pensions and health care (Mello 2007; Grütjen 2008). Pensions and health benefits were distributed through different institutions according to beneficiaries' employment status, including employees in the state sector, private sector employees, self-employed people, and peasants. Since the 1990s, however, the income level of citizens has increasingly replaced employment status as the main criterion for welfare provision (Buğra and Keyder 2006; Saraceno 2002). The necessary labor tenure entitling a worker to a pension has significantly increased, and eligibility conditions have been tightened (Cosar and Yegenoglu 2008). Various poor relief mechanisms have rapidly expanded to cover larger segments of the population, and free health care services are now provided to the poorest citizens through means-test procedures (Elveren 2007; Günal 2007). Hence, over the last decade Turkish citizens have witnessed a true poor relief boom in Turkey.

Structural Explanations of Contemporary Welfare System Change

In contrast to the literature on the first shift, the existing and expanding literature on contemporary changes in welfare provision, that is, the second systemic shift, so far has focused mainly on structural factors, largely neglecting grassroots political factors. The dominant structuralist paradigm on social assistance expansion emphasizes demographic and economic changes, and argues that the shift in welfare systems was in essence a natural result of aging, labor informalization, unemployment, globalization, deindustrialization, the rise of poverty, and the rise of the service sector, all conditioned by existing institutional frameworks in Europe (Pierson 2001; Jaime-Castillo 2013; Hemerijck 2012; Iversen 2001; Gough and Wood 2004; Matsaganis 2012; Vanhuysse and Goerres 2011) and elsewhere (Ansel 2014; Farnsworth and Irving 2011; Franzoni and Voorend 2011; Hong and Kongshøj 2014; Lupu and Pontusson 2011;; Sugiyama 2011; Kersbergen and Vis 2013). Similar to the "logic of industrialization" thesis used to explain the rise of the postwar welfare state, many scholars explain the rise of income-based welfare policies by what can be designated as the "logic of de-industrialization"—a thesis that can be broken down as follows: (1) before the 1980s, there existed informal safety nets that covered the informal sector, including illegal housing, land opportunities, and traditional solidarity mechanisms for the rural and urban poor; (2) since the 1980s, with the rapid rural-to-urban migration, jobless economic growth policies and the commodification of urban land, structural poverty has significantly increased while informal safety nets have also eroded; (3) this has necessitated income-based social assistance systems to expand and cover the growing informal groups "as a natural response" to the new order of things (Buğra and Keyder 2006; O'Loughin and Friedrichs 1996). Scholars argue that the rise of informalization, contingent work, aging of populations, and increasing dependency ratios have made it difficult to cover larger segments of the population through employment-based provisions, which are becoming difficult to finance, thus necessitating an income-based social assistance expansion (Gough and Wood 2004; Estevez-Abe, Iversen, and Soskice 1999; Esping-Andersen 1996; Pampel and Williamson 1985). Within this expanding structuralist paradigm, Esping-Andersen (1999) himself shifted his emphasis to social risks away from his previously central class-political factors.

Neoliberal scholars believed that the economic crisis of the 1970s was caused by excessive government welfare spending for workers (Quadagno 1987). It was also argued that old welfare systems disturb market incentives and bring along additional tax burdens to capitalists whose persuasive power vis-à-vis other classes and governments grew considerably in the preceding decades (Esping-Andersen 1996). The increasing costs of protected labor and the growing burden of taxation needed for welfare provision led the capitalist class to push states toward welfare system transformations and monetarist policies. This was also because welfare systems impeded the competitive edge of national economies in a global market as a disincentive to work and invest (Bosworth 1980; Fiedler 1975; Haveman 1978; McCracken et al. 1977). Thus, it is often argued that globalization reprimands generous governments and uncompetitive markets, and that international institutions such as the International Monetary Fund, the World Bank, and the European Union have constantly put pressure on individual governments in the direction of retrenchment of employment-based welfare programs (Huffschmid 1997; Goldberg 2002; Huber 2005; Lewis and Surender 2004).

Explanations for the Turkish welfare system changes have been mainly informed by these existing structural arguments and have largely disregarded grassroots political factors (Agartan et al. 2007; Buğra and Keyder 2003; Elveren 2007). First, these structural explanations concerning Turkey claim that the costs of the employment-based provision have become unbearable for Turkish governments. Also, population groups excluded from the formal welfare system, that is, those not registered in the employment-based system, were covered by informal social safety nets up to the 1990s. These safety nets included free housing and land opportunities provided by the government, supportive relationships maintained with rural relatives, and traditional solidarity mechanisms developed among the urban poor. With the rapid rural-to-urban migration, jobless economic growth policies, and the commodification of urban land, structural poverty has significantly increased, yet informal social protection mechanisms have also eroded since the beginning of the 1990s. This has necessitated the income-based poor relief system to cover the growing informal groups, an argument that might be considered part of the "logic of de-industrialization thesis" (Buğra and Keyder 2006; O'Loughin and Friedrichs 1996).

Many have seen the recent welfare transition as part of a neoliberal turn that is not simply a policy response to structural and economic changes, but a part of the class warfare of the rich against the poor. This is particularly true of the cutbacks in employment-based programs, which is part of a concerted political attack on the formal proletariat. Yet the existing literature on the second welfare system shift, in general, as well as in the Turkish case in particular, has still suffered from two main, related drawbacks. First, existing studies have generally underexamined the possibility that contemporary welfare system changes have been affected by governments' political concerns about containing and mobilizing changing grassroots groups. As such, the "contemporary role played by social movements in shaping social welfare has too often been neglected in the discipline of social policy" (Mooney et al. 2009; also see Bebbington et al. 2010), especially in the Global South (Gough 2008). Only a few have referred to grassroots politics in examining the second transition from employment-based policies to income-based poor relief policies (Pierson 2001). Second, scholars who consider grassroots activism mostly examine the influence of welfare system changes on grassroots groups. They are interested in how social movements respond to *changing* welfare policies, rather than how welfare policies respond to *changing* social movements (Pierson 2001; Martin 2008). When grassroots groups are taken into account, it is mostly related to the way in which social movements resist the elimination of employment-based benefits, sometimes managing to force the government to step back (Weiss 1998). However, as Pierson argues, the transformation of welfare systems cannot be reduced to economic and structural changes but should be seen as a complex interplay of social and political forces.

Government actors face pressures and find motivations both for welfare austerity and populism that are shaped by the changing dynamics and compositions of social forces at large (Pierson 2001).

Political Explanations of Contemporary Welfare System Change

Questions about whether contemporary welfare system changes have been affected by grassroots movements have remained largely underexplored. The masses' policy preferences have a buttressing effect on many welfare states and there is theoretical reason to expect that citizens' opposition to cuts in social programs would be consequential (Erikson, MacKuen, and Stimson 2002; Stimson, MacKuen, and Erikson 1995; Wlezien 1995; cf. Burstein 1998). Yet demonstrating a causal chain between social movements and welfare outcomes in a systematic way has often been difficult (Skocpol and Amenta 1986; Giugni 1998). This is partly because of a lack of data on social movements. Grassroots sociopolitical activity data beyond labor strike statistics is little available. The main problem derives from the structuralist limitations dominating the existing literature. To overcome this limitation in the theory, political concepts and perspectives are needed in the analysis of the welfare transformation. Specifically, the concepts of political containment and political mobilization from the previous literature should be revisited and then applied to understand the second welfare shift. In this sense, the effect of social movements should be considered to explain contemporary welfare system change. Although these concepts are derived from the literature on the rise of employment-based welfare systems, the main theoretical inspiration connecting grassroots politics to income-based social assistance is the literature stimulated by Frances Fox Piven and Richard Cloward in the 1970s. The US welfare system has always been largely founded on income-based policies, and thus the US experience can be enlightening to understand the current global changes in welfare systems elsewhere. Hence, this book uses the concepts of political containment and mobilization and, considering the Turkish case, tests the Fox Piven and Cloward hypothesis that public welfare is driven by social unrest, rather than social need. The hypothesis, which will be explained below, states that in times of social turmoil, social assistance programs expand as a means of establishing control over the disorderly, but when turmoil subsides, they contract (Fox Piven and Cloward 1971).

The ways in which urban unrest in the 1960s affected the expansion of the Aid to Families with Dependent Children in the US was the starting point of this discussion in the US welfare literature. The neo-Marxist theories of the 1970s and 1980s described the welfare state as a control mechanism to contain actual and potential insurgent groups—especially labor movements with rising bargaining power and militancy, as well as racial groups in the US. Fox Piven and Cloward's pathbreaking work, *Regulating the Poor*, claimed that in order to maintain order and legitimacy, the modern state responded to racial and working-class insurgencies by expanding income-based poor relief programs. In times of social turmoil, relief systems expanded as a means of establishing control over the disorderly. However, when turmoil subsided, social assistance contracted (Fox Piven and Cloward 1971). Thus, this theory suggests that the independent variable for relief outcomes is not social need, but social disorder. Following the work of Fox Piven and Cloward, many scholars have analyzed in what ways and to what effect welfare/relief systems responded positively to the urban riots in the United States, so as to pacify socially dangerous populations. Another common subject of analysis was how black rebellions in the 1960s and 1970s enabled disadvantaged groups to gain significant welfare benefits (Issac and Kelly 1981; Jennings 1983; Schram and Turbett 1983; Chamlin 1989; Hicks and Swank 1981; Hicks and Swank 1981; Welch 1975; Fording 1997).

Fox Piven and Cloward's thesis may help us to understand the recent welfare policy changes in Turkey (and in many other countries) that involve the expansion of social assistance programs targeting the poor. Over the last three decades, there have been remarkable changes in grassroots politics at the global level, which have likely shaped welfare reforms. As such, it is necessary to return to concepts of political containment and mobilization to explore the second systemic transition of welfare systems. There is a new, large group of the world's most disadvantaged sectors—people of the global slums, who have acquired wide political significance over the last couple of decades. Fox Piven and Cloward's claim that mass turbulence by poor people's movements produces social spending concessions needs to be examined in light of recent emerging economies. At the time they made their argument, the US welfare system was expanding poor relief. This was not, however, the dominant mode of welfare provision in many other countries, where welfare provision was done predominantly through employment-based policies. Yet, at present, it is taken for granted that income-based poor relief is becoming a worldwide trend. In this regard, Fox Piven and Cloward's thesis needs revisiting and consideration, given the growing political weight of the informal proletariat.

Structural factors are translated into policy through the mediation of political factors. They set up the constraints within which political factors determine the eventual trajectory of welfare changes. These mechanisms involve conflicts among competing political actors, mainstream and nonmainstream. The key factors determining the systemic shift in welfare provision are the threat of social unrest and competition among political parties, which together involve the containment and mobilization of the grassroots. A thorough political explanation of welfare system change must include political containment as well as political mobilization as influential factors. An argument limited to patronage relations, populism, and electoral competition will not be sufficient and will overlook the security concerns of the Turkish state. At the same time, an exclusive focus on political containment would miss out the pressures that parliamentary liberal democracy places on the rulers. Indeed, only a joint analysis of political containment and mobilization can provide a comprehensive understanding of the political determinants of welfare system change.

Global Changes in Grassroots Politics: The Rise of the Informal Proletariat

As the central grassroots dynamic of the expansion of global welfare programs, the informal proletariat of poor slums has become the major grassroots political group in the contemporary world. In *Planet of Slums*, Mike Davis has called global slums the new center of sociopolitical conflict and dynamism. For Davis, the debt crisis of the 1970s, the subsequent structural adjustment policies led by the International Monetary Fund and the World Bank, processes of agricultural deregulation as well as de-peasantization, and finally expanding civil/ethnic wars and conflicts in regional peripheries have created push instead of pull factors, which led to the rapid exodus of rural populations into the cities (Davis 2004). In cities that are unable to absorb this migration via formal networks of employment and accommodation, large slum areas, as places of surplus population, have appeared. Today, there are roughly one billion slum dwellers—a figure estimated to double in the next three decades. In many Third World metropolises such as Kinshasa, Khartoum, Dar es Salaam, Dhaka, Lima, and Istanbul, as well as in First World ones such as Paris or Los Angeles, new slums are located at the spatial margins, enveloping absolute poverty as the permanent urban experience.

Global slum dwellers make up the "fastest growing, and most unprecedented, social class on earth"—the informal proletariat (Davis 2006). This distinction between the formal and informal proletariat comes from Alejandro Portes and Kelly Hoffman (2003). On the one hand, Portes and Hoffman argue that the formal proletariat consists of the workers in industry, services, and agriculture that are protected by existing labor laws. On the other, the informal proletariat is composed of those workers who are not incorporated into fully commodified, legally regulated working relations, but rather survive at the margins through a wide variety of subsistence and semiclandestine economic activities. The informal proletariat is "the sum of own-account workers minus professionals and technicians, domestic servants, and paid and unpaid workers in microenterprises" (Portes and Hoffman 2003, 54). Portes and Hoffman further argue that the formal proletariat of the pre-1980 period has declined over the last few decades (in Latin America, the percentage of formal job creation has dropped from 60% to 20% in 30 years), while the informal proletariat has grown to comprise two-fifths of the global workforce (Portes and Hoffman, 2003). This rising majority works without any social security, largely in the service and manufacturing industries and trade, as well as in self-account jobs or direct subsistence activities, as liquor sellers, street vendors, cleaners, washers, rag pickers, child minders, and prostitutes. Moreover, many studies have shown how these workers, though they operate outside of the legal framework, are in fact linked to the modern sector and to capitalist accumulation in general. For this reason, they are labeled the informal proletariat (Beneria 1989; Yörük 2010). In line with this, the slums have become the home of the informal proletariat (Davis 2006).

Various scholars of urbanization designate this surplus population by different terms, such as the previously mentioned informal proletariat (Portes and Hoffman 2003; Davis 2006), the socially excluded (Munk 2006), the reserve army (Arrighi 1990), passive proletarianization (Mitschein et al. 1989), the new poor (Keyder 2005), or the urban outcast (Wacquant 2008). There are quite similar social experiences and political consequences. The crisis of capitalism in the 1970s inverted the structural positions of formal and informal workers and created informality as the primary form of livelihood and absolute poverty as the demographically dominant urban experience in many cities (Baulch 2006; Room, Lawson, and Laczko 1989; Lipton and Maxwell 1992; Maxwell 2003; Goode and Maskovsky 2001; Kazemipur 2000). These slum dwellers are massively concentrated in shantytowns as global residuum, yet they lack the "strategic economic power of socialized labor," largely utilized by formal workers until the 1980s (Davis 2004). Davis also claims that when, where, or how the social grievances in the slums turn into political turmoil is very unpredictable (Davis 2006). Davis then asks whether the slums with growing misery are great "volcanoes waiting to erupt" against the winners of neoliberalism or whether the competition among the informal proletariat fueled by this impoverishment leads them toward self-destroying intracommunal violence (Davis 2004, 28). In other words, Davis wonders to what extent the informal proletariat is becoming the historical agency or to what extent the protests of the poor shantytown masses are becoming occasionally explosive in response to consumption crises. Moreover, to what extent can these slum disturbances be easily managed by clientelism, populist spectacle, and appeals to ethnic unity? (Davis 2004).

For Giovanni Arrighi, capitalist accumulation inherently and periodically creates legitimation crises as a consequence of the immiseration of the so-called reserve army of the proletariat (the unemployed, disguisedly unemployed, or the excluded), as the state and capital cease to "feed" the surplus population (Arrighi 1990). Long ago, in *Capital*, Karl Marx pointed out the basic antagonism in a capitalist society, referring to a similar group of the population. For Marx, capitalist accumulation, leading to centralization and concentration of capital, creates the conditions under which the active army of the proletariat grows in social power, because they acquire a high degree of bargaining power: As they unionize and come together in large factories, their level of proletarian militancy increases. The active army becomes increasingly demanding, leading the state and capital to allocate increasing resources toward meeting their demands for higher wages, better work conditions, and more control over the production process.

In the meantime, this process generates another outcome: the increasing number and worsening misery of the industrial reserve army.

> The greater the social wealth, the functioning capital, the extent and energy of its growth, and therefore also the absolute mass of the pro-

letariat and the productivity of its labor, the greater is the industrial reserve army. The same causes which develop the expansive power of capital, also develop the labor-power at its disposal. The relative mass of the industrial reserve army thus increases with the potential energy of wealth. But the greater this reserve army in proportion to the active labor-army, the greater is the mass of a consolidated surplus population, whose misery is in inverse ratio to the amount of torture it has to undergo in the form of labor. The more extensive, finally, the pauperized section of the working class and the industrial reserve army, the greater is official pauperism. This is the absolute general law of capitalist accumulation. (Marx 1976, 798)

Marx stressed that the reserve army grows in number and misery and raises demands in order to alleviate its misery. However, as capital and the state increasingly allocate their resources to the active army, they have trouble meeting the demands of the reserve army at the same time. In other words, meeting the rising demands of both parts of the proletariat becomes impossible. This impossibility creates a legitimacy crisis with which capital and the state must cope, and this, for Marx, is the fundamental social antagonism that capitalist accumulation produces.

For Arrighi, the legitimacy crisis emanating out of the structural incompatibility of meeting the rising demands of the active army and the rising misery of the reserve army is a globally ongoing process. This has also been exacerbated by the existing ethnic and national hierarchies. As Arrighi put it:

If you look at the process globally—where the reserve army is not just the unemployed, but also the disguisedly unemployed and the excluded—then there is a status division between the two. Nationality has been used by segments of the working class, of the active army, to differentiate themselves from the global reserve army. At a national level, this is less clear. If you take the United States or Europe, it's much less apparent that there is actually a status difference between the active and reserve army. But with immigrants currently coming from countries that are much poorer, anti-immigration sentiments which are a manifestation of this tendency to create status distinctions within the working class have grown. So it's a very complicated picture, particularly if you look at transnational migration flows and at the situation where the reserve army is primarily concentrated in the global South rather than the North. (Arrighi 2009)

While we know much about the *economics* of the urban informal sector, its definition and measurement, we know little about its *politics* (Sanyal 1991; Agarwala 2009). Scholars mostly examine the declining formal proletarian activism in the face of economic globalization (Castells 2004; Tilly 1995; Zolberg 1995). More recently, there have been a few studies of how informal workers' struggles improved their working conditions in Latin America and Africa (Carr et al. 2000; Chowdhury 2003; Sanyal 1991; Sharma and Antony 2001). There is also an emerging literature on how public policies have responded to the political activism of the emerging informal sectors. Informal workers in India and Mexico appear to have organized themselves along class lines, using electoral power to make social welfare claims on the state, and they have managed to obtain some gains (Agarwala 2008; Heller 1999; Cross 1998). Yet we still lack a systematic analysis of whether policy-makers at the macro level take informal politics significantly into account.

The Informal Proletariat, Identity Politics, and Welfare

Social assistance programs in some emerging countries, including Turkey, are directed toward specific ethnic or racial groups. Scholars have argued that the Workers' Party of Brazil has used Bolsa Familia as a highly effective tool to garner political support from Afro-Brazilians of northern Brazil and the slums (*favelas*) where the government competes with drug traffickers (Moura 2007; Hunter and Power 2007). Specifically, Souza's logistic regression analysis of Brazilian census data demonstrates that Afro-Brazilians are more likely, with statistical significance, to receive conditional cash transfers after controlling for intervening socioeconomic variables (Souza 2006). The Chinese system has shown signs of similar strategies for the political containment of ethnic and urban unrest using social assistance. The social base of public assistance in China has shifted from more privileged social groups toward the urban poor in order to "avoid serious social unrest from those who were left behind by economic reforms" (Gao 2006). In Mexico, the Prospera social assistance program has been directed to the

Indigenous minority as a counterinsurgency strategy against the Zapatista unrest (Yörük, Öker, and Şarlak 2019)

Possible political motivations to direct social assistance programs to specific ethnic/racial/religious groups are related to the identity politics of informal workers. The political struggles of informal workers usually become manifest in growing ethnic, religious, and gender-based inequalities to produce novel threats to political stability. Wallerstein (1976) has claimed that the lower classes of the contemporary world heavily overlap with ethnic distinctions. According to Arrighi (2009), the surplus population of the contemporary world is increasingly acquiring an *ethnic characteristic on the national level* and *national characteristics on the global level* and creating increasing political instability (Arrighi 2009). Wacquant (2008) has emphasized that the contemporary rise of ethnic urban marginality in the American ghettos, Brazilian favelas, and French *banlieues* tends to coalesce urban inequalities, ethnic cleavages, and political unrest. Uprisings in Egypt, Tunisia, Haiti, and Greece in the 2010s are likely to show that the poor people of the world are not passive victims of neoliberalism, but rather they emerge as important political threats capable of paralyzing existing political regimes. Harvard economist Dani Rodrik (1997) argued that globalization created deeper class divisions between the rich and the poor that would politically harm both sides of the divide. He has specifically recommended to the International Monetary Fund and the World Bank that a reorientation from pensions to antipoverty programs would address the political challenges of globalization. As will be shown in the following chapter, these institutions, in fact, adopted this policy shift in the 2000s. It is now worth asking whether welfare provision has been used to contain this political threat and to mobilize the social forces existing within the slums.

Religious movements such as Islamism and Pentecostal Christianity as the "religions of the informal periphery," ethnic militias, street gangs, and revolutionary social movements emerge as the agencies able to mobilize the global residuum. A good indicator of this trend is the strategic analyses of governmental security organizations that Davis mentions, including of the United Nations and the US Department of State, concerned with the rising threat from the slums. For the RAND Corporation, a US Air Force–based think tank, the urbanization of poverty has created the "urbanization of insurgency," and governments should develop counterinsurgency strategies for slums that are now the weakest link in the new world order. Governments are advised to address the sociological phenomenon of excluded populations (Davis 2006). Although social movements in slums tend to be episodic and discontinuous, they still possess the capacity to pose a threat to political stability, especially when mobilized by organized oppositional groups, increasingly on the streets, rather than inside factories (Walton and Seddon 1994). Hence, to what extent can we now predict that growing ethnic conflicts and class-based poverty overlap in the world's slums and produce a novel political agency?

Social Movements and the "Welfare–Terrorism Nexus"

The social policy effects of social movements and conflict in general are largely underexamined in the social sciences. Most of the effects of social movements on welfare policies, if any, are unintended consequences (Gamson 1990; Isaac and Kelly 1981; Giugni 1998). If the shift to income-based policies is a response to the rising political significance of the informal proletariat, this would probably be an unintended consequence. Most of the time, when grassroots groups struggle for a demand, and when they are provided some gains, these gains are not actually what these groups have been struggling for, but rather they result from governments' containment strategies (Rucht 1992; also see Giugni 1994). Yet empirical work that focuses explicitly on the unintended consequences of social movements is quite rare (Deng 1997; Paul et al. 1997).

There are numerous arguments and evidence that show how social policies serve to contain social unrest and how political unrest is linked to the social welfare situation in a country (Burgoon 2006; Paxson 2002). International institutions such as the World Bank, the International Labour Organization, the G20, and the Organization for Security and Co-operation in Europe, however, have only recently begun to express this view more explicitly. Rodrik (1997) argued in his influential essay on globalization and welfare policies, "Sense and Nonsense in the Globalization Debate," that contrary to common belief, growing international trade has brought about increasing government spending on welfare safety nets and income transfers. He argues that the welfare state has always been the "flip side of the open economy" (Rodrik 1997, 26). For Rodrik, globalization creates deeper class divisions between the rich and the poor that would be politically unstable. He suggested that individual governments not retreat behind national protectionist walls, but rather "complement the external strategy of liberalization with an internal strategy of compensation, training, and social insurance for those groups who are most at risk" (Rodrik 1997, 35). He specifically proposed that a reorientation from pensions to antipoverty programs would address the political challenges of globalization. The tendency was also expressed by James D. Wolfensohn, the ex-president of the World Bank, an institution that recently seems to be the most influential international actor affecting the Turkish welfare system. In his essay entitled "Fight Terrorism by Ending Poverty," he argues that civil wars do not necessarily stem from ethnic diversity but instead from a mixture of factors; most important, poverty and exclusion propel ethnic diversities into ethnic conflict. Thus, as a measure for countering terrorist activities and ethnic strife, he suggests that governments should act to "eradicate poverty, promote inclusion and social justice, and to bring the marginalized into the mainstream of the global society and economy" (Wolfensohn 2002, 42).

According to the World Bank, one of the central objectives of these programs could be to prevent the possibility of (economic) reforms resulting in a deprivation of a large share of the population, "or losers who are politically too powerful to ignore" (Barr 1995, 3). There may be opposition to social safety nets by a country's "financial elites" but "they can win political capital amongst the poor" (Pelham, Clay, and Braunholz 2011, 96). Even those authors from the World Bank who are skeptical about the possibly positive results of welfare programs believe that such programs may contribute to political stability when unemployment levels are high (Fretwell, Benus, and O'Leary 1999, 31).

Social welfare spending is a useful governmental tool for reducing civil conflicts, with a dual effect. On the one hand, favorable social policy measures can assimilate oppositional movements and bring about legitimacy for governments by decreasing people's grievances. Authorities can "affect the attitude and voting choice of the poor, who would otherwise oppose the government" (Taydas and Dursun 2012, 273–76). On the other hand, social spending by the government can also reduce the chances of political insurgency by subverting (part of) the motives behind the insurgency.

An emerging literature on what has been called the "welfare-terrorism nexus" provides insight into the relationship between welfare provision and grassroots politics. Developed mostly by conservative scholars, this literature has produced important contributions to help fill the scholarly gap between welfare provision and political and social movements. This literature is particularly interesting because its definition of terrorism overlaps with the definition of social unrest in the social movement literature. In one of the founding articles of this (emerging) literature, Brian Burgoon argues that "social welfare policies may reduce international and domestic terrorism" by "diminishing grievances underlying extremist action." Analyzing 93 countries with cross-sectional and time series data since 1983, he concludes that "a country's welfare efforts negatively correlate with transnational or total terrorist incidents on its soil, as well as transnational terrorism perpetrated by its citizens" (Burgoon 2006, 176). These results are valid even when including alternative controls, such as civil as opposed to interstate conflict; civil rights as opposed to democracy; measures of income inequality or horizontal inequality; or GDP per capita. Burgoon asserts that welfare efforts reduce poverty, inequality, and socioeconomic insecurity, and thus they diminish incentives to commit, support, or tolerate terrorism. Other scholars agree and argue that poverty and inequality stimulate feelings of injustice and thus can stimulate the mobilizing capacity of terrorists, fueling civil and ethnic conflict (Auvinen and Nafziger 1999; Gurr 1970; Fearon and Laitin 2003; Chen 2003; Paxson 2002; Li and Schaub 2004). Burgoon further argues that "terrorist" groups, including, most importantly, radical Islamists and radical leftists, provide economic and social security for the poor whenever governments do not provide it, in order to garner popular support. As Burgoon (2006, 182) suggests:

At any given level of poverty, development, or inequality, many religious communities provide shadow social services that make them imperfect substitutes for social policy in addressing poverty (Gill and Lundsgaarde 2004; Chen 2003). Examples of this phenomenon can be found across a range of denominations and countries—from child care and elderly assistance among Orthodox Jews in Israel, to maternity and sickness benefits among catechist groups in Ghana, to cash assistance and social services among Muslim groups in the Palestinian Territories, to poor relief from Muslim and Hindu organizations in India, to cash payments and services among Christian churches in the United States (Townsend 1994; Landau 1993; Gruber 2003). If welfare and (some) religious organization are imperfect substitutes, more generous social policy should reduce citizens' "demand" for substitute services, in turn diminishing reliance on religious and other organizations that recruit members partly on material bases.

Empirically assessing the influence of social policies on homegrown terrorist activities in 15 Western European countries between 1980 and 2003, Krieger and Meierrieks (2009) argue that social policies such as health, unemployment benefits, and active labor market programs indirectly reduce terrorist activities by ameliorating poor short-run and long-run socioeconomic conditions. They also show that different typologies of welfare capitalisms, as originally categorized by Esping-Andersen, have different capacities to cope with terrorist activities. This shows that the effectiveness of the welfare state on counterterrorism not only depends on the level of social expenditures but also on the level of de-commodification. In a similar vein, Erica Chenoweth suggests that terrorist activities can be diminished by increased welfare spending, which would increase the legitimacy of the government as well as "ameliorate the major grievances of terrorists" and "reduce residual public sympathies for violent political expression" (Chenoweth 2007, 3).

Social policy can reduce what Frances Stewart calls "horizontal inequality," that is, economic inequality that coincides with ethnic or religious divisions in a society, by leveling out income differentials between different social groups and thus lowering the likelihood of terrorism (Stewart 2002). It has a larger ideological function that is independent of its capacity to alleviate poverty (Burgoon 2006). Social policy develops "citizens' *perceived* (as opposed to objective), economic security" (Burgoon 2006, 183) and creates ideological attraction for government policies as opposed to radical groups' imperfect substitute for economic security and equality. Therefore, even for the many "groups in some countries for whom social policy does little to diminish economic insecurity . . . there is little reason to believe that they will ever be worse than neutral for insecurity" (Burgoon 2006). Thus, even when social policy programs do not alleviate material conditions, these programs should still be implemented in order to generate an ideological imagination of a "caring state" that would discourage support for political extremism.

In light of these existing studies, I seek to explain the recent transformation of the Turkish welfare system, in which social assistance policies have replaced employment-based provision of welfare, as part of a global trend. Most scholarship, both about Turkey and about other countries, has explained this shift as a response to demographic and structural changes including aging populations, the decline in the economic weight of industry, and the informalization of labor. Structural changes underlie changing welfare policies, but there are fundamental political causes of the transformation, which have mediated structural pressures, shaping the specific policies, determining the timing of their enactment, and influencing the way benefits are distributed.

The relationship between recent changes in welfare provision and grassroots politics has been studied by different social movement scholars. Most of this literature, however, has looked at the ways in which social movements (or terrorism/conflict, in other terminologies) responded to welfare state changes. For example, while formal workers' movements have resisted cuts in employment-based benefits, income-based social assistance is used to reduce the politicization of the poor by radical groups. Yet, in these existing studies, grassroots politics has been considered as the dependent variable, while changes in welfare policies have been the independent variable. I look at the opposite causal direction and analyze how the transformation of the Turkish welfare systems has been shaped by the actions of grassroots groups and government responses to these actions.

My approach is informed by scholars who have argued that during the 20th century state authorities expanded welfare provision not so much in response to social needs, but rather in order to contain or mobilize potentially dangerous populations of urban workers. Employment-based welfare is being replaced by social assistance in large part because state authorities now see the informally employed urban population as more important—and more dangerous—than formally employed workers. In particular, Turkish authorities are shifting welfare provision to the urban poor especially in order to contain discontent among the growing population of Kurdish migrants in Istanbul and other Turkish cities. The governing Justice and Development Party has particularly targeted Kurds for social assistance in order to win support—and diminish opposition—among this highly organized and contentious population. A shift in welfare policies from employment-based social assistance policies to income-based social assistance policies is a global phenomenon, and Turkey and other emerging economies have been in the forefront of this trend. The findings of this book, therefore, will have broader implications, contributing to our understanding of the global trends in welfare provision.

CHAPTER 2

The Transformation of the Turkish Welfare System

A common perception among welfare scholars is that the welfare systems in many countries, including Turkey, have largely retrenched during the post-1980 neoliberal era (Korpi and Palme 2003; Elveren 2008; Dorlach 2019). Turkish welfare system expenditures as a percentage of gross domestic product, however, have increased from 2.2% in 1980 to 12.5% in 2016 (OECD 2019) (see fig. 1). In this chapter, I will illustrate that during the last four decades, the Turkish welfare system has undergone a transformation from employment-based social security policies to income-based social assistance policies, while the welfare state in general has expanded in total budget and coverage (Buğra and Keyder 2006; Yörük 2012; Göçmen 2014).[1] This development has essentially involved a transformation in the main eligibility criteria for welfare provision.

Under employment-based social security policies, the welfare system provides benefits and social protection to formally employed citizens and their dependents. The level of protection and benefits depends on beneficiaries' type of employment—private sector, public sector, or self-employed. Under income-based social assistance policies, income level is the main

---

1. Employment-based social security programs are welfare programs that grant benefits only to citizens who are formally employed. These programs provide benefits including old age pensions, sickness insurance, health care insurance, and unemployment compensation. Thus, the eligibility criterion for these programs is employment status. Income-based social assistance programs are programs that grant cash or in-kind benefits, as well as social services, to citizens determined to be impoverished. Thus, the eligibility criterion for these programs is income level.

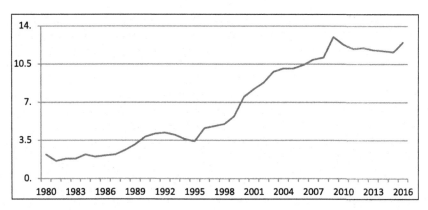

Fig. 1. Turkish total public social expenditures as percentage of GDP (1980–2016)

criterion, regardless of one's employment status. If a citizen's household income is determined through means testing to be lower than the poverty threshold, then the citizen is determined to be eligible for certain welfare benefits such as social assistance and free health care. In short, the transformation of the Turkish welfare system since the 1970s can be characterized by two general trends: (1) an overall expansion of welfare provision in terms of coverage and expenditures, and (2) a shift in the main criterion of welfare provision from employment status to income level.

Until the 1990s, the logic of welfare provision in Turkey was primarily based on providing formally employed workers and their families with social insurance for pensions and health care (Grütjen 2008). This system excluded the majority of those employed in informal rural and urban economies from receiving any benefits. Since the 1990s, however, income level has become as important as employment status in determining welfare provision. Means-tested social assistance programs, designed to provide the informal poor with in-kind or cash transfers, as well as free health care, have rapidly expanded (Buğra and Keyder 2006; Elveren 2008; Günal 2008). These programs have coincided with declines in welfare generosity for the formal sectors, as the necessary labor tenure entitling a worker to a pension has significantly increased and eligibility conditions have tightened (Cosar and Yegenoglu 2009). Thus, the Turkish welfare system, once based only on employment status, has expanded into a system with close-to-universal coverage, based partially on employment status and partially on income level.

In the post-1980 era, the shift in Turkish welfare policies has coincided with a macro-level shift in economic policies, similar to trends occurring in many other developing countries. After the 1980s, the national developmentalist economy of the postwar period, which was based on import-substitutionist industrialization, was replaced by an economic system focused on exports and guided by a neoliberal economic policy (Keyder 2004; Yeldan 2006). The import-substitutionist industrialization policies began with the 1960 military coup, supported by the United States, which aimed to generate a national bourgeoisie and a working class, whose relations would be regulated under the Keynesian logic of the 1962 constitution. This developmentalist system created an extensive employment-based welfare system that provided many rights to formal sector workers. However, the 1980 military coup, also strongly supported by the United States, was followed by a rapid succession of neoliberal policies that opened Turkish markets to global economic flows and restructured capital-labor relations favoring the bourgeoisie.

A quantified analysis of welfare legislation also exposes the nature of Turkish welfare policy changes. I have classified social welfare legislation into quantitative indices, according to the direction of change those laws entailed, creating an index of post-1980 welfare policy laws enacted by the Turkish parliament: (1) laws that expand employment-based social security programs and rights, (2) laws that retrench employment-based social security programs and rights, and (3) laws that expand income-based welfare programs and rights. No legislation thus far has retrenched income-based social welfare benefits. In other words, the first category consists of laws that enhance the welfare rights of the formal proletariat, the second of laws that cut the welfare rights of the formal proletariat, and the third of laws that increase the welfare rights of the poor—the informal proletariat. This indexing does not consider the extent of change that a law brings about and represents each law with one unit of change in either direction. Obviously, some laws have more significant ramifications than others. Nevertheless, rather than quantifying the significance of each law, I indicate the direction that each law signals, as this provides a clearer view of trends over time. I have indexed 134 social welfare laws into one or more of the above categories. The laws do not necessarily lead in any of the three directions, and some signal more than one direction (e.g., improving both employment and income-based benefits). The results of the indexing are presented in figure 2.

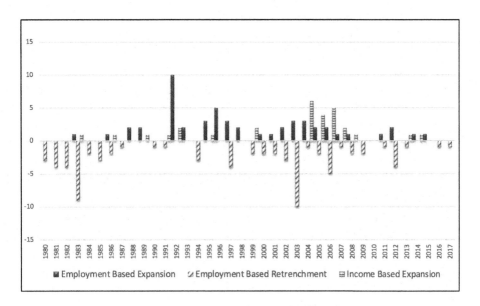

Fig. 2. Patterns of employment-based and income-based welfare law enactment

Figure 2 indicates three distinct patterns in the trajectory of welfare policy law-making:

1. Employment-based benefits were mainly retrenched in the 1980s and 2000s.
2. Employment-based benefits expanded in the 1990s, especially in the early and mid-1990s.
3. Income-based benefits were introduced in the late 1980s and early 1990s but significantly expanded in the 2000s.

This chapter traces the trajectory of employment-based social security policies and income-based social assistance policies. Welfare provision has gradually transitioned from exclusively employment-based policies to an amalgamation of income and employment-based policies. This has involved a relative decline in employment-based policies in terms of coverage, budget, and generosity, accompanied by a boom of income-based social assistance policies since the 1990s.

The Postwar Development of Employment-Based Social Security Policies in Turkey

As in many other developing countries, the modern Turkish welfare system was established after World War II. This system was primarily based on employment-based social security policies. Previously, the late Ottoman Empire period legacy of poor relief, as well as a few policies targeting workers, had already constituted a fragmentary set of social welfare policies. Nevertheless, the establishment of the Ministry of Labor and Social Security in 1945 initiated the process of developing an institutionalized, centralized, and extensive welfare system in Turkey. Various welfare institutions, employment policies in state-owned enterprises, agricultural subsidies, and government policies concerning informal housing culminated in an extensive welfare system consisting of formal and informal components (Buğra 2008). By the late 1970s, employment-based benefits reached large segments of the population (almost half), as family members were covered through dependency relations (Özbek 2006).

In 1945, the Ministry of Labor and Social Security was established, with the objective of managing rising unemployment, regulating worker-employer relations, stimulating job security, and administering housing and health benefits for workers. The postwar welfare system depended on different institutions to distribute social security and health care benefits according to beneficiaries' position within the labor market. According to Buğra and Keyder (2006, 212), this welfare system maintained a corporatist character, providing "differential health and pension benefits to formally employed heads of household according to their status at work." Private and public sector workers were covered by the Social Insurance Institution (SSK) founded in 1946; employees in the state sector by the Retirement Fund founded in 1954; the self-employed by Bağ-Kur founded in 1971; and agricultural workers and peasants by two (relatively insignificant) institutions established in the 1980s. This system was mainly organized by central government institutions and largely depended on formally employed heads of families (Gough 1996; Saraceno 2002). While these institutions were formally independent from the government, they also benefited from public status, meaning that contributions to these funds were mandatory and usually deducted from payrolls. However, this configuration led to a fragmented and hierarchical structure, not only because the quality and reliability of welfare services differed between institutions by favoring those in civil services and modern sectors but also because it excluded almost 40% of the population from welfare provision (Buğra and Keyder 2006).

In 1954, the Retirement Fund (Emekli Sandığı) was established in order to provide social security and health insurance for civil servants. The fund assumed the task of providing social security in case of retirement or the inability to work, and for workers' dependents in case of the death of a civil servant. The fund was charged with paying old-age and disability pensions for civil servants, as well as pensions for widows and orphans of employees in the state sector. Later amendments to the fund also dictated the responsibility of providing free health care for state sector employees and their dependents.[2]

The Social Insurance Institution was designed to provide retirement pensions, free health care, and sickness insurance for workers in the formal sector. Until the consolidation of all security institutions in the 2000s, the SSK system was funded by collecting premiums from workers and employers. The Social Insurance Institution provided health services through countrywide hospitals owned by the institution (Buğra 2007; Özbek 2006). In 1964, a new law expanded the coverage of social security to include a wide variety of workers from workplaces of varying sizes and different sectors. Social security rights also expanded, and eligibility conditions were loosened. Health insurance, for example, was expanded to cover dependents of the insured worker. In addition, the retirement age for women was lowered from 60 to 55. New calculations of retirement pensions resulted in higher pension amounts, and allowances that workers received in case of disease or disability (previously limited to 20 months) were rendered unlimited.

The expansion of the Social Insurance Institution into a generous welfare system occurred after the new 1961 constitution following the 1960 coup d'état. This constitution embraced import-substitutionist developmentalism (a trade and economic policy that replaces foreign imports with domestic production), defined vari-

---

2. The fund owns a large quantity of real estate properties, stocks, and bonds, as well as commercial enterprises (most importantly hotels), which allows for more efficient management of financial resources. A 1969 law increased the pensions of civil servants from 50% to 70% of their last salary. This law also included another 100,000 people in the Retirement Fund system and equalized benefits for members of the military and civil bureaucracy (Güvercin 2004; Özbek 2006).

ous social and economic rights of workers, and encumbered governments with the responsibility of expanding these rights. Article 41 of the constitution, for example, declared that "economic and social life will be regulated with the purpose of developing the standards of living which would befit the principles of justice, full-employment, and human dignity for all." Similarly, Article 42 states that "the state will protect employees and encourage employment by taking necessary social, economic, and fiscal measures with the purpose of increasing the living standards of employees and improving working standards." In a similar vein, Article 43 affirms that "everyone has the right to social security. It is the obligation of the state to establish social security institutions in order to realize this right" (Özbek 2006; Güvercin 2004).

Import-substitutionist   developmentalism,   which   embraced employment-based welfare benefits, was crystallized in the Five-Year Development Plans modeled after USSR developmentalism. Since 1963, nine subsequent development plans were published by the State Planning Institution. The first development plan materialized the welfare and social security system outlined in the 1961 constitution. In the section entitled "Economic and Social Objectives," the plan stated that "in the following fifteen years, the fragmented and narrow social security would be consolidated and expanded into an extensive social security system." The plan introduced this need for social security as a measure to overcome social injustice. Concrete steps in the 15-year plan included the establishment of a comprehensive social security system that would introduce an unemployment insurance fund and provide retirement and health insurance for all, including the self-employed, artisans, and peasantry in the social security system through payment of insurance premiums (Özbek 2006).

In 1971, a separate institution for the social security of the self-employed, artisans, and independent laborers was established, as envisaged in the First Five-Year Development Plan eight years previously. This institution, called Bağ-Kur, was initially intended to provide old age, disability, and death insurance for its beneficiaries. In 1985, health insurance was also included in the services that the Bağ-Kur system would provide. Inclusion of the peasantry in the social security system through Bağ-Kur took place relatively late, in 1983, at which point adult peasants with no other social security were covered (Güvercin 2004; Özbek 2006).

The Neoliberal Trajectory of Social Security Policies in Turkey

Between the 1950s and the 1980s, the Turkish welfare system mainly provided basic benefits and services (such as pension and free health care) to citizens according to their employment status. The logic of welfare provision in Turkey was almost exclusively based on providing formally employed workers and their families with social insurance for pensions and health care (Mello 2007; Grutjen 2008). Pensions and health benefits were distributed through different institutions according to beneficiaries' employment status, including state and private sector employees, the self-employed, and peasants.

After the 1980s, neoliberalism dramatically restructured employment-based social security provision in Turkey. While the generosity of benefits has significantly declined as a result of austerity measures (except for a brief period in the 1990s when electoral competition and workers' unrest halted the neoliberal trend), the coverage and expenditure of social security institutions have continued to expand as a result of the growth of the urban capitalist economy. As such, the neoliberal period in Turkey has seen the expansion of both employment-based and income-based policies, though the latter has been expanding more rapidly than the former. As a percentage of the total population, coverage of employment-based programs has significantly increased. Yet, as a percentage of the urban population, these programs' coverage has remained stable or even declined over the course of the last four decades, as Turkey has undergone rapid urbanization, raising the urban percentage of the total population from 29% in 1970 to 71% in 2009.

After the 1980s, eligibility conditions for employment-based policies tightened, and benefits significantly declined. Alongside increasing insurance premiums and decreasing pensions, the necessary labor tenure entitling a worker to a pension has significantly increased, and eligibility conditions have tightened (Coşar and Yeğenoğlu 2009). In the meantime, income-based social assistance benefits have become dramatically more extensive and generous. Indeed, Turkey has experienced a kind of social assistance boom especially since the 2000s. The income level of citizens has become an increasingly important criterion in determining whether or in what ways citizens may access public welfare. A new system of extensive social assistance and health care structures that target the poorest citizens and operate independently of employment status has become a substantive part of the Turkish welfare system (Agartan et al. 2007; Buğra 2008; Buğra and Keyder 2006; Yılmaz 2013; Yoltar 2009).

Finally, the public health care insurance system, which was previously based solely on employment status, has evolved in a trajectory through which income level has become a central criterion for health care insurance. The General Health Insurance system enacted in 2006 established that income level (in addition to employment status) would be the second criterion in determining the necessity and amount of insurance premiums. Thus, the health care system, which, together with retirement pensions, constitutes the backbone of the entire welfare system, has come to be increasingly based on income level. Hence, Turkey has seen a sharp increase in income-based social assistance policies, as well as a decline in benefits and a hardening of the eligibility criteria of employment-based policies vis-à-vis an expansion of income-based social assistance policies, which have become increasingly generous. In addition, new participation rules in the health care insurance system are dependent on income level.

The economic policy underlying the restructuring of the social security system consisted of structural adjustment, with export promotion through direct export subsidies, commodity trade liberalization, regulation of the foreign exchange system, and capital inflow. Together with a high inflation policy, which resulted in 75% inflation in 1989, real wages and pensions declined significantly during the 1980s. The share of wage labor in private manufacturing-added-value declined from 38% to 15% between 1979 and 1988. Union density declined by 65% (Cam 2002), and real wages hit bottom in 1989. During the period following the 1980 coup, employment-based benefits, alongside many economic advantages of the working classes in Turkey, began to erode. This erosion matched the global neoliberal trend that marked the post-1980 period. In Turkey, neoliberal policies were initiated by the 24 January Decisions, an economic policy plan announced by the government in 1980. These decisions ended the import-substitutionist policies characteristic of the period between 1960 and 1980:

> On the one hand, the government accepted an export-led growth strategy and sustained the external competitiveness of the Turkish economy through exchange rate policy and export subsidies. On the other hand, the 1980s witnessed a deliberate contraction in real wages, which aimed at producing an exportable surplus and

enhancing export competitiveness through lower labor costs. (Central Bank of the Republic of Turkey 2002)

The radical reforms in the Turkish political economy occurred first through the legislation of the military junta that ruled between 1980 and 1983, followed by those of the neoliberal Motherland Party government. The junta outlawed all political parties, leftist unions, strikes, and collective bargaining, passing new laws that would devastate the collective rights of formal sector workers. Between 1980 and 1983, the Labor Unions Law (no. 2821), Collective Bargaining Law (no. 2822), Political Parties Law (no. 2820), Associations Law (no. 2908), and Meetings and Protest Rallies Law (no. 2911) dramatically limited the strike and collective bargaining rights of workers, outlawing any relationship between political parties and labor unions and hardening the conditions for raising democratic demands. With these laws, solidarity strikes and non-wage-related strikes were outlawed, and governments were given the right to postpone strikes in order to protect national interests. The concept of national interest was defined ambiguously so as to cover, for example, national economic interests relating to export performance, thus enabling the government to easily suppress strikes (Buğra 2008, 200). These laws also placed extremely high sector and workplace thresholds (50% and 10%, respectively) for collective bargaining eligibility. Law No. 2316 enabled the control of the possessions of labor unions by state security institutions. Laws 2320, 2457, and 2762 placed upper limits on severance payments. Law No. 2422 of 1981 deteriorated the conditions of health and old age insurance for workers—workers began to pay 20% of health care costs, insurance premiums increased, and retirement pensions were lowered. A law enacted in April 1982 limited the levels of bonus allowances given to public and private sector employees. In 1981 and 1982, Laws No. 2429 and 2818 decreased the length of holidays for workers, and Laws No. 2495 and 2577 placed severe limitations on strikes. With Law No. 2645, the majority of executive board positions in the Social Insurance Institution (the social security institution for workers) was transferred from workers' representatives to assigned government officials. In 1983, Law No. 2929 removed the requirement that public enterprises employing a large number of workers have one worker representative. Law No. 2845 ordered that strike-related crimes be tried in State Security Courts (antiterrorism courts). And, in 1983, the Emergency State Rule, Law No. 2935, placed additional limitations on union rights.

After the junta, the Motherland Party government continued to enact antiworker policies. For example, it passed a law allowing the government to audit labor unions, followed by another law enabling public enterprises to employ contract workers. In 1985, the Free Trade Zone Law (no. 3218) established a 10-year strike ban in free trade zones. Law No. 3308 allowed large-scale enterprises to employ 10% of their workforce from vocational high schools, making it easier for the government to suppress strikes. In 1986, the government set up special security forces to take charge during labor strikes. Law No. 3246 set the minimum retirement age to 60 for men and 55 for women. Previously, there had been no age limit for retirement, which was based on the number of days for which insurance premiums were paid. Law No. 3299 inhibited labor organizing by expanding the coverage of firm-type contracts. Law No. 3300 terminated the Social Insurance Institution's housing loan services and placed the institution under strict governmental control. And, in 1987, Law No. 3395 enacted a number of changes to the calculation of retirement pensions, severely lowering pension amounts.

Due to an odd combination of intense electoral competition, labor unrest, and Kurdish insurgency, neoliberal policies were paused during most of the 1990s. Wages in the public sector increased by 143% while the rate of inflation was 75% between 1989 and 1993. Real wages increased by 90% between 1988 and 1991, accompanied by significant increases in civil servant salaries, public sector wages, social budget spending, and farm subsidies (Boratav 2000; Cam 2002).

> There was a major shift in the public expenditure accounts towards more socially desirable ventures. An overall increase in both the share and level of public salaries, and investments on social infrastructure enabled the working masses to attain improved living standards. (Boratav 2000, 2)

This populist period ended in 1994, when a deep crisis hit the economy. Since then, "the Turkish economy can be said to be operating under conditions of a truly open economy—a macroeconomic environment where both current and capital accounts are completely liberalized" (Boratav, Yeldan, and Köse 2000, 2). A deregulation of financial markets, a high inflation policy, declaration of the convertibility of Turkish lira, and layoffs were the main responses to increased wages. Through this "financial liberalization" and the inflow of speculative capital, the domestic economy experienced high levels of liquidity, which financed growing public expenditures (Oyvat 2011; Cam 2002). Between 1994 and 1999, after a brief period of populism, real wages and pensions began to decline, and the Turkish economy reverted to the export promotion of industrial sectors based on savings on wage costs (Oyvat 2011).

As figure 3 shows, the neoliberal trajectory of the Turkish welfare system reflects two major trends in real wages: first, the real wages of workers have declined significantly since the late 1970s, and second, this decline has followed a very tortuous path. These fluctuations correspond to critical points in the history of Turkey's grassroots politics. While Turkey's developmentalist era (1950–80) witnessed an increase in both real wages and productivity, the neoliberal era has witnessed an increasing gap between the two. This gap was temporarily closed during periods in which labor unrest escalated. While neoclassical economics argue that real wages should follow productivity levels, the case of Turkey shows that real wage levels follow productivity levels only insofar as labor unrest escalates. When labor is strong, the gap between real wages and productivity levels narrows and otherwise the gap widens. Chapter 3 will explain the dynamics of workers' movements while chapter 4 will explain how such contentious activism will alter the welfare state.

A similar trend can be observed in private-sector wage shares in private-sector industrial added-value between 1980 and 2000. Turkish trade volume per GDP is negatively correlated with wage shares, indicating that the success of the export-oriented growth strategy characterizing the Turkish economy in the neoliberal era was dependent on low wages (Oyvat 2010). Real pension levels for private sector workers increased during the 1970s, declined in the 1980s, and sharply expanded in the early 1990s, in the early 2000s, and in the year 2015.

The minimum retirement age has been subject to a number of changes and fluctuations since the 1950s. Until the 1980s, the minimum retirement age had been on a downward trend; it then experienced a reversal, excluding a brief populist period during the early 1990s (see fig. 5). The 1950 Pension Law No. 5417 originally set the minimum retirement age at 60, for both men and women. Subsequently, it was lowered to 55 for women, with the enactment of the 1965 Social Insurance Law No. 506. In 1969, Law No. 1186 eliminated the minimum retirement age altogether, allowing both men and women to work only a minimal number of years

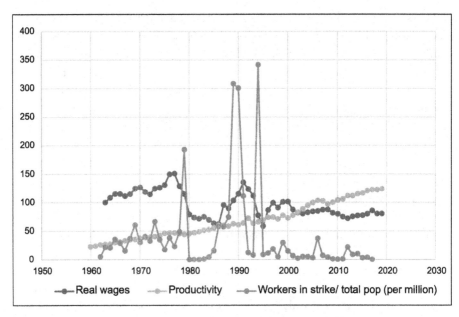

Fig. 3. Labor productivity, real wages, and strikes in Turkey (1960–2019)

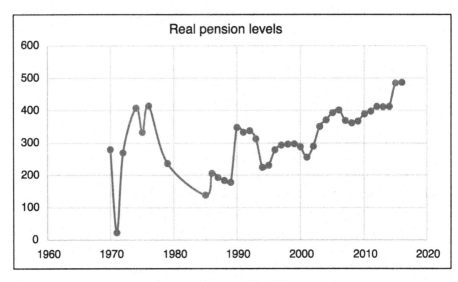

Fig. 4. Real minimum pension levels from the Social Security Administration (1970–2016)

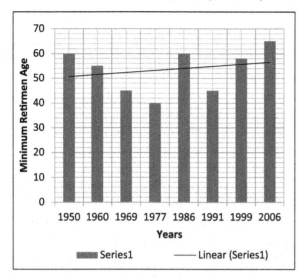

Fig. 5. Changes in minimum retirement age for female employees (1950–2006)

before being eligible for retirement. Employees might retire after only 25 years of employment, regardless of their age (Brook 2006). In 1976, this limit was lowered to just 20 years of employment. In 1986, the minimum retirement age was again set at 60 but was eliminated once more in 1991 before being reimposed in 1999. In 1999, the minimum retirement age was set at 58 for women and 60 for men, and in 2006, it was raised to 65 for everyone. The Social Security Reform of 2006, however, will gradually raise the minimum retirement age to 68 by the 2040s.

Another major change to the retirement system has involved a sharp increase in the number of days one needs to contribute to social security premiums in order to be eligible for pension benefits. In 1999, the law raised the minimum number of days from 5,900 to 7,000. Recent social security reforms have further increased this number from 7,000 to 9,000 days, effective by 2023. In addition, these reforms have lowered minimum retirement pension amounts while placing upper limits on maximum pension amounts. In the meantime, premium levels for all categories have increased.

Yet another change to the retirement system is the significant decline in retirement pension amounts. The pension of the retiree is calculated by multiplying the average salary from the last five years before retirement with a specific coefficient called the "accrual rate" (*Aylık bağlama oranı*). The pension amount is proportional to this coefficient. The accrual rate used to be 2.6 for private sector workers and the self-employed, and 3.0 for state sector employees. With the 2006 reform, this coefficient has decreased to 2.0 for everyone, resulting in a 33% decrease in pension amounts for employees in the state sector and a 23% decrease for workers in the private sector and the self-employed. In other words, "workers now have to work more years for the same pension" (OECD 2006).

After the 1999 and 2006 social security laws, the Turkish old age pension system has been less generous. Gross pension wealth has significantly decreased, along with the benefit/cost ratio, the ratio between pension wealth at retirement, and the sum of contributions paid into the system. This is primarily due to increases in the minimum retirement age. The social security contribution period has increased while the duration of pension receipt has decreased. There has also been a sharp decline in pension amounts as a percentage of annual average earnings. This percentage for men who were born in 1960 and who would retire in 2006 is twice as much for those who were born in 1980 and who would retire in 2043. In sum, these three trends indicate that those in the social security system have been required to pay higher amounts of old age pension premiums for a longer duration of time and will receive lower amounts of old-age pensions when they retire.

While social security benefits have been reduced during the neoliberal period, coverage of the Social Insurance Institution for workers has gradually increased. For employees in the state sector and the self-employed, however, this coverage has either remained constant or has declined (see fig. 6). The increase in coverage for workers (the most dramatic of which occurred during the 2000s) has much to do with the rapid expansion that the Turkish economy and industry have undergone since the mid-1990s. This expansion has resulted from the export-oriented growth strategy that successfully created a competitive advantage due to the excess supply of cheap labor (more than 40% of workers in the formal sector were earning minimum wage by 2020), the proximity of European markets, and the rise of a strong financial sector.

Government expenditures for social security institutions have grown significantly, especially since the 1990s (fig. 7). This is an expected pattern, as social security institutions collected premiums during early periods after they were established. Thereafter, expenditures grew rapidly as members of these institutions grew older, leading to expanding retirement benefits and health care costs. This, in turn, has led to increasing retrenchment efforts

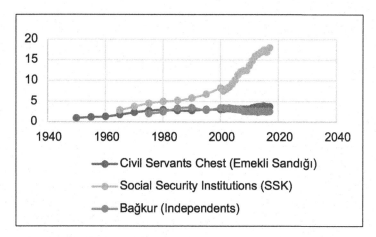

Fig. 6. Coverage of social security institutions as percentage of population (1955–2017)

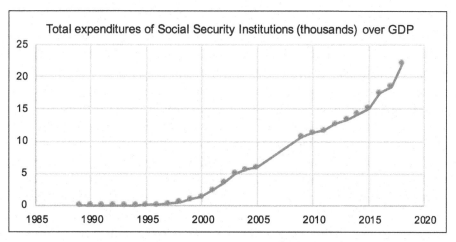

Fig. 7. Total Expenditures of social security institutions as percentage of Turkish GDP (1989–2018)

by the government. In a nutshell, the neoliberal transformation of social security policies is characterized by a long-term decline in social security benefits and eligibility conditions for those benefits, a limited reverse trend in benefits and eligibility conditions during the early and mid-1990s, and an overall long-term upward trend in the coverage and spending of social security institutions, indicating a formalization of the labor force.

The Rise of Income-Based Social Assistance Policies in Turkey

Since the 1990s, most welfare policies have been restructured in order to provide coverage according to citizens' income level (Elveren 2008). Turkey has drastically expanded means-tested social assistance and free health care programs for the poor, greatly increasing the number of beneficiaries and the share of allocated government budgets. Social assistance expenditure increased from US$860 million in 2002 to US$9.34 billion in 2016 (Ministry of Family, Work and Social Services 2017). This has included sharp increases in free health care, conditional cash transfers, food stamps, housing, and education and disability aid for the poor. The largest social assistance program in Turkey is the free health care card program for the poor (Green Card program), which was introduced in 1992. Coverage of the Green Card program increased from 4.2% to 12.7% of the population from 2003 to 2009 and remained at about 10% of the total population during the 2010s. In addition to receiving benefits from the central government, families are also still eligible to receive many types of in-kind and cash assistance programs from municipal governments, which expanded exponentially during the 2010s. As a result, the monthly average in-kind and cash benefits from the central government for a poor family increased to US$260, equaling 70% of the minimum wage in Turkey (Özgür 2014).

The General Directorate of Social Assistance and Solidarity also significantly increased allocations to conditional cash transfer programs, food stamps, housing, and education aid during the 2000s. In 2009, conditional cash transfers covered one million beneficiaries with health-based conditions and 2.1 million with education-based conditions. Between 2009 and 2016, CCT expenditures increased from 483 million liras to one billion liras. Additionally, the Social Insurance Institution increased old-age pension and disability aid, while the Social Services and Child Protection Agency increased programs for orphans and poor families. In 2011, the Ministry of Family and Social Policy was established to administer central government programs and to introduce new social assistance benefits. Furthermore, there was a proliferation of social assistance programs implemented by municipalities in almost every city. Since the early 2000s, social housing programs have been initiated to target the poor, providing cheap credit to purchase homes. By 2013, such programs covered over three million families. The Ministry of Education, which now distributes all school course book materials free of charge to all primary and secondary

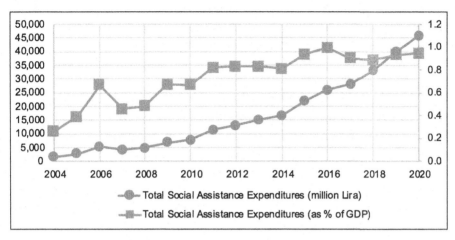

Fig. 8. Total social assistance expenditures in Turkey in lira and as percentage of GDP (2004–2020)

education students (a total of 15 million pupils), also serves 600,000 students each year with free transportation and school lunches. In addition, affirmative action policies for the disabled were enacted into the constitution, which has greatly increased their participation in the labor market. The coverage of disability benefits has tripled and the generosity doubled since 2002. If a poor family provides nursing to a disabled family member, it receives US$350 per month—an amount almost equal to the minimum wage (Özgür 2014).

During the neoliberal period, income-based social assistance policies have grown much more dramatically than the employment-based social security policies. Coverage of employment-based and income-based programs (see figs. 6 and 9) indicates increasing levels of political effort and financial resources meant to gradually diminish the centrality of employment-based welfare policies and to expand the demographic coverage of income-based policies. This effort can be seen in policy-making preferences as well as social policy outcomes. Buğra and Keyder (2006) have also described the transformation in the Turkish welfare system as part of a global trend whereby a nonegalitarian corporatist character has moved into a more redistributive direction, placing "greater emphasis on the provision of social assistance for the least privileged groups" (citing Seekings 2005, 211). As such, the new welfare system has begun to provide coverage according to both income level and employment status. Previously limited

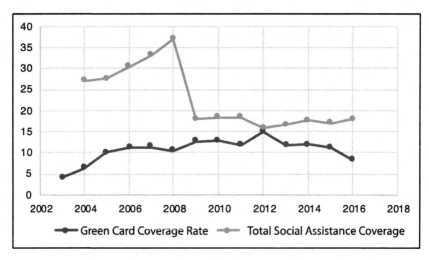

Fig. 9. Changes in the percentage of the population benefiting from all social assistance and from the free health care (Green Card) program (2003–2016)

only to formal sector employees, the new system now covers the majority of the population, targeting employees according to employment status and informal sector employees according to income. This transformation has involved changes in health, social assistance, and pension systems.

Established in 1986, the Social Assistance and Solidarity Fund was the first national and widespread social assistance institution in Turkey. Since its establishment, this fund has become the only central government institution to significantly expand social assistance programs in Turkey. According to Buğra and Keyder (2006, 12), the authors of the legislation based the fund on traditional Ottoman ethics:

> It was clearly hoped that a fundamental characteristic of the Ottoman charitable foundations, the mélange of public and private funds without proper delineation, could be used in order to mobilize private donations with the initiative and under the guidance of the state and alleviate the burden of welfare provision on the budget. Hence, the Fund was conceived as an umbrella organization covering over 900 local foundations, managed by representatives of the central government at the district level with the aid of boards of directors that include prominent members of the local population.

Originally planned to target a small population, the Fund has assumed a much more substantial position in the Turkish social welfare system. After the 2001 economic crisis debilitated the poor population, the Fund distributed widespread social assistance through the Social Risk Mitigation Project. Supported by the World Bank, this project included a health care component providing conditional cash transfer programs to pregnant women, preschool children, and children attending compulsory schooling. Such provisions required beneficiaries to have regular medical checkups. The education component of the project offered assistance to mothers of school-age children, provided that the children attend school. The Fund also allocated resources providing medicine, prostheses, and hearing aids for the poor. Currently, one-third of the Fund's budget is spent on educational assistance, including scholarships and the provision of school supplies, meals, and snacks for school children. During the 2000s, elementary school students were provided with free textbooks. The Fund also distributes in-cash and in-kind assistance for the poor, including coal and medicine (Buğra and Keyder 2006).

The centrally coordinated Social Assistance and Solidarity Fund's primary purpose was to distribute relief to the poor. Between 2003 and 2007, the Fund provided 7.5 million people (more than 10% of the total population) with social assistance, amounting to a total of 6.1 billion Turkish liras ($4.7 billion).[3] During the 2000s, the number of health-conditional cash transfer recipients increased fiftyfold, and the number of education-conditional cash transfer recipients increased thirtyfold.[4] Meanwhile, most municipalities began distributing free meals to the needy in soup kitchens, and hundreds of thousands of families were provided with daily meals in their homes. The social pension program grants monthly salaries to poor people who are over the age of 65 and not registered with any social security organization. And the disability program provides cash and health support for disabled people in need.

---

3. The total amount of educational material aid for children of poor families increased from 10.22 million in 2003 to 183.74 million Turkish liras in 2009, increasing the number of recipients from 855,907 to 2 million. The amount of education aid for students with disabilities increased from 1.9 million Turkish liras in 2003 to 31.4 million Turkish liras in 2009, expanding coverage from 6,900 to 27,205 recipients.

4. Between 2003 and 2009, these numbers are even more impressive: from 59,000 in 2003 to 2,118,821 in 2009.

The Social Assistance and Solidarity Fund administers most of its social assistance programs through provincial offices. These programs are based on means-tested benefits, and program eligibility is determined by boards upon investigation of caseworkers. As is the case with the Green Card, the eligibility criteria for most of the Fund's social assistance programs have been standardized: applicants must be unregistered with any social security office, and the per-capita household income must be lower than one-third of the minimum wage. However, meeting both criteria results in a dilemma, making it impossible to determine income for someone working in the informal sector. To resolve this dilemma, local boards resort to indirect ways of determining income, including house visits and neighborhood-level investigations. Caseworkers collect detailed data on local communities and the socioeconomic statuses of families. They also use an electronic database (Social Assistance Information System, or SOYBIS) that contains data on the social security and home ownership statuses of citizens.

The primary social assistance program in Turkey is the Green Card (Yeşil Kart) program, or free health care for the poor. Founded in 1992 as a means-tested health service system, the program covers health care expenses of those not supported by any social security institution. It provides outpatient treatment, medical examinations and tests, medicines, prenatal care and delivery, and emergency medical care. While those in the social security system make small copayments when receiving health services, Green Card holders do not. Financed by the Ministry of Health, the Green Card program greatly expanded during the 2000s, covering 4.2% of the population in 2003 and 12.7% in 2009. During this period, total government expenditures for the program increased from 917 million to 4.1 billion Turkish liras. In 2007, the program accounted for 85% of the total social assistance budget. The eligibility criteria for the Green Card are the same as those for the Social Assistance and Solidarity Fund: the applicant's household's per-capita income must be less than one-third of the minimum wage, and the applicant must have no formal social security coverage. Recipients hold Green Cards for a maximum of 12 months but may renew after another means test.

The health insurance system is separated from the social security system by the social security reforms of the 2000s, which established the General Health Insurance system. The organizing principle of the General Health Insurance system detached health care insurance from the employment status of citizens and included income level in addition to employment status as requirements for eligibility (Günal 2007). As already mentioned, the General Health Insurance Law unified health care provision previously offered by different institutions, including provision for state sector employees, workers, the self-employed, and the poor. In the previous system, state sector employees, workers, and the self-employed were members of different institutions and thus received varying types and degrees of health care services. The new system eliminated this fragmented structure and created a Social Security Institution to cover all citizens. Separate health care insurance systems were replaced by the premium-based General Health Insurance system, with premium amounts determined by both income level and employment status (Ağartan et al. 2007).

The new General Health Insurance system provides mandatory and universal health coverage for all citizens and requires that every resident pay obligatory health insurance premiums. This system includes three categories of citizens:

1. Citizens (and their dependents) who are formally employed and have their premiums paid by their employers;
2. Citizens (and their dependents) who are not formally employed and, if identified as poor through a means test, have their premiums paid by the government; and
3. Citizens (and their dependents) who are not formally employed and, if not identified as poor through a means test, pay their own premiums.

Effective since 1 January 2012, the new system dictates that the main function of formal employment is to allow for official income determination. Employers pay separate premiums for employees' health care and old age pension insurance under the General Health Insurance Law of 2006. In addition, the General Health Insurance system requires those in the second and third categories (i.e., those in the informal sector) to pass a means test, whereas previously only Green Card applicants were subject to income determination. The new General Health Insurance system encompasses the existing free health care program for the poor, or the Green Card system, and the eligibility criteria for having premiums paid by the government are the same as for those for Green Card holders. Many citizens are informally employed yet ineligible for free health care. Thus, scholars have warned that the obligatory nature of the General Health Insurance system will likely produce a large number of informally employed citizens accumulating premium arrears (Buğra 2008). Many people in this category will therefore not be able to benefit from health care services because of their debt.

Since the 1990s, local governments and nongovernmental organizations have come to play an increasingly important role in social assistance provision in Turkey. Municipalities in almost every city have enacted social assistance programs that reach a vast number of residents (the metropolitan municipalities of Istanbul and Ankara, for example, have led this trend by establishing local poor relief institutions). These social assistance programs include means-tested cash transfers, coverage of health care expenses for the poor, mass circumcision events (a Muslim tradition) for children of poor families, fuel aid, soup kitchens, free evening meals during Ramadan, and rehabilitation for homeless children (Özbek 2006). Municipalities do not, however, provide these social assistance benefits on a permanent or regular basis. Therefore, nongovernmental organizations have occupied a growing role in social assistance provision by assuming a complementary function to local and central government assistance. Organizations such as the Light House Association (Deniz Feneri Derneği) and the Association for Supporting Civic Life (Çağdaş Yaşamı Destekleme Derneği), for example, provide assistance to hundreds of thousands of people every year.

A nationally representative, 2,635-respondent survey designed by the author and conducted by the KONDA research company in December 2019 indicates a rapid expansion of the social assistance system in Turkey. The KONDA Barometer survey revealed striking results concerning the contemporary nature of the Turkish social welfare system, showing that welfare provision has reached a very large segment of the population. According to the survey, more than 80% of respondents belong to a social security program through their employment or family members. A comparison of the 2006 KONDA survey and the 2019 survey illustrates that the scope of the social insurance system for employees has expanded. In addition, the most recent survey indicates that, as of 2019, the social assistance system has reached approximately one-third of the population, mostly covering the urban and rural informal populations, while more than 40% of the population is shown to have received social assistance at least once in their lifetime. Contrary to the general belief that neoliberal globalization would bring an end to the welfare state, the results of the study show that, similarly to other emerging economies such as Brazil,

China, India, and South Africa, Turkey's welfare system expanded precisely during the neoliberal era.

Although the expansion of the Turkish welfare state may seem to be a positive development, details underlying this expansion raise serious questions. One such concern is that, although coverage and expenditures have expanded, the generosity of the welfare state has declined considerably, as seen in pension and retirement age policies. Another concern is that, while social security programs such as SSK, Bağ-kur, and Emekli Sandığı increased the scope of the welfare state, the major enlargement of welfare provision was due to the social assistance system. Almost half (47.6%) of Turkish citizens are part of the SSK system, 10.9% part of Bağ-Kur, and 10% part of the Emekli Sandığı, while 8.7% have Green Cards and 18.6% no social insurance whatsoever. Social welfare programs, on the other hand, are considered income-test based welfare programs and thus are nonegalitarian, discriminatory, nonuniversal, stigmatizing, and ultimately nonpermanent, as has been observed in the literature. Consequently, these programs have both low permanent poverty reduction effects and very limited effects on establishing an equal and competent citizenship system. In addition, the temporary and flexible nature of social assistance programs allows them to be used for questionable political purposes.

TABLE I. Percentage of Respondents Who Have Received Social Assistance, by Category

Type of social assistance	Percentage
Conditional cash transfer	9.7
Scholarship (central government)	8.3
In-kind assistance (municipal government)	6.0
Birth aid	5.5
Other	5.5
Green Card	4.6
In-kind assistance (central government)	4.3
Social pension	3.7
Unemployment insurance	2.4
Disability aid	2.1
Scholarship (NGOs)	1.7
Widow's aid	1.5
In-kind assistance (NGOs)	1.2
Soldier aid	1.2
Care support	1.1
Scholarship (municipal government)	1.0
Orphanage aid	0.4

Note: Multiple responses were allowed.

According to the 2019 KONDA survey, the perception, expectation, and support of the public toward social policies is extremely high in that all class, ethnic, and politically based groups almost universally support the improvement of different social policy programs related to pensions, social benefits, and social services. In highly politically polarized countries such as Turkey, this consensus suggests that the welfare state is now seen by citizens as a duty of the state and a right of citizenship, implying that future "austerity" policies in the social welfare system will have a significant political cost.

Conclusion

Over the last four decades, the Turkish welfare system has shifted from exclusively employment-based policies to a mixture of employment-based and income-based policies. Although it is commonly thought that the Turkish welfare system has eroded during the neoliberal era, the welfare state has in fact expanded significantly since the 1980s. In other words, the main transformation in the welfare system is not in overall retrenchment, but in a shift of the main selection criterion (from employment- to income-based determinants) for welfare provision recipients. Before the 2000s, the Turkish welfare system was based on a fragmented corporatist social provision system in which state sector employees, workers, and the self-employed received different qualities of services and benefits from different institutions. The new welfare system of the 2000s, on the other hand, created a social security and general health insurance system that *theoretically* covers all citizens so that services for the informal poor are now equal to those of formal sector employees. Until the 1990s, the welfare system provided formal sector employees and the self-employed with social security, including health care, pensions, and job security. Since then, these social security policies have undergone a relative decline compared to the rising income-based social assistance programs. This is a result of the relative retrenchment of less generous employment-based policies with stricter eligibility conditions. In the meantime, there has been a boom in income-based social assistance policies. Conditional cash transfers, free health care for the poor, and other in-kind and cash assistance mechanisms have rapidly grown to cover larger segments of the population. More importantly, the legal transformations of welfare policies indicate that an increasingly significant segment of Turkey's population is covered by income-based welfare policies. With the new General Health Insurance system, one quarter of the population is obliged to pass a means test in order to be eligible for government subsidies and to determine the level of insurance premiums. The results of the 2019 KONDA study show that, compared to the rest of society, Kurds and Justice and Development Party voters are much more intensively targeted by social assistance programs such as the Green Card program. These groups receive higher levels of social assistance when econometric variables that determine social assistance programs are controlled for. In light of these results, social assistance in Turkey functions to ensure social order and benefit party politics by addressing the needs of the poor. Thus, as history indicates, the welfare state, rather than establishing the welfare of the people, may instead aim to discipline and control them. The expansion in the welfare state parallels an increase in social needs, as well as an increase in party competition and contentious social events. The following chapters analyze both the possible causes of this shift and focus on contentious and electoral political factors.

CHAPTER 3

Contentious Politics in Turkey, 1970–2017

Until the global wave of social unrest wreaked havoc on the capitalist world system in the 2010s, there was a general tendency to think that massive social movements of the working classes were "ancient" phenomena that belonged in the Golden Age of Capitalism. The political right in Turkey has acclaimed this as the end of anarchy, while the left has remained in a deep nostalgia for the powerful and militant proletariat immersed in socialist ideology. Yet, the Turkish case shows that since the 1970s, while social movements in general have continued their powerful existence, the center of grassroots politics in Turkey has shifted from the formal proletariat to the informal proletariat and from non-Kurds to Kurds. This chapter will review the structural processes that have underlined the social power of both formal and informal working classes and identify the mainstream and radical political actors that have politicized, mobilized, and contained the contentious political power of workers. Thus, the trajectories of grassroots political groups—including the formal proletariat, the informal proletariat, Kurds, Islamists, socialists, and the far right—can be put into a narrative framework.

Since the 1970s, an informal proletariat has gradually replaced the formal proletariat as the demographic and political center of the grassroots in Turkey. The Turkish economy's shift from import-substitutionist national developmentalism to an export-oriented neoliberal growth strategy has allowed this relative decline of the formal proletariat and the demographic growth of the informal proletariat. The informal proletariat has grown not only in numbers but also significantly in political power in comparison to the formal proletariat. Existing ethnic, religious, and political divides interact with growing poverty in metropolitan slums to create an informal proletariat as the new center of grassroots political activism. Here, independent political factors including political interests and competition among mainstream political actors and radical groups (socialists, Kurds, and Islamists) have been crucial in determining the fate of grassroots activism. Competition among mainstream political parties for national power increased the mobilization of both the formal and informal proletariat and gave them significant bargaining power. As a result, since the 1990s informal proletarians have become the central political force as political competition has forced the mainstream political actors to garner their political support, and the radical Kurdish and Islamist movements have found a mass base in the slums.

This chapter will portray the changes in grassroots politics in Turkey based on empirical data from primary sources. Extensive newspaper archive research has allowed the creation of a dataset of grassroots political events, the Global Contentious Politics Dataset, that occurred in Turkey and elsewhere since 1970 (glocon.ku.edu.tr). This dataset provides trajectories of grassroots politics over the last five decades, including the activities of the formal proletariat, the informal proletariat, the left, the Islamists, and the Kurds. As scholars have already observed, quantitative time-series data on grassroots politics that would include a spectrum of contentious political events—formal and informal labor, ethnic, religious, student, right-wing, left-wing, feminist, and so forth—has often been lacking in the literature. As in many other countries, scholars of labor movements in Turkey have largely used government-collected strike statistics to measure labor unrest (Akkaya 2006). However, official strike statistics do not suffice for a full understanding of labor unrest, because they miss nonstrike forms of unrest (slowdowns, riots, demonstrations) and exclude political and wildcat strikes. Also, scholars do not have access to historically quantifiable data on political movements, including leftist, Kurdish, and Islamist ones. Thus, these limits greatly enhance the use of newspaper archives as a reliable source of indicators on grassroots politics in Turkey over the last four decades (Silver 2003).

To create a reliable empirical source on grassroots politics, newspaper articles have been collected from the archives of the Turkish daily *Cumhuriyet* (Republic). *Cumhuriyet* was chosen because it is one of major national newspapers in Turkey that have extensively reported news about grassroots political activities since the 1970s. Events reported in *Cumhuriyet* was obtained by analyzing news articles published every other day on the basis of a systematic sampling strategy. For formal proletarian activities, strikes, rallies, boycotts, protests, riots, and demonstrations organized by trade unions and political groups that organize within the formal proletariat have been included. For informal proletarian activities, the events organized by the political groups working within the informal proletariat as well as the events that spontaneously occurred in slum areas are considered. Also included are informal workers' protests and resistance against slum demolitions. Some events are covered as both formal and informal proletarian activities, for example, a May Day rally. Unless organized by the Kurdish political organizations, events are marked as being "non-Kurdish." Events organized by the Kurdish parties, including the legal political parties and the Kurdistan Workers' Party (Partiya Karkeren Kurdistan—PKK), and events taking place in the Kurdish regions are referred to as Kurdish political activities unless otherwise indicated.

This dataset is not intended to produce an exhaustive count of all, or even most, incidences of political events, since *Cumhuriyet* reported on only a fraction of the events that occurred. During times of social movements, newspapers report social events more than usual (Silver 2003). Hence, the dataset presents the changing levels of formal and informal as well as Turkish and Kurdish events over time and space during the welfare transformation: the waves of political activities. A comparison between the labor strike data in the dataset between 1989 and 1993 with the official strike statistics for that period (Akkaya 2006) illustrates that the dataset is able to correctly identify the officially recorded strike waves, attesting to the validity of the methodology. Finally, each incidence that an event is reported is included in the dataset, which enabled a differentiation of events in terms of their importance on the basis of the assumption that newspapers report important events several times.

Figure 10 presents the times series distribution of all grassroots events between 1970 and 2010. The most immediate conclusion from this figure is that grassroots activism did not fade away in the neoliberal period and that the average number of contentious political events in the 1970s and 1990s were almost similar, despite the spectacular peak in the late 1970s. Examining the details of this pattern and present times series figures for grassroots activities of all major players (formal proletariat, the informal proletariat, socialist, Islamist, and Kurdish movements) will illuminate the relationship between structural trends and political processes that shape the dynamics of grassroots politics in different decades.

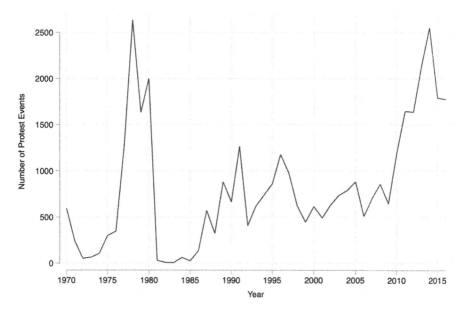

Fig. 10. Total number of grassroots political events per year (1970–2017)

The Politics of the Formal Proletariat

During the two decades prior to the military coup in 1980, the formal proletariat in Turkey significantly expanded in numbers and in militancy. Figure 11 demonstrates the grassroots activities of the formal proletariat in Turkey between 1970 and 2010. The graph shows that there was a rapid increase in formal proletarian activities in the 1970s before the military coup of 1980 halted such activism. Yet the largest ever labor activism occurred in the early 1990s when the formal proletariat reacted against neoliberal policies adopted after the coup in a wave of labor unrest known as the Spring Actions (Bahar Eylemleri). After the Spring Actions, the formal proletariat largely lost its significance as a grassroots political power. Analyzing the processes that both enhanced and undermined the structural bargaining power of formal sector workers and political factors that translated this power into varying degrees of associational bargaining power and labor militancy[1] will explain why.

---

1. Erik Olin Wright (2000) classifies workers' bargaining power into associational and struc-

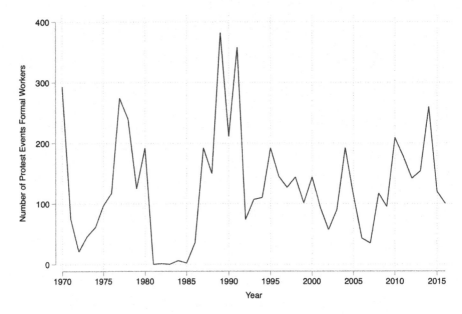

Fig. 11. Grassroots political activities of the formal proletariat (1970–2017)

The formal proletarian movement in Turkey is very much related to the developmentalism that characterized most of the 20th-century republican state policy. Between 1923 and 1950, the Republic of Turkey was governed by a Bonapartist single party regime (Parla and Davidson 2004). The Republican People's Party (Cumhuriyet Halk Partisi—CHP), founded and led by Kemal Atatürk until his death, functioned as the party-state until the 1950 elections. In 1946, the Democrat Party (Demokrat Parti—DP), representing an alliance of big landowners, the agricultural bourgeoisie,

---

tural bargaining power. Associational bargaining power derives from the collective organization of workers in unions and political parties. Structural bargaining power comes from the location of workers in the economic system. Beverly Silver (2003) classifies structural bargaining power into marketplace and workplace bargaining power. Marketplace bargaining power results from "the possession of scarce skills that are in demand by employers," "low levels of general unemployment," and "the ability of workers to pull out of the labor market entirely and survive on non-wage sources of income" (Silver 2003, 13). Workplace bargaining power stems from "the strategic location of a particular group of workers within a key industrial sector," and it depends on the extent of damage that stoppage in production might generate in the sector and other sectors as well. This workplace structural bargaining power is determined by the skill levels of workers, the system of production, type of product, scale of the workplace, and the interconnectedness of the sectors.

and the urban commercial bourgeoisie, was founded as an opposition party. In a short time, the Islamic/conservative-leaning populism of the party garnered the support of the peasantry as well. In the first free elections in Turkish history, in 1950, the DP won 52% of the votes while the CHP could gain only 39%. During the 1950s, the DP oversaw large-scale, agriculture-based economic growth driven mainly by the support of Marshall Plan aid and the liberal free trade regime that the US hegemony instigated (Keyder 1987). Toward the end of the decade, the DP success faded and a growing opposition of an urban-based social coalition was formed around the old CHP. This coalition was composed of the emerging industrial bourgeoisie (whose interests were not prioritized by the DP), the civil and military bureaucracy, intellectuals, students, and growing sections of the new formal proletariat (Savran 2010). In 1960, the military, as the armed force of this coalition, staged the first coup d'état in Turkish history, deposing the Democrat Party and resulting in the execution of Prime Minister Adnan Menderes and two ministers.

The 1960 coup was a critical juncture in Turkish history, deeply transforming the social and economic structures of the country. The urban-based coalition under the hegemony of the industrial bourgeoisie initiated developmentalist policies based on import-substitutionist industrialization. These policies empowered the flourishing national industrial bourgeoisie and a concomitant productive formal working class (Kuş and Özel 2010). In general, the coup enabled the shift from agricultural/commercial capitalism to industrial capitalism in Turkey (Savran 2010).

This transformation was reflected in the constitution enacted after the coup, laying the ground for a semicorporatist welfare system. Formal sector workers were the main grassroots group that supported this new power coalition in this highly peasant society. Thus, in order to garner and sustain grassroots support for the new economic system, the formal proletariat was granted high levels of concessions, including the right to strike, as main pillars of an employment-based welfare regime, as will be detailed in the next chapter (Savran 2010). This maintained the demand condition of the import-substitutionist industrialization strategy by increasing the purchasing power of workers.

The United States enthusiastically supported this project, which complied with the developmentalist strategy of US hegemony. Influenced by the United States, an AFL-CIO type labor union confederation, Türk-İş, was strengthened by the state. The confederation was seen by all political parties as "an opportunity to cut off any militancy of rank-and-file union members and control the union movement through ties with its leadership. [Competing parties] sought to tap into the emerging Turkish working class as a source of electoral support" (Mello 2007, 7). Along with this co-optation strategy, workers were given the right to unionize and strike and obtained significant gains in real wages and welfare rights, including retirement pensions, health care, child benefits, and housing benefits. The unions were also given opportunities such as "official recognition, monopoly of representation, compulsory membership and state help in ensuring a regular source of income for unions" insofar as they were able to control rank-and-file worker militancy, "through the corporatist logic of exchange and in return for its promise to keep 'above party politics'" (Cizre 1992, 718).

These corporatist policies generated real structural bargaining power (workplace and marketplace) for the labor employed in heavy industries. As workers increased their skill levels and control over production in general, they acquired more capacity to disturb the production process whenever labor disputes occurred. Also, the rising demand for labor decreased the level of unemployment, alleviating the labor market pressures on workers (Ahmed 1994). According to Mello (2007, 7), the import-substitutionist industrialization strategy "combined with important changes within Turkish society associated with urbanization and rapid industrialization expanded the organizing opportunities for labor activists, and contributed to the growing importance of organized labor within Turkish politics." Rapid urbanization stemmed from the import-substitutionist industrialization strategy, which necessitated the rise of labor supply, increasing the urban population rate from 25% in 1960 to 45% in 1980. As Feroz Ahmad stated:

> By the end of the 1960s, the character of Turkey's economy and society had changed almost beyond recognition. Before the 1960s, Turkey had been predominantly agrarian with a small industrial sector dominated by the state. By the end of the decade, a substantial private industrial sector had emerged so much so that industry's contribution to the GNP almost equaled that of agriculture, overtaking it in 1973. This was matched by rapid urbanization as peasants flocked to the towns and cities in search of jobs and a better way of life. (Ahmad 1993, 134)

As a result, between 1960 and 1980, the size of the working class in Turkey significantly expanded. Those under the social security system consisted of private sector workers (through SSK), public sector employees (through Emekli Sandığı), and the self-employed that lived mostly in urban areas and a small group of peasants (through Bağ-Kur). The number of wage earners increased from 3 million in 1965 to 6.2 million in 1980, while the population increased from 32 million to 44 million in the same period. The ratio of wage earners to total income earners increased from 22.5% in 1965 to 33.4% in 1980. In 1970, 35% of heads of households were wage earners, while this proportion increased to 42.1% in 1980. The ratio of those under the social security system to urban population increased in the 1970s to 28%, decreased to 22.73% in 2000, and increased again to 25.78% in 2009 and 36.17% in 2016 (Koç 2003).

The Politicization of the Formal Proletariat

The corporatist structure was developed in the 1960s in order to garner the support of formal workers for the hegemony of the industrial bourgeoisie, which initiated a development strategy based on import-substitutionist industrialization. Controlled empowerment of the proletariat was regarded by the state as the optimum way to synchronize economic development and political stability. During the 1970s, the mobilization of formal sector workers became the main source of both political threat and support for governments. I will illustrate in this section that, as a result, the formal proletariat started to use its structural bargaining power to demand radical economic and political changes, surprising the designers of the corporatist system who did not originally expect formal workers to become radicalized to this extent (Savran 2010).

This radicalization of the formal proletariat did not occur as a natural outcome of structural processes that improved the bargaining power of workers, but mainly through the mobilization of political actors. Following the 1960s, the structural bargaining power of the formal proletariat was extensively mobilized into labor militancy by a growing leftist movement and by the leftwing trade unions that carried out organizing activities within the formal working class. During the late 1970s, the number of strikes, number of workers on strike, and days lost in strikes sharply increased, and over time the radical left grew as a hegemonic power among

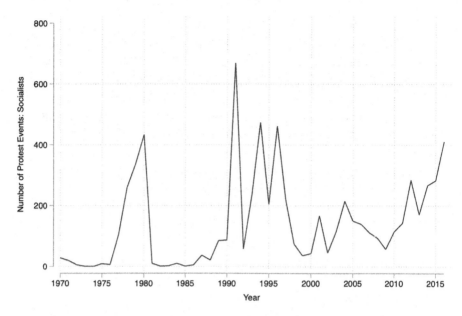

Fig. 12. Grassroots political activities of the socialist movement (1970–2017)

the working class. Eventually, the late 1970s witnessed a violent civil war between paramilitary forces and the radical left largely supported by organized workers (Keyder 2004; Rustow 1994). As Mello (2006, 156) summarized,

> Broader structural changes, the availability of resources, and changes of political opportunity structures only matter insofar as activists interpret these as either openings or threats, and then use the resources available to them in order to mobilize popular contention.

Figure 11 and figure 12 illustrate that the trajectory of socialist movement correlates largely with that of formal proletarian activities. There is a rapid escalation of the socialist movement in the late 1970s. The 1980s were a period of grassroots political silence following the military coup in 1980, and in the mid-1990s there is another wave of socialist mobilization. The socialist movement in Turkey in the 1970s originated from the National Democratic Revolution (Milli Demokratik Devrim) tradition. The National Democratic Revolution strictly rejected the parliamentary path to socialism and it was admired mostly by the militant youth of the period (Yurtsever 2002). Three radical leftist organizations—the People's Liberation Army of Turkey (THKO), the People's Liberation Party (THKP), and the Communist Party of Turkey–Marxist-Leninist (TKP-ML)—which have become the historical lineage of the radical leftist movements since, rejected the parliamentary path and put the National Democratic Revolution strategy into practice. However, departing from the National Democratic Revolution tradition, they also shifted the responsibility away from the army officials that were expected by the National Democratic Revolution tradition to lead the revolution, into organized independent revolutionaries who would form rural and urban guerrilla units. The THKO adopted a strategy of people's war expanding from rural to urban areas. Formulated as a politicized military war strategy, the THKP adopted a focoist urban guerrilla strategy to be followed by a protracted people's war. The TKP-ML was a Maoist organization that envisioned a people's war originating from rural areas. This strategy was seen as the first sharp split in the Turkish left from Kemalist ideology by declaring unconditional support for the Kurdish national liberation movement.

In 1971, the military staged a coup d'état, imprisoning and executing many of the socialist leaders. This intervention decelerated the labor and leftist movements only until 1974, however. After which, leftist organizations' and trade unions' political influence grew rapidly among the formal proletariat as well as among professionals, intellectuals, students, the peasantry, and even among police and army officials. In the late 1970s, the Soviet-leaning Communist Party of Turkey (TKP) and a spectrum of China/Albania-leaning smaller radical revolutionary parties constituted the main players of the socialist left. The TKP, Halkın Kurtuluşu (People's Liberation), and Dev-Yol (Revolutionary Path) were the three most powerful radical leftist organizations in the late 1970s. The TKP, despite being illegal, assumed a less radical strategy than those aligning with China and Albania. In the second half of the 1970s, the TKP rapidly grew and became the most organized party among the working class. The party became a mass party by working with the unions, students, peasants, women, and intellectuals. With the mobilization of these political actors, the last quarter of the 1970s turned out to be a period of civil war between socialist militants and paramilitary forces. Many people on the left came to expect a socialist revolution by the end of the decade. The International Workers' Day Rally on 1 May 1977 was the high tide of leftist and working-class movements, gathering half a million people in central Taksim Square in Istanbul. This represented 1.2% of Turkey's population and 3.8% of the total urban population.

The main focus of these socialist strategies was to politicize the formal proletariat in Turkey, which started to gain political power even in the 1960s (Tuğal 2006). The Saraçhane meeting in 1961, Kavel Resistance in 1963, Paşabahçe Strike in 1966, and the establishment of the Confederation of Revolutionary Labor Unions (Devrimci İşçi Sendikaları Konfederasyonu—DİSK) in 1967 helped create a militant formal proletariat during the 1960s. DİSK was founded by leftist trade unionists after large-scale metal workers' strikes in an attempt to oppose the state-sponsored union confederation Türk-İş (Etöz 2002) and rapidly became the harbinger of political unionism in the 1970s (Cizre 1992; Mello 2010).

By the early 1970s, militant socialist activity dramatically increased. DİSK became popular and powerful, student movements became more militant, and land occupations by the peasantry grew in number. The strengthening of the socialist movement was the main reason for this cross-class mobilization. DİSK, heavily influenced by socialist unionists, organized most of the new union membership during the 1970s: the membership of DİSK increased from 67,000 in 1967 to 500,000 in 1980, while Türk-İş membership increased from 497,000 to 700,000 (Mello 2006, 158). The first time in which the formal proletariat was involved in mass scale labor militancy was the 15–16 June labor unrest in 1970. The government of that time enacted a law that made it difficult for workers to move between unions. The objective was to prevent the leftist union DİSK from gaining power, and it was supported by Türk-İş. As a response, on 15 June 1970, DİSK leaders started to march in Istanbul, spontaneously drawing workers from factories who joined the march, swelling the crowd to 75,000 workers. The second day, the events grew even further and the government declared martial law in Istanbul and the neighboring industrial city, Kocaeli. Five workers were killed and many union leaders were arrested. After the events, the Supreme Court canceled the new labor law, elevating the 15–16 June events to one of the founding actions of formal proletarian militancy in Turkey.

After the early 1970s, there was an "increasing militancy, the fragmentation and radicalization of the labor movement" (Cizre 1992, 718). Workers recognized that militancy would bring increased political and economic returns (Mello 2007). As such, public sector workers managed to enjoy the benefits of the corporatist structure as the socialists became powerful in these sectors. As Mello (2010, 8) mentions, the degree of radicalism and socialist tendencies in labor unions depended largely on the type of industry and private/public divide. Unions organizing in public sector enterprises are the least inclined to socialist and radical political unionism (Bianchi 1984; Dereli 1968).

The rise of the labor and socialist movements increased radical rightwing attacks against the left, attacks organized mainly by the militants of the Nationalist Movement Party (Milliyetçi Hareket Partisi. This led to such an increase of armed clashes between state-backed paramilitary groups and left-wing militants that Turkey found itself on the verge of a civil war by the late 1970s. The escalation of the leftist threat and armed clashes led to the announcement of martial law in 1979, even before the military coup in 1980 (Lipovsky 1992).

In addition to the radical grassroots political mobilization by unions and socialists, the intense political competition for national power among center-right and center-left political parties during 1960s and 1970s brought significant electoral bargaining power for the formal working proletariat. A grand competition for national power between the center-right Justice Party (Adalet Partisi—AP) led by Süleyman Demirel and the center-left CHP led by Bülent Ecevit (see fig. 13) gave the expanding formal proletariat an extensive advantage, as the parties needed the popular support of the workers.

After the coup d'état in 1960 that overthrow the Menderes government, the CHP under the leadership of İsmet İnönü won the elections, and remained in office until 1963 when the young and ambitious new leader of the AP, Süleyman Demirel, gained an electoral victory. In the mid-1960s, a young ambitious leader, Ecevit, became the leader of the CHP. As the minister of labor, he was a popular figure and had maintained close relations with trade unions. Under the leadership of Ecevit, the CHP adopted the famous Democratic Left rhetoric, a populist social democratic nationalist ideology that would profoundly dominate the center-left during the decades to come (Lipovsky 1992). As a response, Demirel increasingly articulated a rhetoric of anticommunism vis-à-vis the new slightly center-left orientation of the CHP. This strategy was effective, in combination with a strong populism directed toward the poorest sectors, especially the peasantry: the AP again won the 1969 elections, increasing its votes to 47%.

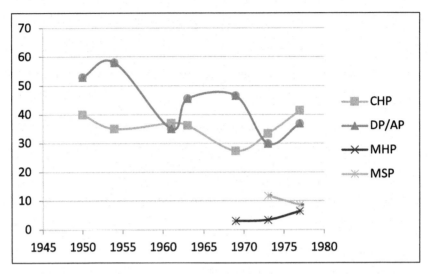

Fig. 13. Vote percentages of the main parties in Turkish elections (1950–1980)

Along the way, both parties adopted the same general strategy to increase support. Both parties tried "to harness the electoral support of the working class, while simultaneously stifling the growth of political unionism" (Mello 2010, 12). The competition resulted in a series of laws that established a generous welfare regime for formal sector workers. The AP instigated the first series of inducements during the late 1960s. These policies provided social security payments in the form of retirement pensions and benefits for workers' health, family, children, and housing. By the end of the 1960s, this system had created extensive privileges and rights for the working class, including increases in real wages (Cizre 1992). The Social Security Law in 1964, the unionization right for employees in the public sector through an amendment to the labor law in 1964, and various health and job security laws in 1974 were concessions designed to both contain the radicalism of workers and to mobilize the popular support needed for the competition for national power. Bianchi (1984) also adds that concessions to state-sponsored Türk-İş increased especially after the rise of leftist DİSK as a political power. Moreover, the Türk-İş gained the privilege of participating in decision-making on macroeconomic policy-making and minimum wage commissions in the 1960s. This inducement was granted partly as a way to gain the electoral support of unionized workers and to control rank-and-file workers through the compliant union bureaucracy

(Mello 2007). The AP government guided the Türk-İş toward bread-and-butter issues and job unionism as opposed to political unionism (Cizre 1992; Kuş and Özel 2010; Mello 2006), and thus, "in return for the organizational and welfare concessions, the state imposed legal and de facto constraints on the unions to secure their commitment for maintaining social peace" (Cizre 1992, 718).

The Türk-İş confederation often sought material benefits, making use of the competition between political parties that were in substantive need of electoral support from workers (Mello 2010). Yet, in addition to the formation of DİSK as a radical split from Türk-İş, a social democratic faction, too, formed within Türk-İş in the early 1970s. This faction originated from the center-left orientation adopted by Ecevit's CHP, which increased efforts to gain leverage over the confederation. By the mid-1970s, the number of labor unions that aligned themselves with social democracy reached 24, which comprised 40% of all union members. In 1977, the more radical DİSK leadership was replaced by social democrats, who would then support the CHP. As such, the CHP garnered support from both DİSK and social democratic Türk-İş unions in the 1977 elections in which the party gained 41% of the vote and became the largest party (Lipovsky 1992). This social democratic populism toward the proletariat became the crux of the political success of the CHP during the 1970s (Keyder 1987, 47):

> In the poor *gecekondu* neighborhoods of Izmir and Istanbul, for example, the CHP's vote increased from 22.6% and 21.8% in 1969 to 44.2% and 47.5% in 1973 (Ayata 1991: 91). Furthermore, between the years 1969–1973, there was a dramatic shift away from electoral support for the Justice Party [Adalet Partisi (AP)] in the coal mining regions of Zonguldak, with gains going mostly to the CHP. Specifically, the AP's vote declined from 55.6% to 38.2%, while the CHP's increased to 39.8% from 30.7%, and in 1977 the CHP's vote increased further, to 45.7%.

The coup in 1971 could not stop the growth of the radical left and the labor movements despite a brief weakening that occurred in the immediate aftermath of the intervention. Ecevit's Democratic Left rhetoric served to contain the political instability as it backed up the popular support of workers and middle classes whose interest in leftwing ideologies increased over time. During the decade, the vote rates of the CHP grew steadily and significantly. In the 1973 elections, the CHP won 34% of the votes, while the AP gained only 29%. The socialists

> failed to transform their parties into mass political organizations. The majority of their members and of the socialist groups came from the intelligentsia and non-working class strata: most of the workers supported the CHP. The splintering of the socialist movement, the strained relations between the various parties and their mutual recriminations created a situation in which the supporters of the socialists were obliged to vote for left-wing RPP [Republican People's Party, CHP in Turkish] candidates. (Lipovsky 1992, 63)

The political upheaval led by the socialists and the political competition among the CHP and AP caused the 1970s to be remembered as a decade of political chaos. Working-class support for the CHP and peasant support for the AP were insufficient to form long-standing single-party governments. Both parties gained fluctuating but almost equivalent political power and popular support, leading to an alternating series of short-lived coalition governments formed by each party. On some occasions, the newly rising Islamist National Salvation Party (Milli Selamet Partisi) and the Nationalist Movement Party joined the coalition governments as well.

In addition to Türk-İş and DİSK, where the AP and CHP were strong, two more confederations, Hak-İş and the Confederation of Nationalist Trade Unions (Milliyetçi İşçi Sendikaları Konfederasyonu), were also founded under the influence of the National Salvation Party and Nationalist Movement Party. All confederations tried to differentiate themselves from Türk-İş by increasing the level of workers' politicization, as opposed to the "above party politics" rhetoric of Türk-İş. As such, the political competition between the center-right, the center-left, the Islamists, the far right, and the socialists resulted in a fragmentation of the labor movement, in which all political groups tried to mobilize the support of workers, leading to the "politicization, polarization and radicalization in the labour sector" (Cizre 1992, 723).

During the 1970s, corporatism was not the preferred strategy of state and capital because it became too expansive considering the declining economy and subsequent crises. Yet the power and militancy of the formal proletariat as well as the political competition among political parties made it impossible to bring an end to corporatist developmentalism

(Mello 2010). As Cizre explains, "While TISK [Confederation of Turkish Employer' Unions] was pressing for more decisive policies against labour, neither the CHP-led coalition governments (1973–74, 1977–78), nor the right-wing nationalist-front coalition governments dominated by the Justice Party (1974–77, 1978–80) were strong enough to impose further state controls on labour to avert and contain the growing militancy of a politicized and polarized labour movement, especially in the socialist DISK." TİSK (Confederation of Turkish Employer' Unions) was calling the rising benefits and escalating strikes "a social disaster" (TİSK 1977, quoted in Cizre 1992, 724). Toward the end of the decade, electoral competition devolved into a political crisis in which no party was able to form a government and the parliament was unable to elect a new president. The combination of an ever growing labor militancy, rising socialist power, and the escalating violence between the socialists and the far right was viewed by the army as a reason to wage the 1980 coup d'état. The coup would bring an end to this regime-wide crisis and would mark the start of the neoliberal era for Turkey. This intervention would bring an end to political competition for national power as the source of populism and destruction of socialist and union power as the source of labor militancy.

On 12 September 1980, the Turkish army staged a coup d'état. The junta closed the parliament and banned all political parties, arrested their leaders, and invalidated the constitution. During the seven years of martial law, 650,000 people (1.5% of the population) were arrested; 1,683,000 people were blacklisted from public sector jobs; 7,000 people were tried on capital punishment charges; the main leftist trade union, DİSK, was closed and its leaders were imprisoned; 23,677 associations were closed; 30,000 workers were dismissed for their political activism; 14,000 people were deprived of their citizenship and 388,000 people were deprived of their passports; 30,000 left the country as political refugees; 50 people were executed, 171 people were determined to have died because of torture, and 300 people died in suspicious ways. Police operations started against all leftist organizations and a total of 98,000 people were put on trial with the accusation of being a member of illegal organizations ("Darbenin bilan-çosu," *Cumhuriyet Gazetesi*, 2000).

The coup was a measure not only against a possible socialist revolution but also against possible working-class resistance to intended neoliberal policies. The coup d'état created suitable political conditions to implement the neoliberal structural adjustment policies that had been proposed by the IMF. During the 1980s, these policies managed to establish an economic and social atmosphere that gave an advantage to capital vis-à-vis labor. Halit Narin, the president of the Employers Union Confederation of Turkey, acclaimed the coup by saying that "until now, the workers have laughed, from now on, we will laugh." He made a good prediction. One of the first actions of the junta would be to freeze wages and outlaw strikes. In a series of similar interventions, the military junta and the following neoliberal government of the Motherland Party (Anavatan Partisi—ANAP), with strong backing from the United States, brought about the dismantling of import-substitutionist industrialism and politically sustained a worsening income distribution.

The government immediately implemented the so-called January 24th Decrees to bring a swift neoliberal transition from import substitutionism to export-oriented growth. This move faced minimal resistance from the workers and the socialist left whose political power was destroyed by the coup, resulting in a 58% decline in real wages and a 51% private sector wage share between 1976 and 1986. The high growth rate after the 1980s did not result in formal job creation and the rate of unemployment has increased during most of the years since then (Adaman and Keyder 2006) (see fig. 14). As Keyder claims,

The share of wages and salaries in national income dropped from around 30 per cent in the 1970s to roughly 20 per cent in the 1980s. Wages in manufacturing had increased, more or less in line with productivity, over the three decades after 1950; by contrast, the level of real wages remained in 2000 what it had been in 1980, having dropped below that for long periods in between. Manufacturing employment in the public sector fell from 250,000 to 100,000 between 1980 and 2000, due to downsizing and privatization. Workers in the state-owned industries had constituted the core of the labor movement of the 1960s and '70s—organized trade unionists who received relatively high wages and good benefits. With privatization, deregulation and flexible employment, the advantages they had enjoyed in a protected manufacturing sector rapidly eroded. Subcontracting, the spread of smaller enterprises and piecework became standard practices; especially as the service sector gained ground, informal and diversified conditions of work increased. (Keyder 2004, 2)

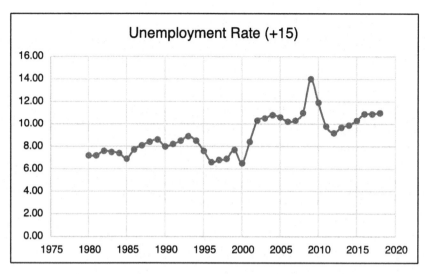

Fig. 14. Unemployment rate in Turkey (1980–2018)

The coup d'état wiped out the associational bargaining power of formal workers in Turkey by demolishing the trade unions, the left-wing political parties, and the radical left. Between 1980 and 1989, the Turkish state and capital made use of this declining associational bargaining power of formal sector workers in order to lower the wages and social welfare rights of the workers (Yeldan 2006). Yet this smooth transition to neoliberalism was halted at the end of the 1980s. The formal proletariat had not yet significantly lost its structural bargaining power during the 1980s because there was no critical change in the skill levels of workers, nor a sharp increase in the labor supply or change in the nonwage earnings of workers. Moreover, formal workers did not lose their workplace bargaining power either because of the enduring capacity to inflict high levels of damage to capital by stopping production. All of these were related also to the rapid growth in export-led industries and a parallel increase in employment. Toward the end of the decade, the formal proletariat started to use its continuing structural bargaining power to resist neoliberal policies.

In 1989, the largest ever wave of labor unrest in Turkish history began. Since the unrest started in the spring of 1989, it has been called the Spring Actions. The labor unrest started with the miners' movement and strikes and then spread to almost all state-owned enterprises and private sector concerns. For a period of almost three years, thousands of labor strikes of different scales and durations occurred. Workers developed nonstrike forms of protest as well, including passive resistances such as sickouts (collective visits to medical centers), refusing to shave, occupying factories, and so forth. Although the 1970s was the heyday of formal proletarian protests in Turkey, it is important to note that the greatest labor unrest wave in Turkish history occurred during the few years that spanned the late 1980s and early 1990s, almost a decade after the military coup (Doğan 2010; Voyvoda 2011). This militancy was possible because of the still enduring structural bargaining power of workers in addition to suitable electoral political conditions (explained in subsequent chapters).

After the severe repression of the early 1980s, workers took advantage of a general political opening in Turkey in the late 1980s. Electoral competition among mainstream parties contributed to this. Also, some scholars have argued that the military intervention and state repression contributed to the unity of the labor movement to some extent as an unintended consequence. Corporatist Türk-İş and Islamist Hak-İş became the main beneficiaries of the coup, while the socialist DİSK was harshly repressed. They actively supported the coup with the hope that their main rival would be eliminated. State repression to level out ideological differences between unions eliminated the conflict between these unions and members of these unions managed to raise strong demands in a militant way, most of the time in wildcat strike actions (Koç 1999; Mello 2010).

The Spring Actions were defeated by the government using repression. Most of the strikes were banned by the government, using the Gulf War and national security as a pretext. After the defeat of the Spring Actions, the neoliberal process was resumed and accelerated again, as reflected by the fact that the rate of unemployment started to dramatically increase only then. The expansion of neoliberal capitalist accumulation became possible after the waves of labor unrest subsided in the early 1990s. As soon as the labor strikes came to a halt, public enterprises started to lay off those workers who had been active in organizing the strikes, and, in a short while, these public enterprises themselves started to be privatized.

The Politics of the Informal Proletariat

During the neoliberal period starting in the 1980s, the Islamist and Kurdish political movements became the main political actors that mobilized grassroots opposition to the neoliberal project. Since the 1990s, an informal proletariat has replaced the formal proletariat as the center of grassroots politics, and the main hegemonic struggle has shifted into winning the support of the informal proletariat in the struggle to delegitimize neoliberal policies. The informal proletariat of Turkey's slums became the main object of political party competition. As this section will explain, becoming a huge source of popular support for contending political parties, the informal worker also emerged as the main political threat to the state due to the influence of Islamist and Kurdish radical groups.

During the three decades following the military coup, an informal proletariat has replaced the declining formal proletariat as the center of grassroots politics. As seen in figure 15 below, the informal proletariat has become increasingly active, with the levels of informal proletarian events in the 1990s close to those of formal proletarians in the 1970s.

There are important structural processes, such as neoliberal export-oriented policies or the internal displacement of Kurds, that have both enhanced and undermined the social power of the formal and informal proletariat. As the Turkish economy was incorporated into global economic networks through neoliberal policies, the formal proletariat has been unmade and replaced by an emerging informal proletariat. Since the 1990s, neoliberal economic policies have encouraged and depended largely on temporary flexible employment schemes. Subcontracted and informal labor has become the crux of a new accumulation regime in manufacturing and services in both the private and public sector (Cam 2002). Rapid urbanization after the 1990s also contributed to the demographic rise of the informal proletariat. Turkey's major cities have absorbed waves of mass migration from Turkey's peripheral regions since the 1950s. However, it is important to differentiate between migration before and after the 1990s in terms of the conditions that caused them. Up until the 1990s, population movements to urban areas were primarily driven by economic concerns, particularly by employment opportunities in big cities. In other words, this migration wave was mainly a pull migration (Taş and Lightfoot 2005). However, migration after the 1990s was mainly a push migration caused by a combination of factors. First, there was a more rapid mechanization of agriculture than before and a parallel decline in agricultural subsidies. As a result, between 1980 and 1997, the number of tractors tripled in the country and the number of livestock fell from 49 million to 32 million, predominantly in Kurdish areas where the effects of neoliberalism were felt

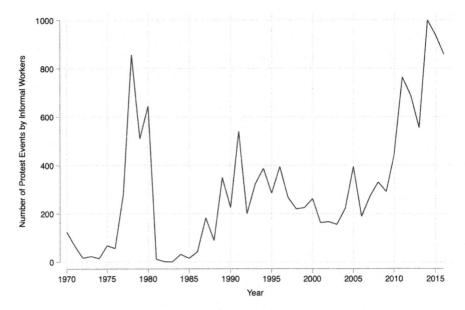

Fig. 15. Grassroots political activities of the informal proletariat (1970–2017)

the most. This created an exodus of rural workers (with poor fortunes and prospects) from all regions of the country to the urbanized western parts of Turkey (Adaman and Keyder 2006; Cam 2002).

The second source of rapid migration during the neoliberal era was the internal displacement of Kurds during the 1990s. Under the Emergency State Rule imposed in the southeast, Turkish military forces evacuated and burned more than 3,000 villages in Kurdish regions and initiated a policy of internal displacement to block growing rural Kurdish popular support for the Kurdistan's Workers Party. Millions of Kurdish peasants were forced to migrate, initially to the cities within their region, but later on to western parts of the country (Kurban and Yükseker 2009; Ayata and Yükseker 2005). According to a recent survey conducted by the KONDA Research Institute, 4.8% of Turkey's population and 23% of the Kurdish population was internally displaced during the 1990s. Considering the population of Turkey during this period, this means that approximately 2.3 million people were uprooted and displaced. The internal displacement of the Kurds after the 1980 coup has been one of the largest internal displacement operations in the world (along with those in Nigeria, Somalia, Sudan, Zimbabwe, and Colombia).

While the internal displacement of Kurds was intended as a military measure against the Kurdish insurgency, it had unintended consequences in terms of the social, political, and economic processes that would take place during the following decade. First, internal displacement has radically changed the class structure of Turkey and the ethnic composition of the working class. Second, it has urbanized the Kurdish movement and, ironically, made Istanbul the city with the largest Kurdish population in the world, with three million Kurds out of a population of 12 million. Third, this has transformed the pace and content of Kurdish migration, making it quantitatively and qualitatively different from previous migration waves (Keyder and Yenal 2011).

Unlike earlier generations of migrants, the newcomers to Turkey's major cities were pushed from their lands because of political and military-security concerns instead of being pulled by the cities' social and economic opportunities. Among migrants, the Kurds were the most disadvantaged group because internal displacement created a condition of dispossession for them. They were forced to leave their villages, houses, and arable land behind, relying mainly on kin and community networks to survive under extremely unfavorable conditions in the economic and spatial peripheries of the cities (Ayata and Yükseker 2005). Furthermore, this forced migration occurred in a neoliberal economic environment in which there were very limited opportunities for formal permanent jobs. Constituting a cheap labor source without professional qualifications and ready to work in any job they could find, displaced Kurds became a major part of the informal labor market in cities like Istanbul. Due to neoliberal policies, including the privatization of state-owned enterprises and the rise of outsourcing, formal employment has declined as a social reality as well as an expectation for the new migrants. According to a recent KONDA survey, the rate of informality is more than two times higher among Kurds than among non-Kurds (KONDA 2019). In addition, improvements in automation and new management techniques, introduced to minimize labor costs, have reduced formal employment still further in nonagricultural sectors. Even between 1986 and 1996, when the neoliberal project was again slowed, 300,000 workers lost their jobs in public enterprises (Cam 2002, 100). Since the 1990s, the globally competitive sectors of the Turkish economy—textiles and apparel, construction, shipbuilding, and electrical equipment production—have depended largely on subcontracting chains based in the informal economy and on an informal working proletariat crowding the slum areas of major cities. Overall, the rapid proletarianiza-tion of the Kurds and the growth of the informal proletariat have turned out to be two converging processes: the war in the southeast has changed the ethnic composition of the working class in Turkey by proletarianizing the Kurdish population, and Kurdicizing the expanding informal prole-tariat. As a result, slum areas in Turkey have grown dramatically while gaining a new ethnic characteristic (Yörük 2012).

Urban Kurds have been increasingly included in the labor force as part of the informal proletariat that has replaced the diminished formal prole-tariat, whose structural bargaining power had been too strong to allow the neoliberal project to be implemented. The weak bargaining power of Kurds has made them a cheap and flexible labor source for the new accumulation regime, an important factor contributing to the immense success that the Turkish economy has recently achieved in the global economy. Turkey has done much better than other comparable countries as an emerging econ-omy and a center of capitalist production and accumulation.[2] The inter-nal displacement of Kurds is the most extensive and rapid dispossession and proletarianization operation in Turkish history, supplying an excess of cheap, informal, insecure, disposable, and fully proletarianized labor. It has created the material conditions for successful neoliberal accumulation by providing the backbone of the informal labor market for textiles, con-struction, food production, dock work, and seasonal agricultural produc-tion that have led economic growth in Turkey. In sum, the unmaking of Turkey's formal proletariat and its structural and associational bargaining power, as well as the subsequent creation (through internal displacement) of a significantly ethnicized informal proletariat without structural bar-gaining power, have rendered the Turkish economy an important zone of flexible accumulation in the world economy.

After the 1990s, the growing informal proletariat has become the cen-ter of grassroots politics. Already in the 1970s, the informal proletariat was politically active and important to a certain extent. Two important radical organizations of the 1970s, Halkın Kurtuluşu (People's Libera-

---

2. Turkish exports increased from $3 billion in 1980 to $13 billion in 1990, to $50 billion in 2000, and to $113 billion in 2010. Gross national income (GNI) increased from $93 billion in 1980 to $235 billion in 1990, and from $580 billion in 2000 to $1,103 billion in 2010. This corresponds to a GNI per capita of $2,120 in 1980, $4,350 in 1990, $9,120 in 2000, and $15,170 in 2010 (World Bank 2011). In 2008, Turkey was ranked third in construction business worldwide, and fourth in textiles and clothing.

tion) and Dev-Yol (Devrimci Yol—Revolutionary Path), were the successors of THKO and THKP-C. They were strong in slum areas where an informal proletariat was also emerging out of migrant populations. These slum dwellers were developing kinship and family networks, and the leftist groups helped turn these networks into class-based solidarity institutions. This encompassed various solutions to the material needs of the residents of these neighborhoods, including militant methods for bringing municipal services (e.g., occupying public buses), parceling out the land and collective construction of squatter houses, reconciliation of interfamily conflict, gathering solidarity funds, provision of health services, and protection of the neighborhoods against security forces or far-right groups. These activities contributed to turning the slum areas of big cities into liberated zones by the end of the 1970s.

While the formal proletariat was already radicalized by socialist movements in the 1970s, the informal proletariat of the slums was radicalized by the Islamist and Kurdish movements in the 1990s and by the Kurdish movement in the 2000s. During the 1990s, it was the Islamists who mobilized anti-neoliberal grievances, while in the 2000s, because of the deradicalization of the Islamist movement that enabled the imposition of neoliberal hegemony in Turkey, it was the radicalization of the Kurdish movement that became the main force resisting this hegemonic establishment. In the 2000s, the Islamists formed the government and started to contain the Kurdish slum radicalization. That is, the left-leaning Kurdish movement has replaced Islamists as the main center of anti-neoliberal mobilization targeting the informal proletariat. The Justice and Development Party (Adalet ve Kalkınma Partisi—AKP) only gained hegemony to the extent that the informal proletariat gave consent to government policies and lost power to the extent that the informal proletariat was mobilized by the opposition.

Islamism as a political movement in Turkey has its origins in the 1970s. The long-standing political leader of Turkish political Islam, Necmettin Erbakan, established the first Islamist party, the National Order Party (Milli Nizam Partisi), in 1970. Erbakan's success mainly depended on support from two sectors during the 1970s. The first group was composed of small provincial entrepreneurs who were opposing westernization, secularism, state industrial policies, the growing labor militancy, and the leftist movement. The second sector were conservative peasants and artisans who sympathized with Erbakan's anti-Western rhetoric and his economic statism that promised an economic system based on communally owned private enterprises (Öniş 2007; Tuğal 2007).

After the coup in 1980, the state organized and mobilized Islamic social and political forces in order to contain the remaining threat from workers and Kurds: "The military junta subscribed uncritically to the American policy of encouraging Islamism as a buffer against the socialist movement" (Keyder 2004, 3). During the 1980s and 1990s, this project in Turkey aimed at creating an Islamic political atmosphere among the masses able to challenge the dangerous leftist and Kurdish ideologies while being minimally abrasive to the dominant Kemalist structures. This controlled Islamism aimed at a synthesis of Turkish nationalism and religious conservatism (Tuğal 2007).

This set the political stage for the Islamic movement to flourish and mobilize broader segments of the population. However, this project backfired in a different direction. State-sponsored Islamism organized into an independent political movement and a radical Islamist party, the Welfare Party, by the 1990s. The cadres of the movement assumed positions in various ranks of the state bureaucracy, in education, health, justice, and state finance, and produced a mass base composed of the newly urbanized informal workers (Shively 2008). The effects of neoliberal structural adjustment policies, rapid migration especially of Kurds, and the Islamic Revolution in Iran enabled the Islamist movement organized around the new Welfare Party to appeal to the growing informal proletariat of the slums (Öniş 2007). The Islamic Revolution in Iran

was an electrifying message for the impoverished young workers streaming towards the cities in hope of jobs. Under conditions of increasing inequality, the left was politically and ideologically absent after the 1980 military crackdown. The squatters of the neo-liberal period, who encountered the consumerist wealth of the city without being able to partake of it, could look neither to the social-revolutionary option that had mobilized earlier generations nor to the hope of joining an expanding industrial working class. In this environment, a militant, socially radical Islamism had much to offer. Religious responses multiplied to fill the political vacuum, while faith based welfare substituted for the formal social security system gutted by expenditure cuts. . . . The Welfare Party was also very vocal on the Kurdish question, promising to recognize the

Kurdish language and culture; this won it substantial support not only in the south-east of the country but also among the huge numbers of Kurdish migrants to the central and western cities. (Tuğal 2007, 10–11)

During the 1990s, center-left and center-right parties as well as the radical left ceased to mobilize the grievances emanating out of neoliberalization. Failure to provide any democratic and left-wing solution to the political and economic turmoil surrounding the subalterns of the country, the Social Democratic Populist Party (Sosyal Demokrat Halkçı Parti - SHP) turned back to the rigid secularist position of the early Republican People's Party (CHP). This position has been strengthened and has remained the main political strategy followed by the social democrats since the mid-1990s. Indeed, during their coalition government, the social democrats did nothing but silently watch what happened to those whose support brought the Social Democratic Populist Party to power (Öniş 2007). The Kurds were oppressed with state terror, dozens of Alevi intellectuals were massacred in Sivas in 1993, and the formal proletariat was ruined under neoliberalization. This resulted in an alienation of the social democrats from the subalterns and rapidly and permanently turned them back into an elitist and secularist Kemalist position—its historically original position. The revolutionary left, smashed by the military coup, was still too weak to mobilize the informal proletariat, and in this vacuum the Islamists grew as the main political power to garner the political support of the growing informal proletariat ruined by neoliberalization (Özbudun and Hale 2009; Şenyuva 2009).

Furthermore, the Welfare Party also appealed to the employers of these informal proletarians. The bourgeois factions that had supported the Islamist party in the 1970s also transformed from small, nationalistic provincial entrepreneurs into big capitalists integrated into global capitalist networks. These small enterprises in provincial cities swiftly adapted to the logic of post-Fordism, used subcontracting chains and enjoyed cheap, flexible, nonunionized informal labor in labor-intensive sectors located in buyer-driven commodity networks. These small capitalists turned into the so-called Anatolian Tigers (closely resembling the emerging capitalist classes in East Asia), and their cities, such as Kayseri and Gaziantep, have become regional industrial centers (Gümüşçü and Sert 2009). These conservative but simultaneously more outward-looking capitalists provided a much stronger bourgeois support for the Welfare Party than the inward-looking Islamist entrepreneurs of the 1970s. These Muslim capitalists later organized themselves into a business organization, MÜSİAD (Independent Industrialists and Businessmen's Association), that became a counterweight to TÜSİAD (Turkish Industry & Business Association), the organization of Istanbul-based secularist capitalists (Yavuz 1999).

During the 1990s, the Welfare Party managed to garner support from the emerging sectors of the bourgeoisie and the informal proletariat of the now globalized Turkey, by using a seemingly contradictory, and perhaps thus more powerful, ideological framework. The famous Just Order (Adil Düzen) system that became Erbakan's founding ideology "emphasized the virtues of private enterprise, appeals to workers' rights and social justice predominated. In a 'just' Islamic economy, workers' representatives would be assigned a crucial role, there would be full employment and wages would be universally set by the state" (Tuğal 2007, 12). The Islamist movement radicalized the informal proletariat in the 1990s. Slum dwellers gave practical support to the Islamic Welfare Party in its struggle against the secularist establishment, by providing electoral power and street militancy (see fig. 16).

This growing political power of Islamists was also translated into electoral success. Islamist votes increased from 8% in 1987 to 16% in 1991 to 22% in 1996, bringing the Welfare Party to office. However, the Welfare Party also eventually minimized the egalitarian rhetoric and declared the Just Order as "the real pro-private sector order" and that "there would be no strikes or lockouts under the Islamist order, since there would be no need for them" (Tuğal 2007, 13).

The Islamists' road to national power began with running municipal governments in the 1990s. In 1994, the Welfare Party, riding the votes from the slum-dwelling informal proletariat, won the municipality elections in several big cities, including Istanbul, Ankara, Diyarbakır (the biggest city in the Kurdish region), Kayseri (the new center of industry), and Konya. This indeed supported the emerging middle class fears and bourgeois discourse that was based on a deep grievance about the slums as *the* source of backwardness and tradition and the social force that would ruralize the urban areas in Turkey (Gümüşçü and Sert 2009). Yet the Welfare Party embraced the slums with a rhetoric that combined justice and tradition, supported largely by welfare populism (discussed later), as well as by increasing the quality of urban services, especially in long-neglected areas.

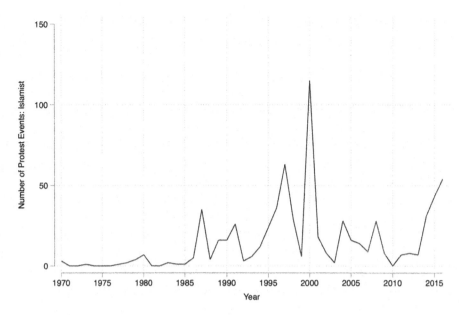

Fig. 16. Grassroots political activities of the Islamist movement (1970–2017)

These policies resulted in a major success for the Welfare Party in the 1995 general elections (Tuğal 2007). In this context, Recep Tayyip Erdoğan, the mayor of Istanbul, established his popularity and paved the way for his decade-long and ongoing rule of the country. As indicated by the declining trend in the 2000s in figure 16, Erdogan's AKP would deradicalize the radical Islamist movement through what Cihan Tuğal has called a "Passive Revolution" (Tugal 2009).

Since the early 1980s, the Kurdistan Workers' Party has led a Kurdish uprising against the Turkish state that continues today. The Kurds constitute 18% of the current population in Turkey, and there has been an intermittent Kurdish nationalist movement since the foundation of the republic in 1923. The PKK's original goal was to create an independent, socialist Kurdish state in Kurdistan, a geographical region that comprises parts of southeastern Turkey, northeastern Iraq, northeastern Syria, and northwestern Iran, where the Kurdish population constitutes the majority. After the mid-1990s, the objective shifted to the attainment of Kurdish cultural and identity rights that have been fiercely denied by the Turkish state since the 1920s. During the 2000s, the main Kurdish movement focus became the decentralization of state power and the establishment of regional governments in a system called "Democratic Autonomy" to secure the rights of minorities.

The PKK started the guerrilla struggle against the Turkish state in the Kurdish areas of the country in 1984. The popularity of the PKK among the Kurdish people, which was then mostly a peasant population, rapidly grew in the late 1980s, and the PKK became capable of mobilizing huge numbers of the Kurdish masses in the 1990s. In 1987, the Turkish government declared Emergency State Rule and set up a Special Governorship of Emergency Rule, which would be effective until 2002. Considering the martial law imposed between 1978 and 1987, the Kurdish region had been placed under extraordinary security measures for a total period of 24 years.

Between 1989 and 1993, the PKK called hundreds of thousands of Kurds for armed and civil disobedience, and almost every city in the Kurdish region simultaneously staged mass protests against the state. The rebellion in Nusaybin, a town close to the Syrian border, marked the beginning of this Serhildan, the Kurdish intifada, and the riots spread to other cities in the southeast and then to the other cities in the entire Kurdish region. This long-standing popular unrest and the accompanying escalation of guerrilla warfare made it clear that the Kurds had become a serious threat for the Turkish state.

Grassroots political activities among the non-Kurds and outside of the Kurdish regions have declined, while there has been an increase among the Kurds and in the Kurdish regions (see fig. 17 through fig. 21). There was an increase in grassroots activities in rural areas, while there was a decline in activities in city centers. This increase in rural activities was largely caused by the fact that Kurdish guerrillas fight and organize in rural areas. The Kurdish movement originated in rural areas and most of the fighting between the PKK and the state security forces has occurred in rural areas. The PKK also garnered much of its support from the rural areas, especially in the 1990s. Figure 20 and 21 show that there has been a shift in grassroots political activities from non-Kurdish to Kurdish regions of the country.

In the early 1990s, the Turkish government faced two big grassroots political challenges at the same time: the Kurdish unrest in the east and the labor unrest (the Spring Actions) in the west. This was a coincidence because there was no significant ideological or organizational link connecting the Kurdish unrest in eastern Turkey and the labor unrest in western

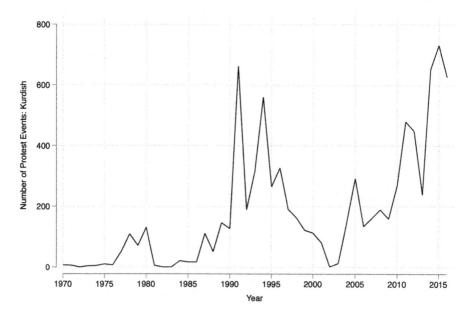

Fig. 17. Grassroots political activities of the Kurdish movement (1970–2017)

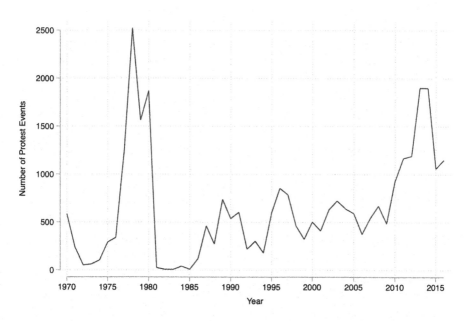

Fig. 18. Grassroots political activities of non-Kurdish origin (1970–2017)

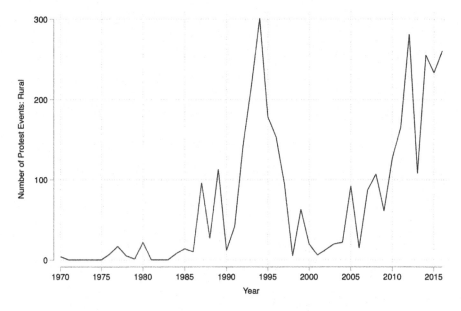

Fig. 19. Grassroots political activities in rural areas (1970–2017)

Turkey. Yet this historical coincidence has influenced the trajectory of the working-class movement and the Kurdish movement in a permanent way since the late 1990s.

In response to the labor unrest, after a period of populism, labor strikes were banned, using the first Gulf War as a pretext. As a response to the growing level of rural grassroots activity in the Kurdish region, the Turkish state initiated a large-scale policy of internal displacement. These developments have worsened conditions for formal proletarian activism. The rise of subcontracting and informality has made it ever more difficult to organize workers through unions. However, it has also opened a new zone of struggle that is difficult for the state to control. In the late 1990s, this largely Kurdish informal proletariat residing in the slums of metropolises started to create the embryo of a political threat to the state. The Kurdish informal proletariat gained its associational capacity with the emerging urban-based, legal left-wing Kurdish political parties. Not only the Kurdish political parties but also the radical left have recognized this shift of the center of social movements toward the slums. Therefore, as in many other countries, the slums in Turkey have turned into places that are unpredict-

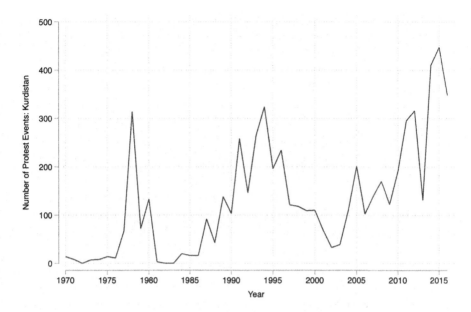

Fig. 20. Grassroots political activities in the Kurdish region (1970–2017)

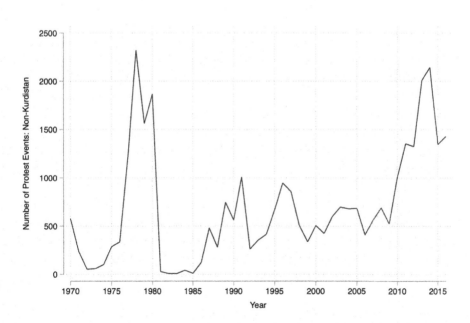

Fig. 21. Grassroots political activities outside of the Kurdish region (1970–2017)

ably prone to social explosions. As the figures above demonstrate, Kurdish issues have become one of the main centers of grassroots political activism. The first signs of this transformation came with the Gazi Neighborhood Riots in 1995 and May 1st celebrations in 1996, both in Istanbul. At the Gazi events, the security forces could not keep control of the Gazi slum, and on 1 May 1996, the slum unrest exploded into a huge riot in the city center. The informal proletarians had become the instigators of these riots, and of many others that followed.

Since the 1990s, the informal proletariat of the slums, and particularly the Kurdish poor, have become the main players of grassroots politics in Turkey, providing both potential threats as well as potential bases of popular support for political parties. Thirty years of Kurdish armed struggle, urbanization, proletarianization, and impoverishment have expanded the Kurdish political movement into the slum areas of big cities. The urban Kurds have increasingly radicalized and carried out massive protests and uprisings during the decade in the Kurdish region as well as in the metropolises in the western parts of Turkey. The ethnic threat to the regime has also morphed into electoral competition.

Kurdish grassroots mobilization has been organized by a constellation of political groups, which has been designated as the "Kurdish political movement." Starting in the 1990s, the Kurdish movement in Turkey has been organized through illegal and legal wings, similar to how the Euskadi Ta Askatasuna (ETA)–Herri Batasuna in Spain and the Irish Republican Army (IRA)–Sinn Féin in Northern Ireland have been organized. A number of subsequent Kurdish parties have been founded because the Supreme Court has outlawed each of them in turn. One can say that Kurdish grassroots mobilization is significantly centralized, hierarchical, and well organized. In each city, district, and neighborhood, the legal Kurdish political parties have functioning branches. In addition, the movement is also organized through nongovernmental organizations, and these organizations, including the ones that provide social assistance and solidarity, are able to galvanize the Kurds into one voice. As a result, the Kurdish political movement has become one of the largest radical grassroots social movements in the contemporary world, able to bring millions of Kurds into the streets, and garner the votes of half of the Kurds in Turkey, whose population has reached over 18 million.

In the 1991 elections, the candidates of the Kurdish party of the time, the People's Labor Party (Halkın Emek Partisi), joined the elections under the auspices of the SHP, and 10 Kurdish candidates were elected to the parliament. This coalition between social democrats and Kurds decreased the votes of the social democrats in the non-Kurdish regions of the country, while the votes increased significantly in the Kurdish regions. Yet, as the social democrats ceased to accommodate the Kurdish deputies, they resigned from the party, and joined the People's Labor Party, which was soon banned by the Supreme Court. The Kurdish deputies joined the new Kurdish party, the Democracy Party (Demokrasi Partisi—DEP), which was founded after the People's Labor Party.

However, in 1994, these Kurdish deputies were arrested in the parliament because they swore the parliamentary oath in Kurdish. The Democracy Party was also closed down and the deputies spent the following decade in prison. Then, the Peace and Democracy Party (Barış ve Demokrasi Partisi) was founded in 2008, and the latest People's Democracy Party (Halkların Demokrasi Partisi—HDP) was founded in 2012. All of these Kurdish parties, except for the HDP, received 5-6% of the votes in general elections, while the HDP has gained 12–13% popular support since the mid-2010s.

During the 2000s, the governing AKP has been intensely competing with these Kurdish parties in the entire Kurdish region of Turkey as well as in the slum areas of metropolises. This increase in Kurdish political power has also resulted from a series of successful electoral alliances with the socialist left in Turkey. The collective electoral campaigns have worked very well in the Kurdish region as well as in poor slums of metropolises since the 2007 elections. The HDP achieved major gains in the national elections of June 2015 when it won 13.12% of the votes, enough to end the long-standing majority-party rule of the AKP. With the AKP reduced to minority rule status, President Recep Tayyip Erdoğan could not realize his long-term dream of consolidating his power by changing the constitution toward a presidential system. The HDP's electoral success is also the historical peak of any pro-Kurdish party or radical left party in Turkey thus far. Previous pro-Kurdish parties had participated in elections since the early 1990s, but their vote shares remained at 4–6%. In the June 2015 elections, however, the HDP not only became the AKP's main political rival in the Kurdish region and in metropolitan working-class neighborhoods, but also the first pro-Kurdish party in Turkey to garner the majority of Kurdish votes.

The legal and illegal wings of the Kurdish movement, together with hundreds of NGOs, youth and women's organizations, and political organizations of the Kurdish diaspora in most European countries have together managed to mobilize Kurds, both to provide electoral support and instigate frequent uprisings in Turkey's urban areas. Since the late 1990s, uprisings, protests, and police patrols and operations have become constant futures of the Kurdish populated city slums, both in the Kurdish southeast and western regions. Kurdish parties have risen to become the governing AKP's main radical political rival in both areas, especially as the cease-fire agreed between the PKK and the Turkish state since the early 2000s has improved its chances of success in democratic politics. This growing power of the Kurdish opposition has become the main challenge to the AKP's neoliberal hegemony. In sum, during the 2000s, the AKP has competed with the Kurdish parties to win the support of Turkey's Kurdish informal proletariat. While socialist Kurdish parties have partly replaced the radical Islamists of the 1990s in responding to the grievances of the (Kurdish) informal proletariat against neoliberalism, the AKP has turned Islamism into a force for containing the political activism of the slums.

The AKP's response to this rise of Kurdish power has been inconsistent and ambivalent. The party first gained the support of the Kurdish masses by promising to bring about a democratic solution to Turkey's Kurdish problem. However, this was followed by a period of repression during the mid-2000s. Later, between 2007 and 2009, the AKP introduced both a discourse and policy of democratic relaxation regarding the identity rights of Kurds in Turkey through a program called the "Kurdish Overture." This program included state TV broadcasting in Kurdish for the first time and the legalization of teaching the Kurdish language. Since 2009, however, the AKP has launched increasing numbers of police operations targeting Kurdish parties. For example, the police have arrested more than 7,000 members of the Peace and Democracy Party since 2010 and the governing AKP has withdrawn its Kurdish Overture policies. For example, in March 2012, the AKP outlawed the Kurdish Newroz (New Year) celebrations. Despite strict security measures taken by the government, hundreds of thousands of Kurds gathered in Diyarbakir on Newroz, ignoring the government's demands and indicating the extent to which the Kurdish movement is able to mobilize. Indeed, coercive policies more generally have only resulted in increasing Kurdish popular support for Kurdish parties. In short, the HDP, as a representative of Kurds in Turkey, has increasingly managed to mobilize Kurdish slum populations, making it a serious competitor for votes in these areas with the governing AKP.

The ruling party's success against the Kemalist elites left behind a radicalized secularist popular base. Their disappointment with Kemalist leaders' failure to challenge the AKP led to militant street activism as the sole remaining form of political opposition, culminating in the outbreak of the Gezi protests in June 2013 (Yörük and Yüksel 2014). Shortly after the Gezi protests, Erdoğan's rule was challenged once more in December 2013 through the largest corruption scandal in Turkish history, which involved some ministers and Erdoğan's family and himself. This episode was part of a larger political battle between the governing AKP and the Gülen Community, with which the AKP itself allied against the Kemalist bloc until recently (Gürel 2015). This struggle between Fetullah Gülen and Recep Tayyip Erdoğan eventually culminated in a failed military coup on 15 July 2016. After the coup attempt, Erdoğan deepened his one-man rule through repressive policies targeting all forms of political opposition, and increasing his direct control over the media, universities, the judiciary, and the economy. As such, Turkey's ranking in the World Press Freedom Index declined from 98 in 2006 to 151 in 2016. Erdoğan also launched a full-scale offensive against the Kurdish opposition that had recently gained unprecedented power. While he consolidated his personalistic rule, the country was being hit by terrorist attacks, a renewed ethnic conflict, a deepening economic crisis, and ever widening authoritarianism.

Conclusion

It has been commonly thought that in the neoliberal era, grassroots politics in general are no longer a central force shaping politics and policies. This widespread assumption has indeed little empirical basis. Empirical analysis of grassroots political events that have taken place in Turkey since 1970 has shown that, over the last four decades, grassroots politics in Turkey have not vanished but undergone a transformation: the center of grassroots politics has shifted from the formal proletariat to the informal proletariat and from non-Kurds to the Kurds. The analysis of the grassroots politics dataset generated from newspaper archives has provided strong support for the initial hypothesis.

Until the 1980s, the formal proletariat had gained substantive structural bargaining power as a result of import-substitutionist developmentalism. This structural bargaining power was translated into an associational bargaining power through trade union militancy and the mobilization of the socialist left. Moreover, the intense political competition between the center-left and the center-right has provided the formal proletariat with extensive electoral power. The military coup in 1980 swiftly suppressed the power of the formal proletariat and created a grassroots political silence for almost a decade. This silence was broken by the largest wave of labor unrest in Turkish history, the Spring Actions that occurred in the early 1990s. The eventual weakening of the formal proletariat came with the suppression of the Spring Actions.

The Kurds facilitated the conditions of a competitive informal labor market, and the single-party government of the 2000s provided the necessary political initiative to implement neoliberal policies without populist pressures. The 1980s and 1990s remained as a transition period, and the full-scale neoliberal project could only start in the 2000s. In the 1990s, an informal proletariat that was crafted through neoliberal export-oriented policies emerged as the new grassroots political actor. Under the influence of Islamist and Kurdish radical groups, this informal proletariat from the slums has become the main object of political party competition as a vast source of both popular support as well as political threat. In other words, poverty has been mobilized into politics, used by ethnic politicians, religious and leftist organizations, or the state itself. Specifically, from the 1990s to the 2000s, the Kurdish movement in Turkey has remained as the epicenter of political opposition against the governments that implemented neoliberal policies. This has occurred as the Islamists have been absorbed into neoliberalism by the governing AKP, and the urban Kurds have been mobilized into radicalism by the Kurdish political parties. As Tuğal has stated, the Islamist Welfare Party of the 1990s had a strategy of mobilizing the subaltern grievances emanating from neoliberalism among the informal proletariat toward Islamic radicalism in order to capture state power. The Islamist AKP of the 2000s replaced this radicalizing strategy with an alternative strategy of containing the grievances from neoliberalism into political patronage in order to maintain state power. In this process, the Islamist movement captured state power, became deradicalized and neoliberalized, while the Kurdish movement became the main oppositional force, radicalized and anti-neoliberal. Structurally, the Kurdish war and the internal displacement of the Kurds during the 1990s proletarianized the Kurds and Kurdicized the proletariat in Turkey. This has facilitated the almost unprecedented "success" of neoliberal capitalist accumulation in Turkey by creating a huge supply of cheap and informal labor. Politically, the AKP has endeavored, first, to mobilize the popular support of lower classes in Turkey in its competition with the CHP and the military and, second, to contain Kurdish parties and the political instability resulting from the grievances of poor Kurds. The Kurdish movement has emerged as the most significant competitor of the AKP in slum areas and this has impeded the AKP's capacity to win over the informal proletariat to its neoliberal agenda. Beyond this impediment, which is already set in motion by the Kurds against the AKP's neoliberal hegemony, the Kurdish movement's search for a strategic alliance with the Turkish radical left, as well as its demand for democratic autonomy for the Kurds, has created a potential for furthering the anticapitalist mobilization of the slums. While the Islamists were more radical and mobilized the grievances among the informal proletariat against neoliberal developments in the 1990s, they became neoliberal and contained the proletarian grievances against neoliberalism in the 2000s. Thus the Kurdish party emerged as the main political actors able to mobilize the slums against the neoliberal economic and political hegemony. Yet, since the current Kurdish party and its radical leftist allies are much weaker than the governing AKP, containment of the Kurdish grievances has taken precedence over mobilization of the same, and this explains the relatively smooth passage to neoliberal hegemony in Turkey during the 2000s.

CHAPTER 4

The Politics of the Turkish Welfare System's Transformation

With roots tracing back to the 19th-century poor relief structures of the Ottoman Empire, the welfare state in Turkey has been shaped by both intra-elite political struggles and conflict between elites and popular groups. This chapter will show that political competition among elites and government strategies to contain social unrest have contributed to this transformation, as the locus of grassroots political mobilization has shifted from formal to informal working classes and from Turks to Kurds. The expansion of the Turkish welfare state during a period of neoliberalism is directly tied to rivalries among mainstream parties and the impact of grassroots politics, as well as the political mechanisms that mediate and transform economic and demographic pressures into social policies. These mechanisms, involving conflicts among competing mainstream and nonmainstream political actors, reveal that political efforts to contain the political radicalization of the informal proletariat and to mobilize its electoral support have driven the expansion and distribution of social assistance policies.[1] For the most part, expansion of the welfare state in Turkey

---

1. This distinction between the formal and informal proletariat comes from Alejandro Portes and Kelly Hoffman (2003). On the one hand, Portes and Hoffman describe the formal proletariat as the workers in industry, services, and agriculture that are protected by existing labor laws. On the other, the informal proletariat is composed of those workers who are not incorporated into fully commodified, legally regulated working relations, but survive at the margins through a wide variety of subsistence and semiclandestine economic activities. The informal proletariat is "the sum of own account workers minus professionals and technicians, domestic servants, and paid and unpaid workers in microenterprises" (Portes and Hoffman 2003, 54).

has occurred during the leadership of right-wing governments. While the left has rarely ruled in Turkey, its history of welfare expansion nevertheless defies the dominant scholarly and public view that the welfare state is a product of left-wing politics. Recent expansion of the welfare state during the rule of the Justice and Development Party (AKP) can be explained by the party's attempts to contain the radicalism of the Kurdish poor and garner the popular support of the poor masses. While the Kurdish poor are the main grassroots threat for neoliberal governments, the double logic of political containment and mobilization characterizes patterns of welfare system change in all periods since the rise of modern welfare provision in Turkey, with different classes or ethnic groups being both contained and mobilized by successive governments.

The Periods and Causes of Welfare Policy Changes

An explanation of how specific political mechanisms have shaped the Turkish welfare state requires a general understanding of the radical shifts in welfare provision since the 1960s. Table 2 illustrates periods of the welfare state's transformation, with each period characterized by a different combination of structural, global, electoral, and contentious political dynamics. During the 1960s and 1970s, employment-based social security policies were politically linked to the import-substitutionist industrialization development model, which was part of the US hegemonic project for middle-income countries during the Cold War. Based on the provision of extensive welfare benefits for formal sector workers, this project entailed a corporatist system designed to help contain the socialist threat. At the same time, this strategy gave structural bargaining power to the formal proletariat. The rise of a radical socialist movement in Turkey later mobilized this power into associational bargaining power and labor militancy.

Governments of the 1970s attempted to contain this threat by further increasing levels of welfare benefits (such as old age pensions and sickness insurance), union rights, and real wages (Yeldan 2006; Koç 2003). Meanwhile, the intense left-right party competition necessitated the mobilization of working-class support through further welfare provision. The Justice Party (AP) and the Republican People's Party (CHP) of the 1970s engaged in fierce political competition and provided welfare concessions. The double exigency, political competition and social unrest, characterizing this period forced governments to significantly expand the social welfare system, benefiting large sectors of the formal working classes. In the view of governing politicians, the economic crisis of the 1970s necessitated an eventual liquidation of welfare rights and the corporatist system; their plan, however, was obstructed due to socialist mobilization, the power of labor unions, and intense political party competition.

An ultimate solution to the problem of the working classes was the employment of fierce state repression. The 1980 military coup eliminated the political competition and socialist mobilization that, during the 1970s, gave the formal proletariat bargaining power, an advantage that angered 1980s elites. In this political context of state repression, neoliberal policies (including employment-based welfare cuts, wage reductions, and anti-union legislation) were enacted until the late 1980s, with minimal resistance from workers. Despite this fact, workers maintained their structural bargaining power, as workplace and labor market conditions remained much the same. By the end of the 1980s, political competition among center-left and center-right parties intensified, providing workers with renewed populist political support and, in the early 1990s, facilitating the rise of militant labor unrest. At the same time, unrest among the Kurdish population escalated rapidly (especially with the rise of the PKK, or Kurdistan Workers' Party, insurgency), pushing subsequent governments to provide simultaneous welfare concessions to both industrial workers and poor Kurds.

The coincidence of the unrest emanating from both Kurdish informal proletarians and formal proletarians fueled the parallel expansion of employment-based and income-based benefits during the first half of the 1990s—a pattern that defied the neoliberal trend. The fact that the nationwide Green Card program was launched in the Kurdish region is a powerful example of this pattern. By the 2010s, Kurds continued to be disproportionally targeted by social assistance programs, though this cannot be explained by higher poverty among the Kurds. Disproportional targeting occurred both on a geographical basis—whereby Kurdish-populated regions received higher levels of social assistance compared to their poverty levels—and on an individual basis—whereby, controlling for poverty and other socioeconomic factors that would determine eligibility, individual Kurds were more likely to benefit from social assistance programs (Yörük 2012).

While the 1980 coup curtailed the socialist mobilization of the 1970s, a coup in 1997 temporarily halted Islamist mobilization. However, a key

TABLE 2. Periods of Turkish Welfare Policy Changes

Period	Welfare policy change	Key structural condition	Global hegemonic policy recommendation	Nature of party competition	Key parties involved	Nature of grassroots politics
1960–80	Expansion of Employment-Based Policies	Import-Substitution Industrialization, National Developmentalism	Expansion of Employment-Based Policies	Strong Dual Party Competition, Coups in 1960 and 1971	AP and CHP	Formal Proletariat and Turks
1980–89	Retrenchment of Employment-Based Policies	Export-Oriented Neoliberal Policies	Retrenchment of Employment-Based Policies	Strong Single Party, Followed by a Coup in 1980	ANAP	Grassroots Tranquility
1989–2001	Expansion of Employment-Based and Income-Based Policies	Export-Oriented Neoliberal Policies	Retrenchment of Employment-Based and Expansion of Income-Based Policies	Competition among Many Weak Parties	DYP; SHP, ANAP, RP, Kurdish Parties	Formal and Informal Proletariat, Kurds
2002–19	Retrenchment of Employment-Based Policies and Expansion of Income-Based Policies	Export-Oriented Neoliberal Policies	Retrenchment of Employment-Based Policies and Expansion of Income-Based Policies	Strong Dual Party Competition	AKP; CHP; Kurdish Parties	Informal Proletariat and Kurds

difference characterizes the two periods following these military interventions. The 1980 coup completely stifled both social unrest and political competition. Hence, social expenditures remained minimal until the wave of labor unrest and intense party competition that characterized the early 1990s. The 1997 military intervention weakened radical Islamist mobilization; the removal of the Welfare Party from the government, however, paved the way for escalated political competition among center-right and center-left parties, leading to a period of fragile coalition governments (fig. 22). Hence, while the threat of social unrest (and thereby the need for political containment) diminished, the intensity of political competition (and thereby the need for popular support) increased. As a result, social expenditures as a percentage of GDP rapidly increased between 1997 and 2001, rising from 4.8% to 8.1% during the coalition government of the Democratic Left Party, the Nationalist Movement Party, and the Motherland Party. It was only after the 2001 financial crisis that the government implemented radical neoliberal policies, eventually leading to the defeat of all three coalition parties in the 2002 elections.

During the early and mid-1990s, welfare provision and material benefits for workers remained higher than a neoliberal transformation would entail and international financial institutions would require, mainly because political competition in an environment of weak/fragmented parties and rising social mobilization fostered populist policies. Thus, welfare policies did not comply with international policy recommendations that proposed cuts to employment-based policies. Because of the revival of social movements and political party competition, the governments' attempts to implement neoliberal policies and cut welfare rights ultimately failed. The emergence of the informal proletariat's renewed political power resulted in an increasing number of social assistance policies. The provision of social assistance through Islamist party municipalities also led to the Islamic radicalization of this now-powerful group. Although neoliberal export-oriented development was the main economic strategy of the time, there was disparity between the logic of market rationalization and actual welfare provision.

In the 2000s, the neoliberal welfare transformation was complete, resulting in the rapid expansion of income-based social assistance policies, as well as significant reductions in employment-based social security policies, the latter of which eradicated the last remnants of the formal proletariat's structural and associational bargaining power. As such, the neolib-

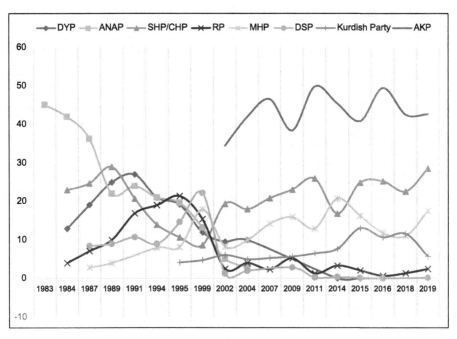

Fig. 22. Percentage of votes by parties in Turkish elections (1983–2019)

eral economic strategy was enforced with minimal economic and political resistance from the formal proletariat. While the formal proletariat's power was diminished, the informal proletariat grew in number, as a result of the rapid exodus of rural immigrants now crowding the cities. This migration was caused by the exhaustion of agricultural income opportunities and the internal displacement of the Kurds. Thus, the rural-to-urban migration during the neoliberal era was a push migration that drove migrants into a highly informal economy. The informal proletariat was partly radicalized by the Islamist movement in the 1990s, and mainly by the Kurdish movement in the 2000s. As a result, the informal proletariat became the government's main source of political threat since the 1990s.

During the 2000s, the competition for national power between the governing AKP and the main opposition, the CHP, became a regime-wide struggle in which the AKP garnered popular support from the informal proletariat. In other words, the AKP assumed two parallel tasks: to contain the radicalization of the Kurdish informal proletarians and to mobilize popular support from the informal proletariat. These parallel concerns resulted in the rapid expansion of income-based social assistance programs chiefly directed to the Kurds. Governments choose which segment of the informal proletariat social assistance will target, depending on which is more threatening or supportive. In the 1990s, for example, social assistance was used by the Islamist Welfare Party to mobilize the poor toward radical Islamism. And when Islamists became the governing power in the 2000s, they aimed to contain the Kurdish informal proletariat. As such, social assistance has become a tool of political containment and mobilization of the informal proletariat.

Turkish social welfare policy legislation has been shaped to a significant extent by grassroots political dynamics. These political activities have either taken the form of political threats to governments or political support for competing political parties. Turkish parliament legislation discussions concerning welfare policies can be traced back to proceedings dating from the 1980s. These proceedings show that both governing party and opposition members in the parliament use welfare provision to contain or mobilize grassroots politics. Twists and turns in these political concerns have created fluctuating patterns in welfare policies.

Neoliberalism during the 1980s: The Retrenchment of Social Security and the Beginning of Social Assistance

The military junta that waged the coup d'état in 1980 ruled the country for three years until elections were permitted in 1983. These elections brought into power an ambitious liberal economist named Turgut Özal, whose political agenda would entirely restructure the economic and social order in Turkey in ways that would establish neoliberal hegemony. Before the coup, Özal served as an undersecretary to Prime Minister Süleyman Demirel and was charged with developing an economic policy program referred to as the January 24th Decrees. These decisions foresaw the relaxation of finance and labor regulations and opened the Turkish economy to global markets. Encouraged by the junta and enabled by the ban on other political party leaders, Özal established a right-wing neoliberal government. Unencumbered by competitors, Özal's Motherland Party (ANAP) gained 45% of the votes in the 1983 elections, forming a single-party government.

The decade following the 1980 military coup was marked by a series of

neoliberal policies targeting the vested rights gained by the formal proletariat during the developmentalist postwar era. Between 1980 and 1989,
the parliament enacted 31 laws that would retrench the employment-based
social welfare provision and rights of formal sector workers. In 1986, the
ANAP government initiated Law Proposal No. 3246, which suggested an
increase in the minimum retirement age to 55 for women and 60 for men.
The ANAP proposed this law as a bitter prescription for curing deficits in
the social security system. ANAP representative Alpaslan Pehlivanli justified this law by arguing that they wanted "wealthy and respected retirees
rather than young and hungry ones" (Turkish Parliamentary Proceedings
Journal, Law No. 3246, 24.12.1985, p. 40).[2] The minister of labor and
social security argued that fluctuations in the minimum retirement age
since the 1960s were a result of concessions given before each election
(Law No. 3246, 24.12.1985, p. 25). The original pension law, no. 5417,
set the minimum retirement age at 60. In 1965, however, it was lowered
to 55 for women. In 1969, Law No. 1186 eliminated the minimum retirement age for both men and women, requiring only that employees work
for 25 years. In 1977, this requirement was lowered to only 20 years.

The 1980 military coup destroyed the possibility of an effective
working-class resistance to neoliberal social security austerity measures and
enabled the ANAP government to reset the minimum retirement age to
55 for women and 60 for men. With other political parties banned, the
ANAP government faced no competition (nor problems stemming from
labor militancy) until the late 1980s. Hence, neither political mobilization nor political containment were key concerns for the government. The
ANAP was thus devoid of heavy political burdens that might hinder structural adjustment policies.

Toward the end of the 1980s, the ANAP government began to systematically expand income-based welfare institutions. One such institution
was the Social Assistance and Solidarity Fund, which would establish the
logical, ideological, and organizational framework for social assistance provision in Turkey during the decades to come. The official objective was to
help needy people in "abject poverty" and to ensure equal income distribution by "taking measures to improve social justice and to encourage social
assistance and solidarity" (Law No. 3294). The ANAP government insisted
that this law, which foresaw the distribution of in-cash and in-kind social

---

2. The quotations from Turkish Parliamentary Proceedings are translated by the author.

assistance, would alleviate poverty. As Ayşe Buğra (2008) has pointed out, the law, which was well suited to "postmodern neo-liberal" conditions, established a poor relief system resembling Islamic/Ottoman-style philanthropy in that it placed no emphasis on citizenship rights.

Parliamentary discussions about the foundations of the Social Assistance and Solidarity Fund reveal that opposition parties, including the center-right True Path Party (Doğru Yol Partisi, or DYP), the center-left Social Democratic Populist Party (Sosyal Demokrat Halkçı Parti, or SHP) and Free Democrat Party (Hür Demokrat Parti), regarded this law as an electoral concession to the poor. Their opposition accused the government of impoverishing the people and using social assistance to manipulate the poor. Their main concern was that the fund would be directly administered by the prime minister, increasing the likelihood that the government might irresponsibly use the fund for political interests. Deputy Faik Tarımcıoğlu from the center-right opposition party HDP summarized the main critique shared by all opposition parties:

> Now it is understood that we are approaching the elections because this law is an investment for elections. Perhaps some really deserving poor would benefit from this law; perhaps some needs would be met. But partisanship and electoral investments are increasingly causing us worry because the proposed law does not issue objective criteria for eligibility conditions. It is based on the assumption that local authorities would prioritize local interests against party and political interests. The preamble is full of emotional expressions, but they are not convincing. (Law No. 3294, 29.5.1986, p. 504)

A DYP representative identified the proposed system as an "archaic system of charity" as opposed to a citizenship right (Law No. 3294, 29.5.1986, p. 509). SHP representative Turan Bayezit emphasized the fact that the legislation was enacted during Ramadan, when religious sentiments were often more easily translated into political gains. He also pointed out that the uncertainty in social assistance application procedures might encourage local governors to use the law for their own political interests. The fact that mayors would also serve on local executive boards further called the objectivity of their decision-making into question. In other words, social assistance might be used as a means of political coercion, ultimately benefiting the interest of the government. The law also did not indicate whether security checks or other regulatory procedures would be executed during application processing (Law No. 3294, 28.5.1986, p. 515).

The opposition parties (especially the social democrats) described the new social assistance fund as a political and economic strategy. Ömer Kuşhan from the SHP accused the government of implementing a double strategy in which economic policies would first "pauperiz[e] the people" before, through social assistance policies, implementing "charity" in order to garner the political support of the poor (Law No. 3294, 29.5.1986, p. 529). Opposition parties mainly complained that the law did not describe the mechanisms of budget allocation, social assistance distribution, and eligibility criteria. Though opposition parties did not oppose the development of social assistance programs, they criticized the government's structuring of the Social Assistance and Solidarity Fund. They argued that because of the discretion and subjectivity involved in the application and distribution processes, this structure would lead to partisanship and electoral advantage for governments, as well as political pressure on the poor. The fact that no auditing mechanism was defined in the law also increased these concerns. HDP deputy Ülkü Söylemezoğlu stated that the law contained too many gaps and uncertainties: "In the beginning, we thought this was because of the inability of the governing party to prepare the law. Now we have understood that this was intentional. The law was left with gaps intentionally in order to bring discretion in implementation" (Law No. 3294, 29.5.1986, p. 33). SHP representative Bayezit also stated that the structure of the social assistance fund was bound to generate "discretion and partiality instead of social solidarity" (Law No. 3294, 29.5.1986, p. 42). HDP representative Osman Bahadir, too, pointed out the risk of "subjective evaluation" in social assistance distribution as formulated in the law, which would leave ample room for "partisanship." He claimed that the ANAP would make distribution of this fund conditional on regional voting rates (Law No. 3294, 29.5.1986, p. 33). The HDP's concerns led the DYP to present a resolution defining specific mechanisms and criteria for social assistance. This resolution, however, was rejected by the government, but, in response to the criticisms concerning Social Assistance and Solidarity Fund legislation, the government promised to issue decrees that would resolve specific problems in the law. In defense of the fund, governing party representative Lütfullah Kayalar argued that social-assistance-based income redistribution had always been part of Islamic tradition (Law No. 3294, 28.5.1986, p. 522). According to another ANAP deputy, the Turkish-Islamic tradition proved superior to that of "the West or the socialists" (Law No. 3294, 28.5.1986, p. 520). For Kayalar, the accusation that the law would be used for electoral support signaled the extent to which the public would appreciate the new system; in other words, the opposition was attacking the law because they wanted to undermine populist endeavors (Law No. 3294, 28.5.1986, p. 512). The ANAP minister asked, "How can the opposition parties explain to their electorate that they oppose a law that would help the poor?" (Law No. 3294, 28.5.1986, p. 516).

Although opposition parties had always focused on clientelistic usages of the Social Assistance and Solidarity Fund, they were also concerned about appearing to be antipopulist before the electorate. Therefore, they consistently backed proposals supporting increases in the levels of assistance and amendments to the structure of the fund. In the case of Law No. 3783, for example, opposition parties proposed ever-higher increases in social assistance benefit levels in competition with each other. Criticism of the fund intensified during discussions of Law No. 3582 in 1988, which required that local municipalities allocate 2% of their revenues to the fund. For the opposition, this law had two drawbacks: first, it would increase funds so that voters would back the government prior to the elections, and second, it would cut the budgets of municipalities, most of which were governed by opposition parties at the time of the legislation (Law No. 3582).

The 1990s: The Intensifying Electoral Competition and the Rise of Social Movements

In 1987, a critical decision by the ANAP government altered the electoral dynamics in Turkey and radically changed the trajectory of neoliberalism and welfare system change. The fourth clause of the 1980 constitution had banned leaders of the main political parties of the 1970s from politics. ANAP and its leader Özal planned a referendum to change the constitution and thereby release this ban on old political leaders such as Demirel, Erdal İnönü, and Necmettin Erbakan. Because of ANAP's political power, this decision proved controversial. For the public, and even for cadres within ANAP, this decision was difficult to grasp. But, as an enthusiastic politician, Özal was taking a political risk; he was also self-confident and believed that the referendum results would not lift the political ban. Özal would then sustain his rule through force of the democratic vote, which would eliminate potential electoral challenges to his government. But the campaign of previous political center-right leader Demirel, as well as the grievances that ANAP's neoliberal policies generated among the populace, resulted in a higher number of affirmative votes. The extensive austerity measures that the ANAP implemented had eroded Özal's popularity among the electorate. On 6 September 1987, "Yes" votes outnumbered "No" votes by a tiny margin, removing the political ban. As a result, the political arena was opened to many popular center-right and center-left leaders.

Following the referendum, the ANAP declared early general elections. For Özal, a win of 49% of the vote was nevertheless a big success, and he attempted to take advantage of the fact that the opposition leaders were unprepared for the election. As it turns out, he was correct. Three months after the referendum, ANAP won only 36% of the general vote, but because of an electoral system that favored majority parties, it received 65% of the seats in parliament. Nevertheless, the opposition parties had gained popular support, thus increasing pressure on ANAP. The political campaign of the old leaders was based upon a critique of ANAP's neoliberal policies, which contributed to the mobilization of formal sector workers. Mainstream political opposition was also reinforced by the labor strike wave (or Spring Actions) that began in the spring of 1989 and rapidly accelerated before the local elections in 1989. The main opposition party—the center-left SHP—gained the largest votes, followed by the center-right DYP. Their gains further eroded the legitimacy of the government. Anticipating that he would lose the next general election, Özal ran for president of the republic and won, leaving the ANAP weakened during the chaotic political struggle that marked the 1990s. Defeat of the ANAP and its neoliberal policies halted Turkey's neoliberal transformation during a decade of political competition and populism. The political chaos of the 1990s began as an unintended consequence of the political risk taken by Özal's ANAP. The old leaders were now clandestinely ruling the new political parties in parliament. Özal attempted to delegitimize their discourse of victimization by testing how far the public was willing to go in order to have their old leaders back. Had he been successful, Özal could have used public opinion to his advantage. Although Özal's risk proved unsuccessful, it changed the trajectory of welfare system transformation and opened a long decade of populism that would undermine the neoliberal project.

A decade-long period of mainstream political instability followed Özal's loss. This decade was marked by intense political competition among a large number of competing weak parties, culminating in subsequent coalition governments and a decade of political chaos (see fig. 22). Among the competing parties were the Social Democratic Populist Party (SHP) of Erdal İnonu, the True Path Party (DYP) of Demirel, the Democratic Left Party (Demokratik Sol Parti, or DSP) of Bülent Ecevit, the Nationalist Movement Party (Milliyetçi Hareket Partisi, or MHP) of Alparslan Türkeş, and the Welfare Party (Refah Partisi, or RP) of Necmettin Erbakan, the leader of political Islam in Turkey. Over the course of the decade, no political party from the center-right or center-left would gain more than 22% of the vote (see fig. 22).

After the 1991 elections, Süleyman Demirel of the True Path Party became the prime minister of the coalition government formed by the SHP and DYP. Between 1983 and 1994, SHP represented social democracy in Turkey. Support for these two parties was reinforced by their backing of the Spring Actions of the formal proletariat. During the second DYP-SHP coalition government, which ruled between 1993 and 1995, the economy suffered a deep crisis. In 1994, inflation rose to 149%, and long-term interest rates remained at over 100% until the end of the decade. This was the first of three major economic crises occurring in 1994, 1999, and 2001. These crises resulted in waves of bankruptcies, debt, inflation, and financial breakdowns. During the 1990s, the average inflation rate rose to 80%, and state debt increased dramatically (to 150% of the GNP in 2001). Turkish banks earned a fortune by borrowing cheap international credit to purchase government assets that would return astronomical interest (Keyder 2004). Subsequent devaluations rendered the Turkish lira one of the least valued currencies in the world, making one US$ equal to 1.34 million Turkish liras in 2005, just before the government removed six zeros from the currency.

As a response to the first major crisis in 1994, the DYP-SHP government announced an ultra-neoliberal economic program called the April 5th Decisions. This program devalued the currency by more than 50%, dramatically lowered real wages, and planned massive layoffs and privatizations. The 1994 economic breakdown was accompanied by the intense war waged against the Kurdish rebels during three DYP-SHP coalition governments. Marked by state terror and accompanied by the internal displacement of the Kurds, the mid-1990s has thus been remembered as a period of political siege (İnce 2010). These repressive policies ended Kurdish support for social democrats. After SHP, the DYP formed another coalition government with the Welfare Party. Erbakan, the long-standing leader of Turkish political Islam, became prime minister. On February 28, 1997, after less than a year, the military issued a memorandum that called for strict actions against antisecularist policies. In June, Erbakan was forced to withdraw as prime minister, and in January 1998, the Supreme Court banned his party. This was a critical turning point for political Islam and would culminate in the establishment of the reformist Islamist Justice and Development Party (AKP).

The Spring Actions, the Kurdish Insurgency, and the Anti-Neoliberalism of the Early 1990s

The neoliberal policies of the 1980s retrenched many employment-based welfare rights without significant resistance. Yet the formal proletariat sustained its structural bargaining power, including both marketplace and workplace components (Silver 2003). This sustained bargaining power led to the largest wave of labor unrest in Turkish history, beginning with the 1989 Spring Actions and lasting until 1991. In order to quell unrest and undermine rising popular support for the opposition, the Spring Actions forced the subsequent ANAP and DYP-SHP governments to grant concessions to public sector workers in the form of dramatic wage increases (Buğra and Adar 2008, 200). Indeed, some of these concessions were even given in 1988, when the precursors of the labor unrest wave (e.g., the SEKA strike) had just begun. In 1988, Law No. 3451 made it easier for labor unions to be involved in collective bargaining and strikes.

Prior to the 1991 elections, the opposition parties (especially the center-right DYP), aware that neoliberal policies created deep grievances among the masses, made a vast array of populist promises concerning social welfare. The DYP, for example, promised the termination of a minimum retirement age and the launch of the free health care card program. These promises made DYP the primary party in the 1991 elections, followed by the ANAP and the SHP.

The DYP and SHP formed a coalition government that would accompany a populist period during a time of Turkish neoliberal transformation. The DYP-SHP coalition implemented welfare policies that expanded both employment-based and income-based welfare benefits. In 1992, this government initiated the most extensive social assistance program in Turkish history—the free health care program for the poor, also called the Green Card program (or Yeşil Kart). During the ANAP government, public hospitals operated by private enterprise logic, with doctors receiving profit shares from hospital revenues. This led to massive grievances among the poor, as many people could not access health care services due to overcrowding (Buğra 2008). The DYP, the main center-right alternative to the ANAP, proposed the free health care program as part of their 1991 electoral campaign pledges. Before the elections, the program was presented as a plan that would provide free access to health care for all citizens. However, after the elections, the actual Green Card program limited access only to the poor, whose eligibility would be determined through a means test. Thus, one of the main criticisms of the program was that, despite campaign promises, it was not universal. In response, the government promised that the law would be temporary, remaining effective only until the establishment of the General Health Insurance System in 1993, when the Green Card could be held by all. This postponement sparked criticism among the opposition. The program covered the costs of inpatient treatment but excluded the medication costs of outpatient treatment; thus, citizens were encouraged to apply to the Social Assistance and Solidarity Fund in order to cover their health care costs. Despite its limitations, the Green Card program set the stage for an institutionalized social assistance system in Turkey to replace the philanthropic structure of the Social Assistance and Solidarity Fund established by the ANAP in 1986 (Buğra 2008).

The Green Card law (Law No. 3816) was enacted in 1992, in a political arena marked by two immense power struggles. Following the 1987 referendum, the DYP and SHP had run a long-standing opposition campaign against the ANAP government, backing the formal proletarian movement that would later be radicalized after the Spring Actions of 1989. In addition, Demirel had promised the lower middle classes that, after 500 days, every family would be able to own two sets of keys: one for a house and one for a car. The third source of support (especially for the DYP) consisted of the poorest sectors of the peasantry and the growing informal proletariat of the slums (Buğra 2008). The DYP, with Demirel as its "father" figure, promised the masses that they would be able to escape poverty and have access to free health care.

After the 1991 elections, the free health care program law was introduced in parliament, albeit in a truncated form. The opposition complained about the use of advertising campaigns and celebrations and carnivals designed to incite populist support for the program. For Gaffar Yakın of the ANAP, the Green Card law would be no more than "political ostentation" after the pledges made before the elections (Law No. 3816, 18.6.1992, p. 36). The opposition also questioned the alleged objectivity of the Green Card's means tests, claiming that it would create systematic control mechanisms for the poor. ANAP's Yusuf Bozkurt Özal referred to clause 7 of the law, which made it possible for local boards to conduct investigations using public records containing applicants' private information (Law No. 3816, 18.6.1992, p. 10). In response, the minister of health claimed that the strict eligibility criteria were designed to prevent the ANAP government's unjust and partisanship-based distribution of Social Assistance and Solidarity Fund aid from happening again (Law No. 3816, 18.6.1992, p. 11).

Another power struggle that marked the political background surrounding the Green Card law was the Kurdish conflict. The Kurdish insurgency against the Turkish state reached its peak in the early 1990s, when the PKK mobilized Kurds living in poor villages and urban slums to riot. These mass riots were part of the Serhildan campaign (also known as the Kurdish Intifada), which posed an immense security threat to the Turkish state. Because of heavy state repression, involving extrajudicial executions, mass arrests, and the internal displacement of millions of Kurds, the mid-1990s are remembered as a dark period in Kurdish history (Günay 2013). The nature and timing of the Green Card law suggests that the Turkish government used this means-tested benefit system to suppress both potential and actual social dissent stemming from the poor, as well as from the ongoing violent and nonviolent forms of Kurdish mobilization. The Green Card law decreed that the program would begin in the eastern and southeastern regions, where Kurds constitute the majority of the population. Furthermore, the Anti-Terror Law enacted in 1991 against the Kurdish uprising included a clause stating that "those citizens, if they are not state officers, who were hurt by terrorist events in the form of loss of lives or property, will receive priority in collecting social assistance from the Social Assistance and Solidarity Fund" (TPPJ Law No. 3713). This clause suggests that the Turkish state incorporated social welfare provision (in particular, social assistance programs) into their counterinsurgency strategy of containing Kurdish radicalism. The utilization of the Green Card for the containment of Kurdish dissent was sharply intensified by the AKP government a decade later (Akyol 2011; Yeğen 2011). Both Mehmet Akyol and Mesut Yeğen believe that the Turkish state has used the Green Card in order to appear merciful to the Kurds. Indeed, as can be inferred from the priority granted to Kurdish regions, the Green Card program targeted the poor from the very onset, especially the Kurdish poor. This prioritization, alongside the strong quantitative associations between Kurdish ethnic identity and Green Card–holding status in 2010, suggests that Kurdish unrest has been a shaping factor in the development of free health care provision in Turkey. Indeed, Turkish governments have instrumentalized the program for the containment of Kurdish unrest by trying to buy off the Kurdish poor (Yoltar and Yörük 2021).

Kurdish popular unrest and the accompanying escalation of guerrilla warfare made it clear that the Kurds had become a serious threat to the Turkish state, which was also facing another major grassroots challenge of labor unrest in western Turkey, the Spring Actions. Although there was no significant ideological or organizational link connecting Kurdish unrest in eastern Turkey to labor unrest in western Turkey, this historical coincidence has nevertheless drawn the shared trajectories of the working class and Kurdish movements since the late 1990s. Challenged by two major social unrest movements (one ethnic and one class-based) occurring during the same period but in different parts of the country, Turkish governments were forced to give extensive welfare concessions that defied most neoliberal blueprints.

The Rise of the Radical Islam and Welfare Provision in the 1990s

In 1991, radical Islamists gained seats in the parliament for the first time after 1980. After the death of President Özal in 1993, Prime Minister Demirel was elected president, with Tansu Çiller, a neoliberal professor of economics, leading the DYP-SHP government. Çiller's government enacted neoliberal labor laws facilitating subcontracting chains, as well as flexible and informal labor contracts. Eventually, the economic crisis in 1994 cut real wages nearly in half. The Welfare Party, led by Islamist leader Necmettin Erbakan, remained in opposition, growing in power until the 1994 municipal elections, when RP became the primary party. This continuation of neoliberal policies brought the Islamist populist Welfare Party into power in 1996 (Buğra 2008; Tugal 2009), when the RP formed a coalition government with the DYP. By the time the RP came into power, the party had already ruled many major municipal governments, and their success in the provision of public services and social assistance increased the popularity of the Islamists (e.g., Recep Tayyip Erdoğan served as the mayor of Istanbul). The party made local governments into institutions of social assistance provision, which enabled it to mobilize the impoverished informal proletariat of the slums (Shively 2008).

Whether or not the Welfare Party, which formed the roots of the current AKP government, pursued welfare populism largely depended on whether the party was in the opposition or in the government. During its governance, the Welfare Party was inclined to expand welfare provision. The party expanded employment-based benefits, partly in order to contain the second-largest labor unrest wave of the 1990s, and partly to establish a base of popular support to use against the secularist army. This was the case for most prolabor International Labour Organization agreements that were to be ratified in the Turkish parliament in 1993. When the party was in the opposition, the nature of its policy-making was shaped by whether or not the acting government was expanding welfare rights. When the RP assumed the role of the opposition party and the government was welfare populist, as in the case of the DYP-SHP coalition government, the RP defended probusiness policies reducing workers' rights, despite the egalitarian tone of the party's Just Order rhetoric.

Parliamentary discussions reveal the double-sided stances of the RP. One such case occurred in 1992, during the enactment of Law No. 3769, which lowered the minimum retirement age. Critical of the government's decision, the RP argued that even employees in Western countries retire after the age of 60. RP representative Ahmet Fevzi İncegöz asked, "Are we more advanced than the West so that we are lowering the retirement age while they are increasing it? If we always imitate the West, then we should imitate their work standards, too" (Law No. 3769, 23.1.1992, p. 170). Similarly, when Law No. 3849 was proposed by the DYP-SHP government in 1992, outlawing the employment of children younger than the age of 15 (as required by the ILO agreements), RP representative Mehmet Elkatmış objected on the grounds that its ratification would lead to "accusation from international institutions and humiliation of the nation" (Law No. 3849, p. 78). In 1993, the RP also challenged Law No. 3917, which required employers' businesses to be confiscated if they did not pay their social insurance premiums. The RP's position was that "this law would put pressure on businesses" (Law No. 3917, 24.11.1993, p. 186). The party later defended privatization Law No. 4232 (passed by the DYP-RP government) on the grounds that privatizations would lead to industrial upgrading (Law No. 4232, 3.4.1997). The RP adopted a similar attitude during legislation on the privatization of state-owned enterprises in 1994. One RP representative emphasized that they were "not principally against privatization and a free market economy," but opposed the privatization of nationally strategic enterprises (Law No. 3987, 4.5.1994).

One important aspect of the RP's welfare policy discussions is that the party often referred to grassroots politics in advancing or criticizing welfare policy proposals. During discussion of ILO Law No. 3848, an RP deputy, referring to the ongoing street protests, asked why workers were being forced to fight for their rights. He claimed that if these rights were not granted, workers would protest illegally, or, "*because of some loopholes in the laws*," they would "*gain some rights that they do not deserve*" (emphasis added; Law No. 3848, 25.11.1998, p. 368). In response to Law No. 3845, which allowed workers to select workplace representatives, the RP representative declared the RP's support, arguing that "there will be peace in society if working life is organized equitably between workers and employers" (Law No. 3845, 25.11.1992).

Law No. 3783 is a good example of the Welfare Party's concerns about political instability. This law increased the amount of social assistance allocated to the elderly poor by Law No. 2022. The DYP-SHP government declared that the decreasing levels of the aid's real value made the proposed law necessary. The RP, on the other hand, regarded this law as a measure designed to suppress social unrest. RP representative Ali Oğuz had the following to say to parliament:

Our religion describes poverty as the closest point to impiety. Why? Imagine a person, unable to escape poverty no matter what he does. He falls into poverty so much that he nearly comes to the point of rebellion. . . . You know the old saying "the doomsdays come because someone eats and the other just looks" [*Biri yer biri bakar kiyamet ondan kopar*, meaning that the greatest conflicts arise from social inequalities]. . . . I am telling this politely: there is a saying in the countryside: "a hungry dog breaks the oven" [*Aç köpek fırın duvarı deler*, meaning that poverty leads people to violence]. What do hungry people do? *They overthrow their state.* That is why we, as members of this parliament, must understand what poverty can lead to. (emphasis added; Law No. 3783, 5.3.1992, p. 677)

RP representatives also referred to the potential for social unrest during discussion of Law No. 3769, which eliminated the minimum retirement age, making citizens eligible for retirement after only 25 years of employment. The DYP proposed the law in response to the increasing demands of citizens who "did not adopt the unjust increase in minimum retirement age" enacted in 1986 (Law No. 3769, 23.1.1992). While the ANAP representative and Adnan Kahveci, a former minister of finance, accused the government of being populist, the RP's Ahmet Fevzi İncegöz claimed that his party actually opposed the law, which they believed would lead the social security system into a permanent crisis. Nevertheless, he declared that they would accept the proposal because of intense worker protests. "Let's consider the example of an electrical fuse," said İncegöz, in the usual metaphorical language of his party members. "If there is an excessive electrical current, the fuse gets blown to prevent explosion. Likewise, it seems that we have come to such a point. We accept this early retirement issue only once in order to use it as a fuse" (Law No. 3769, 23.1.1991, p. 169). In response to privatization Law No. 3987 in 1994, the RP again expressed concern with the sociopolitical grievances that might result. They suggested that unless preventative measures were taken, street protests against privatization might pose a serious threat to national security. Abdullah Gül, a founder of the AKP, former deputy of the RP, and the president of Turkey between 2007 and 2014, said that they would support the law "if it were to facilitate the rationalization of a market economy." At the time, however, enterprises were being sold in order to repay public debts, and the RP was concerned that Turkey might follow in the footsteps of Argentina and Chile—two examples of countries in which privatization and poverty had led to large social uprisings (Law No. 3987, 4.5.1994, p. 443). Another deputy from the RP, Ali Oğuz, warned the government about the law's potential consequences: "Do you not become scared when you see the cheap bread queues? If there were a social explosion tomorrow, not only you but the whole nation would suffer. For this reason, unless you stop working on this law, it may be too late" (Law No. 3987, 5.5.1994, p. 503).

The RP's overwhelming interest in social unrest is significant because the AKP government sprang from the RP, helping to explain the cause of welfare expansion during AKP rule. The Welfare Party referred to grass-roots politics not only when making propositions or voicing objections but also often when evaluating government policies. The RP supported the amendments to policies concerning the working conditions of public sector employees proposed by the DYP-SHP government in 1995 because of the necessity "to follow a wage policy that would sustain social balances in order to ensure social order and peace" (Law No. 4066, 25.1.1995, p. 328). According to RP representative Cevat Ayhan, the government was planning to ratify these amendments only for high-ranking officials, "as a response to the massive street protests of employees to demand their rights." He believed that public employees were "repressed" and were only granted rights when protests and uprisings threatened the social order (Law No. 4066, 25.1.1995, p. 343). Law No. 4066 was proposed under such a threat, when workers took to the streets in massive numbers in 1995. Acknowledging the threat of impending social turmoil, both center-right and center-left parties supported the amendment. The ANAP voiced their concerns about police brutality against protesting public sector employees, and the DSP deputy reminded the government of their previous warnings that "street protests and social explosions were inevitable" (Law No. 4066, 25.1.1995, p. 331).

The matter of social unrest and the threat of grassroots politics played a central role during the consideration of Law No. 4066, so much so that deputy Halil Başol, speaking on behalf of the DYP, made the following request:

> Our public sector employees are protesting in defense of their rights. Yet, as an experienced parliamentarian, I would like to make a sincere request from my deputy colleagues and leaders of political parties. . . . It has often been uttered that "our people will pour out into the streets in order to overcome their difficulties." These sorts of expressions will be of no benefit to any of us, especially to the parliament. We have the Law of Public Protest; we have established the formal manners of claiming rights. We do not oppose those who comply with these manners to claim their rights. Yet, when people participate in illegal rallies against the laws enacted by parliament, it is not proper to say "well, there is nothing to do, public employees are right, there is 100% inflation." (Law No. 4066, 25.1.1995, p. 345)

Başol urged that political parties not encourage workers to wage protests. Referring to himself as an experienced parliamentarian, he emphasized that state interests must be taken more seriously than political party interests.

Even government party members were in agreement with Başol. During the consideration of Law No. 4275, which in 1997 granted public sector employees the right to establish labor unions, a representative of the RP, which was then part of the government, asserted that "public sector employees resisted, struggled, and joined massive rallies" in the past to gain this right. For him, this meant that "if people struggle for their rights, they suffer for a while, but in the end, they achieve these rights" (Law No. 4275, 12.6.1997, p. 143). When amendments were made for workers, the opposition, who saw no need for such amendments, asked, "If workers poured out into the streets in order to demand the termination of the 2% stoppage, why did the government call the parliament for an extraordinary meeting during the holiday period? We cannot understand this" (Law No. 4164, 27.8.1996, p. 15). The answer to the opposition's question was obvious. The second-largest strike wave of the 1990s was staged in 1995 and 1996, when the total number of workers on strike was the highest in Turkish history (Akkaya 2005). The government had apparently made some concessions for formal sector workers (even without direct demands to do so), including over 50% increases in real wages. During this period, the short-lived RP-DYP coalition government passed five laws that expanded employment-based benefits, while no single law was passed to retrench welfare benefits of any sort; in response, CHP deputies accused the government of manipulating public and private sector workers (Law No. 4183, 30.8.1996). After the strike wave came to an end, the government passed three subsequent laws (nos. 4227, 4228, and 4229) that swiftly enabled the privatization of social security institutions' assets, as well as those of other public sector enterprises.

It should be noted that political party competition, especially during the 1990s, blurred the ideological lines between center-left and center-right parties. In order to garner popular support, even ANAP, the most extreme neoliberal party, used social-democratic-sounding discourse. During the consideration of Law No. 4277, which made changes to the Labor Unions Law, ANAP representative Emin Kul spoke as a kind of socialist leader of working-class struggle in Turkey:

This law will make it impossible for labor unions to provide financial aid to political parties, while organizations of capital will be
totally free to enjoy this right. As is known, workers do not have
economic power as individuals; they only have power when they
organize as legal entities in labor unions. But the owners of capital
have unlimited economic power, both as individuals and as legal
entities via their firms. For this reason, I want to point out that
workers, who acquire collective economic power by organizing in
labor unions, must be able to reflect this power in politics and under
equal conditions with capital. That is, the ban on receiving financial aid is understandable; yet workers and their unions, who were
forced to bear the burden of all problems, including the economic
costs, must be allowed to remain outside of this financial aid ban.
This is necessary for them to continue their struggle with capital on
equal terms. (Law No. 4277, 18.6.1997, p. 326)

This *orthodox Marxist* reflection on class struggle was used by the ANAP
as a political move to counter the populist policies developed by the Welfare Party, emphasizing the importance of garnering the political support
of formal workers at that time.

The Roots of Welfare Populism as Counterinsurgency against the Kurds

There have been many other occasions on which the Kurdish issue and
social policy were intermingled in the welfare policy-making of the
Islamists. On some occasions, when the Kurdish question was the more
pressing of the two, social policy measures took precedence, and on others,
when social policy legislation was under consideration, the Kurdish issue
took precedence. In 1995, intense discussions took place concerning the
legislation of changes to the Anti-Terror Law. During these discussions,
political parties voiced their concerns about the internal displacement of
the Kurds and increasing poverty in Kurdish cities, as well as about possible ensuing political instabilities and potential social policy measures that
might be taken. The proposal was originally intended to provide social
assistance for the families of security forces who had lost their lives during
armed clashes. When the Welfare Party suggested including an additional
clause that would also enable internally displaced people to benefit from

the law, their proposal was accepted.[3] This was important because the parliament officially recognized the internal displacement of millions of people through a law that connected antiterrorism and social policy (Law No. 4131, 13.11.1995, p. 217). Discussions regarding the legislation focused on the possibility that internally displaced people living in poverty were highly likely to support the PKK; hence, the government was asked to take further measures to remove internally displaced Kurds from the political influence of the Kurdish movement by means of social assistance provision. The Welfare Party justified its proposal for this new clause by stating that "if war on terror is our aim, it is necessary to annihilate the social conditions that underlie and facilitate terrorism. If internally displaced people are forced to stay in tents in the slums of cities, even during these winter conditions, the government should assume the responsibility of subjecting these people to make wrong decisions" (Law No. 4131,13.11.1995, p. 217). RP representative Ahmet Cemil Tunç claimed that if internally displaced people in cities had been given even small amounts of money, even for a limited time period, counterterrorist efforts would have been much more successful (Law No. 4131,13.11.1995, p. 207).

During the 1990s, both governments and the opposition saw social assistance as a method of supporting the fight against terrorism. The social democratic CHP criticized the proposal to change the Anti-Terror Law because, in their opinion, the Social Assistance and Solidarity Fund would provide only palliative short-term solutions. For CHP representative Algan Hacaoglu, economic development projects in Kurdish regions were a better solution (Law No. 4131,13.11.1995, p. 206). Until the 2010s, social democrats maintained a position that favored economic development over social assistance (Buğra 2008). While all mainstream parties considered welfare provision to be a means of containing long-standing Kurdish unrest, the center-right preferred income-based social assistance, while the center-left leaned more toward economic development involving employment-based welfare benefit policies. Given the informal nature of the Kurdish class structure in Turkey, the center-right seemed to assume a more rational strategy, especially considering that more Kurds tended to support them since the 1990s.

A good example of this contrast between the center-right and center-

---

3. The Welfare Party and ANAP also criticized the timing of the law. It was passed five months before elections, which led the opposition to accuse the government of making electoral pledges.

left approaches to counterinsurgency can be seen in the discussion of Law No. 4325 (titled the "Law on Job Creation in Emergency State Rule Region and the Regions with Priority in Development"), approved in 1998. This law was proposed by the coalition government formed by the center-left (DSP and CHP) and center-right (ANAP and DTP) parties[4]— following the fall of the RP-DYP coalition government after the military intervention in 1997. The law was presented as a means of alleviating regional inequalities in development by targeting the eastern and southeastern regions, where Kurds were in the majority. The law brought about a grand policy proposal that would include tax incentives, free public land for new enterprises, low social security premiums, and many other incentives designed to encourage entrepreneurs to stimulate investments in the Kurdish region. The CHP also proposed a clause in the law that would ensure that one member from each internally displaced family be given priority access to employment in public enterprise jobs. The proposal, which would allow applicants to be hired without requiring them to take job-qualification exams, was supported by the opposition. For the DYP, this law was necessary for national security. The governing partner DYP representative Saffet Arıkan Bedük stated:

> The general purpose of this law is to rapidly develop those regions which have remained the most underdeveloped regions, and for that reason, have been subject to all kinds of political exploitation. Developmental inequalities and income disparities in this region directly relate to peace and security. If we properly analyze the origins of the terrorist events that have taken place in the State of Emergency Region [the Kurdish populated region], we can see that low levels of income, employment, and development have led to acceleration of these events and their continuation until today. (Law No. 4325)

The RP also supported Law No. 4325, claiming that it would "eradicate unemployment and economy-related sources of terrorism." But the party also proposed including other cities in the eastern and southeastern regions where the PKK was not especially strong. RP representative Aslan

---

4. The Democrat Turkey Party (DTP) should not be confused with the Kurdish Democratic Society Party, whose acronym is also DTP.

Polat suggested that without this law, these cities might also attract terrorist activities. Moreover, added Polat, if these regions were not included, their inhabitants could "end up migrating to western cities and crowd the slums." He then issued a strict warning to parliament members: "If you cannot keep these people in their land over there, then you cannot be at ease up here, either" (Law No. 4325, p. 66).

This dichotomy between the discretionary and rule-based mechanisms of social assistance provision has been a constant issue in the harsh political struggle between government and opposition parties from various ideological backgrounds. On every occasion, opposition parties have accused the government of implementing discretionary policies that would allow for clientelism and patronage relations. Many times, as in the cases of Law No. 4131, Law No. 3816 (Green Card), and Law No. 3294 (Social Assistance and Solidarity Law), the opposition portrayed electoral concessions as the driving force behind social assistance expansion.

Neoliberalism with Coalition Governments and the Escalation of Retrenchment

The end of the RP-DYP government in 1997 through a military intervention led the remaining smaller secularist parties to form subsequent coalition governments. Among these governments, the cabinet of Bülent Ecevit was the longest lasting. Formed in 1999 by the center-left DSP, center-right ANAP, and nationalist-right MHP, this government ruled until 2002. In August 1999, the coalition government brought to parliament the new Social Security Reform Law (Law No. 4447), which restored the minimum retirement age.[5] Among many other new retrenchment policies, this law set the minimum retirement age at 58 for females and 60 for males. Workers and labor unions strongly opposed this law. The government was not able to bring the law to the parliament because of nationwide protests. Yet the earthquake of 1999 in the industrial northwestern parts of the country brought the succor that the government needed. Fac-

5. In 1991, Demirel's government had canceled the minimum retirement age altogether and rendered retirement conditional on the minimum number of days of premium payment. In contrast to this populist maneuver of Demirel, Law No. 4447 enacted by the Ecevit government restored a minimum retirement age, which was now set to a significantly higher age than the one that was effective before 1991.

ing a tough stand-by agreement with the IMF, the government was so determined to pass the law that they brought the law to the parliament on the week following this gravest disaster in the history of Turkey. This 7.6 magnitude earthquake hit Istanbul, Izmit, and Bursa and caused around 45,000 deaths (Marza 2004). The opposition also accused the government of taking advantage of the termination of workers' protests caused by the earthquake. Yet the government managed to pass this law and reduced employment-based welfare benefits significantly.

The Virtue Party (Fazilet Partisi—FP), the successor to the RP and then the main opposition party, opposed the law by mainly referring to labor protests. Aslan Polat asked the government: "[How] would you be able to implement this law while 500 thousand people were marching against it?" (Law No. 4447, p. 34). Suat Pamukcu, also speaking of the marches, said, "You see what is happening in the streets. The people are rising up! We are doing everything since yesterday to convince you to withdraw the law. But you recklessly do your best to get some money from the IMF!" All other representatives of the FP, including would-be AKP ministers Abdüllatif Şener, Turhan Alçelik, and Yakup Budak, highlighted the threat to "social peace" that the law was likely to bring about. Ahmet Derin from the FP warned the government by reminding it about the power of organized labor in the early 1990s (Law No.4447, p. 44). Bekir Sobacı from the FP brought up the example of unemployment insurance in Germany as a measure against terrorism (Law No. 4447, p. 47). The DYP also followed suit by bringing up the workers' protests: Mehmet Sadri Yıldırım, Salih Çelen, Mehmet Yalçınkaya, and Oğuz Tezmen and former prime minister Tansu Çiller urged the government to pay attention to the "protests," "clashes," "revolts," and "social explosions" taking place in the streets (Law No. 4447, p. 50). Governing party DSP representative Gaffar Yakın responded to these critiques by claiming that the law was a necessary measure to preserve the system and it could not be risked through populism.

Two years later, Law No. 4688 was introduced, saddling more regulations on public sector labor unions and depriving them once again of the right to strike. ANAP representative Ali Kemal Başaran made a historical comment on how welfare and labor legislation are always based on class struggle. Başaran advised the workers that "there is no labor union that managed to gain all rights to collective bargaining, strike and collective organization once altogether. Labor unions first get established, and then get organized. This stage is followed by the rights to collective meeting,[6] collective bargaining and finally strike" (Law No. 4688, p. 69). Başaran demanded patience from the unions and promised that "collective bargaining and strike[s] might be possible over time."

The opposition again assumed an "ultra-leftist" position vis-à-vis the neoliberal government. FP representative Aslan Polat gave an example to demonstrate the importance of the right to collective bargaining and strike for the workers: the Türk-İş union, even with the weakest collective bargaining in its history, managed to get a 15% wage increase, while public sector employees, who do not have the right to collective bargaining and to strike, were given only a 5% wage increase. Polat continued to say that "this means that you only pay attention to power, only to strike, you do not pay attention to what people deserve" (Law No. 4688, p. 80). Kamer Genc from DYP warned the government that "a popular uprising is inevitable these days. Because there are millions of people left unemployed. What will these people do when they do not have anything to lose? Does this country have responsibility for its people, for its public order?" (Law No. 4692, p. 56).

In advance of the election of 2002, the government slowly gave up this neoliberal stance and increasingly resorted to populism. First, Law No. 4747 in 2002 (entitled Promotion of Employment) brought more advantages to enterprises that employed unionized workers. DYP representative Mehmet Dönen interpreted this law as an explicit concession to labor unions that were then planning to start street actions against the government as a response to the deep economic crisis (Law No. 4747, p. 57).

In 2002, the DSP-ANAP-MHP coalition government finalized its term with an important concession to labor unions after a series of neoliberal policies. The government issued a proposed law, no. 4773, which came to be known as the Job Security Law. This law included a number of policies to protect the job security of formal sector employees. Obviously, considering a government that had passed a good number of laws to undermine employment-based welfare policies, this law was surprising. The opposition parties immediately regarded the law as a concession given to workers three months before the elections. For the DYP representative

---

6. Collective meeting (*toplugörüşme*) is a made-up term proposed by the government in place of the term collective bargaining (*toplusözleşme*), for which the unions were pressing.

İbrahim Konukoğlu, the government used the law as a bargaining tool and threat to both workers and employers (Law No. 4773, p. 345). Mehmet Bekaroğlu from the Felicity Party (Saadet Partisi, the follow-up to the FP, which was banned by the Supreme Court in 2001), ironically claimed that "the beauty of the elections began to be seen three months in advance." For him, the governing parties were "waving a greeting to the electorate" by pretending "how labor friendly they were" (Law No. 4773, p. 359).

Governing parties indeed fell very much out with each other concerning this law, which became a key issue before the coming elections. The minister of labor and social security, Yaşar Okuyan from the ANAP, resigned from his position just prior to the passage of the law. The extreme right coalition partner MHP claimed that Okuyan resigned because of the pressure coming from the employers' organizations in order not to pass the law. The MHP claimed that the law would have been legislated much earlier if the "will of the parliament" were not prevented by some "pressure groups" (Law No. 4773, p. 370). The MHP representative complained that "unfortunately, the balance of power has recently been too much moved to the businessmen. Workers have been left abandoned, their rights have been postponed. Yet, the MHP made it possible to make this law today" (Law No. 4773, p. 372). On the other hand, the center-left DSP representative Osman Kılıç also claimed credit for passing this law: "Today, this law is a test for political parties. If a party does not defend job security, it is not a labor-friendly party" (Law No. 4773, p. 378). DSP deputy Rıdvan Budak, an old labor union leader, criticized business: "Nowhere in the world, can businessmen, capital, threaten the parliament in this way. In his resignation speech, Okuyan claimed that a member of the business circle threatened him by saying that if the job security law passed, they would pay its cost" (Law No. 4773, p. 381). The main target of these criticisms was the government partner ANAP, which defended business interests. Obviously, electoral competition created this need for governing partners to differentiate themselves from each other on class-based terms, leading to the passage of this labor-friendly law. However, this last-minute labor friendliness ceased to be sufficient enough to garner electoral support from workers, who apparently did not forget the crises and crumbling standards of living.

As a result of the intense political competition among many center-right and center-left parties, the coalition government continued to expand social welfare provisions during the years leading to the 2001 financial crisis. Total public social expenditures sharply increased from 4.8% to 8.1% of GDP between 1998 and 2001. Yet, following the 2001 crisis, the government, hoping to reestablish business confidence, implemented policies in line with liberal orthodoxy under the control of the new economic minister, Kemal Derviş. These reforms became feasible since the Islamist opposition was crushed by the military-bureaucratic establishment (e.g., the FP was banned in June 2001). Yet, after three years in office, the tripartite coalition government would pay the cost of its neoliberal enthusiasm with a massive electoral defeat that would pave the way for the rise of the AKP: the DSP gained only 1.21%, the ANAP 5.3%, and the MHP 8.35% of the votes and they were removed from the parliament as a result of the 10% parliamentary threshold.

The Rule of the AKP: The Welfare System Shift Accomplished

The 2002 elections brought the AKP to power. The party originated from the Islamist political movement of the 1990s, yet reinvented itself as a moderate and reformist force (Tezcür 2010; Tuğal 2009; see also Yavuz 1999). Turkey experienced the worst economic crisis of its history in 2001. The currency was devalued by 40%, the stock market collapsed, and overnight interest rates climbed to 7,500% in a matter of days. Foreign liquid capital swiftly escaped the country, leaving behind a chain of debt, bankruptcy, and unemployment. The devastating effects of the crisis (as well as the painful recovery program), the rising poverty, mass unemployment, and the resulting political grievances toward the existing political parties of the 1990s created a unique opportunity for the neoliberal Islamist AKP government to set up the basis for a long-standing hegemony. As Tuğal (2009) points out, although Islamist political organizations were initially crushed by the 1997 military intervention, Islamism continued to expand its influence in Turkey.

The AKP embodies Turkish Islamic conservatism, yet in a much more reformed tone than the former Welfare Party. It has rather embraced a neoliberal economic agenda with the help of Islamist political mobilization (Gümüşçu and Sert 2009; Tuğal 2009). During its term in office, the AKP has relaxed financial markets, accelerated privatizations and layoffs, limited agricultural subsidies, and liquidated the welfare rights of private and public formal sector employees. Its main agenda has been to demolish economic statism so as to attract international capital as well as to undermine political secularism to the end of gaining popular support of the Muslim masses. For Tuğal (2009), what the AKP accomplished is a "passive revolution" against the anticapitalist radicalism of the previous Islamist movement. The AKP government has managed to contain the religious radicalism, anticapitalism, and anti-Americanism that were mobilized by the Islamic movement in the 1990s. With the AKP, religious conservatism has diffused into wider segments of social life: Turkey has become a more religious country with less religious radicalism. Still, the founding leaders of the AKP explicitly displayed their neoliberal tendencies and claimed that they would be the WASPs of Turkey (Tuğal 2007). The AKP represented a coalition of provincial bourgeoisie and liberal/conservative intellectuals and claimed to fill the center-right position that had been left empty since the decline of the Özal's ANAP. Tuğal (2009) has argued that "resistance to neo-liberalism has now been removed, and there is a broader acceptance of 'market realities' among the popular sectors. One reason for the change is that, for the first time in Turkish history, practicing Muslims are spearheading the liberalization of the economy; it is their religious life style that wins them mass consent" (Tuğal 2007, 22).

In 2002, the AKP won the election by gaining two-thirds of the seats in parliament. It was able to form a single-party government, a rare thing in Turkey, which has been ruled by coalition governments during most of the last three decades. The AKP gained the support of a large number of people who were economically and socially hurt by the harsh economic crisis of 2001. The party has represented the interests of the emerging conservative bourgeoisie against the state-supported Istanbul bourgeoisie, and garnered the support of the poor informal proletariat. The successful juxtaposition of neoliberalism, populism, and conservatism has been the defining characteristic of AKP rule. A large community of left-liberal intellectuals also supported the rise of the AKP with the assumption that the AKP's struggle with the Kemalist military establishment would democratize Turkey in general. However, this success also brought about a sharp political crisis among political elites.

After coming to power, the AKP engaged in a long, intense political battle with the secularist nationalist economic and bureaucratic elite—the Kemalists. The Kemalist bloc consisted of the CHP, the military, and the high-level civil bureaucracy, including the high courts, media institutions, and secularist intellectuals backed by the Istanbul-centered industrial and financial bourgeoisie. Both the AKP and Kemalists did their best to minimize each other's political leverage with the mobilization of various judicial, social, and bureaucratic forces. The Kemalist bloc attempted to wage a coup against the government in the initial years of AKP rule. The failure of these attempts gave the AKP substantial leverage to pursue police and juridical operations against the civil and military leaders of the Kemalist bloc. They initiated a series of trials targeting a large number of high-ranking generals, politicians, university presidents, journalists, and leaders of various influential Kemalist NGOs. Many of these individuals were put into prison on charges of being members of illegal organizations seeking the overthrown of the government (Sarkissian and Ozler 2009). As Aytaç and Öniş (2014) state, Erdoğan claimed that it is precisely the institutions of "the political establishment," such as the Constitutional Court and the High Judiciary, that "formed an alliance to prevent people from achieving power." The famous motto of the AKP, "Milli İrade" (The Will of the Nation), referred primarily to the Muslim lower classes as opposed to the secularist economic and political elite.

Immediately after coming to power, the AKP, with the broad support of the poor conservative masses that suffered under repetitive economic crises and lost trust in the mainstream political parties of the 1990s, initiated swift neoliberal policies that undermined employment-based welfare benefits. Law No. 4828 undermined job security and facilitated labor flexibility. Law No. 4827, enacted in 2003, required public sector employees to mandatorily retire by the age of 61—instead of 65 as it used to be. While the government presented this as an improvement for employees and as a way to make the workforce younger, the CHP, the main opposition party after the 2002 elections, accused the government of trying to place its partisans in the highest public offices via forced retirements. Interestingly, one clause of the law stated that there might be exceptions for this new lower age limit, which would be at the discretion of the government. This clause increased the suspicion that the government would keep its partisans employed well past the retirement age.

Law No. 5620 (2007) allowed for hiring temporary public sector workers into permanent job positions. In 2008, Law No. 5754 significantly tightened retirement eligibility conditions, increasing the minimum number of days of premium payments from 7,200 to 9,000 days. Nevertheless, in response to nationwide labor protests against the proposed law organized by labor unions, the government decreased this limit to 7,200 days for private sector workers, while keeping the requirement of 9,000 days for public sector employees and the self-employed (Gerek 2008).[7] A CHP parliamentarian, Kemal Kılıçdaroğlu, who would become the leader of the party in 2010, claimed that the government changed the original proposal for private sector workers only because labor unions brought workers into the streets (Law No. 5754). Therefore, it seems that while the AKP was eager to implement promarket policies, the extent to which these policies were realized always depended on the bargaining power and resistance of the formal working class.

The Politics of Social Assistance during the AKP Government

While the generosity of social security benefits was significantly retrenched during the AKP's rule, Turkey also witnessed a boom of social assistance programs for the poor. Before the 2000s, the Turkish welfare system was based on a corporatist, fragmented social provision, in which employees in the state sector, formal sector workers, and the self-employed were members of different institutions with different qualities of service and benefits. The new welfare system enlarged by the AKP has largely eliminated this fragmented structure. It created a general social security institution and a general health insurance system so that services for the informal poor and formal sector employees have been merged. More important, the quality of health care has significantly improved and has often been seen as one of the main pillars of AKP social policies (Yörük 2012a; Yılmaz 2019). In 2011, the Ministry of Family and Social Policy was established to administer central government programs and to introduce new social assistance benefits. The social assistance expenditure, moreover, increased from US$860 million in 2002 to US$9.34 billion in 2016.[8]

From the 1990s to the 2000s, there is a shift from "too many too weak" party competition to a two-party competition between the AKP and the CHP. The lone holdout among the other parties is the Kurdish party, which has been able to consistently hold on to a large share of Kurdish voters. The competition can be seen in class or ethnic terms. In ethnic terms, the AKP

---

7. See http://bianet.org/biamag/toplum/105621-ssgss-karsitlari-tum-turkiyede-alanlardaydi and https://www.cumhuriyetarsivi.com/oku/?newsId=3353008&pageNo=1&home=%2Fmoni tor%2Findex.xhtml

8. See http://www.aile.gov.tr/haberler/2002de-sosyal-yardimlara-ayrilan-butce-13-milyar-lirayken-bugun-bu-rakam-33-milyar-lirayi-asti-sosyal-yardimlarda-buyuk-bir-cigir-actik

and the CHP are competing for ethnic Turkish voters, while the AKP and the Kurdish party are competing for ethnic Kurdish voters. In class terms, while the AKP and the Kurdish voters are competing for less well-off voters, the AKP and the CHP do not, in fact, really compete for the same voters, as most of the CHP voters are secularists who will not vote for the AKP and most of the AKP voters are hostile to the CHP (fig. 23). There is very little shifting of allegiance between the backers of these parties. It is the Kurdish section of the informal proletariat that is most at play. Islamist and Kurdish parties have been competing for the allegiance of these people in different ways since the 1990s. From the onset, the AKP relied on poor voters and this reliance has grown ever further over the years (fig. 24).

Between 2000 and 2010, the percentage of social assistance spending in total government spending increased by 266% (Üçkardeşler 2015). The AKP has drastically expanded means-tested social assistance, including in-kind or cash transfers, free health care programs for the poor, conditional cash transfers, programs for orphans, food stamps, housing, education, and disability aid for the poor. The number of beneficiaries and the share of government budgets allocated to these programs have dramatically increased (Buğra and Keyder 2006; Elveren 2008; Günal 2008; Yoltar 2009; Yörük 2012b). The enrollment numbers of the free health care card program for the poor (the Green Card program) increased from 4.2% to 12.7% of the population from 2003 to 2009. In 2012, a universal health care system was established, and Green Card holders were included in the new system (Yörük 2012b). In addition to these benefits from the central government, poor families were still eligible to benefit from many types of in-kind and cash assistance programs from municipal governments, which expanded exponentially during the AKP era. As such, by 2014, the regular in-kind and cash benefits from the central government for a poor family added up to $260 per month, while the official minimum wage in Turkey was $370 (Özgür 2014). In 2018, disability aid and old-age pensions covered 1.4 million individuals, social assistance by the Social Assistance and Solidarity Funds covered 3.4 million individuals, and the Green Card program covered 6.9 million individuals.[9] In 2004, the AKP proposed a change in the Metropolitan Municipalities Law that would expand the social assistance capacities of municipalities.

One of the first activities of the AKP government was to enact a law

---

9. Directorate of Strategy and Budget, Turkish Presidency, 2019; http://www.sbb.gov.tr/2020-yili-cumhurbaskanligi-yillik-programi-resmi-gazetede-yayimlandi

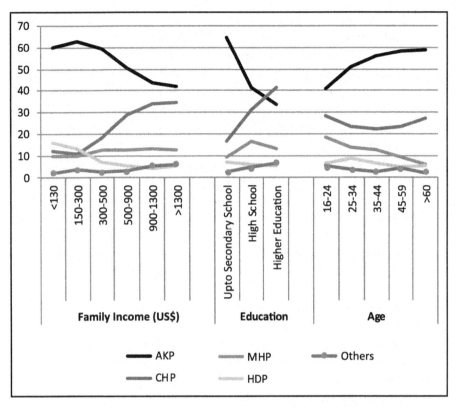

Fig. 23. Vote rates of political parties by monthly family income (USD), education, and age, Turkey

to configure the social assistance policies of the new social security system. AKP representative Mehmet Ceylan emphasized the social threats resulting from increasing poverty: "Increasing poverty in cities cause[s] the exclusion of vast masses of people from economic and social life and their marginalization. This leads to widening of differences in life standards of rich and poor, social polarization, dissipation of the sense of hopelessness, breaking down of public security and peace." He insisted that the law was not a sign of populism, because the elections took place only two months before (Law No. 4784). CHP representative, and later chairman of the party, Kemal Kılıçdaroğlu proposed a family insurance program instead of existing social assistance programs that he regarded as discrete poor relief policies that humiliated the poor (Law No. 4784).

In 2004, the AKP proposed a change in the Metropolitan Municipalities Law that would expand the social assistance capacities of municipali-

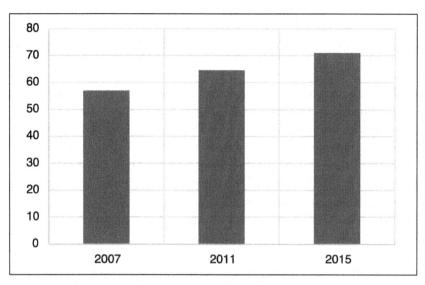

Fig. 24. Changes in rate of votes from households with incomes less than two minimum wages in total AKP votes

ties. CHP representative Mehmet Ali Dincer asked the AKP government: "Don't you also get annoyed by seeing that mayors put people in line and give them food, money, coal? Mayors act as if they are in an advertising campaign." He put forward the usual CHP position about social assistance, referring to the Chinese saying, "Don't give a man a fish, but teach him how to fish." He also suggested giving people at least a regular cash transfer instead of in-kind assistance in order to make sure people do not feel humiliated and indebted to the relief-giving government (Law No. 4784). For the CHP, social assistance can be put to use to prevent social unrest. CHP representative Canan Arıtman stated that the majority of the population used to live in rural areas, while the urban population used to be supported with food from the countryside. For her, this was "the main factor that prevented social unrest." She continued to say that recently the population had been largely urbanized and there was no more support from the countryside. Thus, she argued, "social unrest has become inevitable" (Law No. 4787).

Also in 2004, the AKP government proposed a law to establish the General Directorate of Family and Social Research. The institution eventually evolved into the Ministry of Family and Social Policy in 2011. This was one of the instances that represented the contrast and conflict between the CHP and AKP in terms of social policy. While the CHP proposed a more rational, rule-based, state-centric social assistance system, the AKP defended the existing system by referring to the Islamic roots of charity. Soon, Law No. 5263 concerning the General Directorate of Social Assistance and Solidarity intensified the debate further. İzzet Çetin from the CHP stated that in order not to humiliate people, poor people must be given regular cash assistance to do with as they please, instead of unpredictable, arbitrary poor relief as in-kind assistance, which should "have no place in a modern social policy system" (Law No. 5263).

With this law, the Social Assistance and Solidarity Fund was turned into a legal entity of the general directorate. On behalf of the CHP, Enver Öktem, a former labor union leader, said that "this law was made because the World Bank, giving $250 million credit, conditioned [the loan] that there would be a legal entity." He continued to complain: "Look how powerless we are. In order to get a very small charity from the World Bank, we are establishing a charity institution." Öktem was certain about how global capitalist centers supported and oriented this project. "Because," he added, "the government itself unashamedly named these global capitalist centers, World Bank, IMF, in the law's preamble. What we are supposed to find out is to see which domestic capitalist center, religious sects and rentiers would exactly benefit from this law" (Law No. 5263). He identified this law as a change from a social security system to a social assistance system, with a grand political purpose:

> The government is trying to deeply undermine the social security system. What will be put in place? A social assistance system. What is the difference between two systems? In a social security system, citizens and laborers are the subjects, they own rights and power. In a social assistance system, these rights are turned into compassionate favor. In a system where trade dominates public services, those without money are given assistance, charity. Of course, these assistances have some repayments, to be made in elections by the people. If our people are convinced that the public services, which are indeed rights, are compassionate favors, they will also believe that those who support the benefactor, i.e., the AKP, most, will deserve most social assistance, too. This is the social security and anti-poverty strategy of the AKP government. For their own political interests, they are trying to institutionalize social assistance services, which are temporary solutions for emergency situations. This also shows that poverty will also be permanent. (Law No. 5263)

With this law, the budget priorities of the new institution would be determined by a funding committee under the prime minister's office, whose job definition was kept "too ambiguous." That meant that "a huge charity institution with a huge budget will be left to the hands of a government whose record on charity is not very promising" (Law No. 5263). Enver Öktem claimed that the AKP would use this huge organization, which had local branches in every city, for its own political interests: "Everyone knows that AKP's political tradition made house visits before elections and gave people bread and eggs through municipal budgets in order to get votes" (Law No. 5263). Öktem referred to the Islamic tradition that the AKP was coming from. This tradition, for him, was in close contact with religious sects, their business circles, and their charity organizations: for Öktem, this network corruptively collected charity in order to use it in electoral expenditures. This "reactionary network," whose power was undermined by the 28 February military intervention, was "now reviving under the guise of social assistance and also being covered under government protection" (Law No. 5263).

However, for the AKP, social assistance programs represented "the true social welfare state" (Law No. 5263). Party representative Nevzat Doğan made a "sentimental" speech to defend their programs against the rising opposition demanding right-based regular cash transfers: "We have distributed 1.2 million tons of coal. One can say that 500 kg coal is nothing for a family, it is just charity. But, please try to imagine how a family without coal shivers when it is cold in the winter. Then you will understand what this coal means for these people. Imagine the happiness of a poor child who receives his textbooks for free. I know that you will not speak like that if you see the happiness of this child's father" (Law No. 5263).

CHP representative Haluk Koç replied to this defense with a stronger emphasis on social rights: "It is necessary that social assistance programs are defined as a citizenship right, and as a public claim which can be demanded from the state. Thus, you cannot say things like 'we gave coal, we gave textbooks, look at the kids full of pain.' It is not enough to give social assistance. It is necessary to make sure that beneficiaries do not feel indebted and grateful for social assistance institutions or the people behind these institutions. You are doing social assistance as a charity state, not a social welfare state" (Law No. 5263). During the following years, these themes would continue to be brought up by CHP representatives as well as by the radical socialist deputies, such as Ufuk Uras, who was elected under the list of the Kurdish Democratic Society Party. For Uras, "the AKP, as a party that synthesized neo-liberalism and conservatism, has been putting a charity state in place of the welfare state that has been undermined" (Law No. 5754).

Agah Kafkas, on behalf of the AKP, defended their position by emphasizing the importance of the charity tradition in Turkey: "None of us should offend the hundreds of years of charity tradition of this nation. Fortunately there is charity tradition in this country. These activities keep the society together. In times of crisis, Western societies undergo deep waves of social turbulences, but in our country this does not happen because of this tradition" (Law No. 5754). The minister Beşir Atalay agreed with Kafkas and advocated that a *waqf* (Ottoman philanthropic institutions) tradition had been the historical root of the current system. "In our history," he added, "these kinds of things have always been made by civil society, not by the state" (Law No. 5754).

Haluk Koç stated that in many other countries, poverty had increased to a level that would lead to big social unrest, threatening "the social peace in the world" (Law No. 5754). He went on to refer to one-third of the world living in poverty, while a small minority lived in much prosperity. As in the case for Turkey, "This disparity is likely to bring about big social turbulences. This can be called global terrorism. What we need to do is to protect the reputation, tradition, and logic of the state. This state is needed by you and us alike" (Law No. 5754). He continued to bring up the risk of a political threat that was likely to arise from the AKP's policies: "If a state does not provide minimum levels of health care, education, income for its citizens, then any kind of uprising and rebellion becomes likely to occur. I really want to stress that the superficiality of your social assistance policies will lead to social unrest (*toplumsal çalkantı*). This will be the most important consequence of your policies. Turkish society still has its own ways of help and solidarity and they defer the risk of social unrest. Yet, this does not mean this social unrest will not happen. Your policies may backfire one day, that's why you need to give social assistance as a social right. The wrong thing here is that it is the government who says 'we give the assistance.' But, these policies indeed must be the deeds of the state" (Law No. 5754). The AKP deputy Ali Riza Alaboyun challenged this, saying "these cannot be the deeds of the state," and Haluk Koç continued: "Look, these must be the deeds of the Republic of Turkey. Your government rules the Turkish state, but it is not proper that you present these social programs as your deeds, as part of a charity state" (Law No. 5754).

In 2006, the CHP proposed that the General Secretariat of Social Assistance and Solidarity, the main institution for social assistance, be administered by the Social Security Institution rather than by the prime minister's office, but the AKP refused this proposal. Kemal Kılıçdaroğlu from the CHP responded as follows: "Let me tell you why. You will distribute [millions of dollars] through AKP local branches; you will make electoral investments before elections. Why would you institutionalize these assistance programs? Imagine a prime minister, he visits a poor house in a slum area with his luxurious car in Ramadan month, followed by an army of cameramen. You are creating a 'gratefulness state.' . . . This is the main mechanism by which poverty becomes an instrument of politics" (Law No. 5487). During the legislative consideration of Law No. 5698, which brought changes in social security institutions, Kılıçdaroğlu pointed out the elections-based social assistance implementations of the government. He said that the government distributed coal in the summer before the elections in July 2007 and 5.35 million free health care cards were terminated in the month after the elections (Law No. 5698). Later, Bilgin Paçarız from the CHP also claimed that one million more free health care cards were recently granted before the upcoming local elections (Law No. 5754).

The minister of labor and social security, Murat Basesgioğlu, responded that they would not sacrifice this social security reform for populism. He added that in the new social security system, there would be means tests to determine whose premiums would be paid by the state. These means tests would constantly monitor citizens' incomes and jobs on a daily basis. This would allow the state to control the informal economy. Thus, social security reform would be an important instrument in the fight against the informal economy (Law No. 5754).

In 2004, the Law on Compensation of Harms due to Anti-Terrorist Struggle (no. 5233) issued social assistance provision for the internally displaced people and those civilians who lost their financial resources during the armed conflict between the state and the PKK. AKP and CHP deputies both found the law very positive for the effort to reduce terrorism, and the law was extended in 2006 with Law No. 5562. A CHP representative said that "these [internally displaced] people who were taken out of their villages and homes have been forced to survive in the slum areas of big cities. Many of these families' children do not go to school but get involved in crime. This must be a shame for the state. If this situation continues, there cannot be peace and pain will continue" (Law No. 5562). AKP representative Osman Aslan defended the proposed law as a mechanism to undermine the social and economic bases of the ethnic struggle. Apparently, the law was part of a counterinsurgency strategy. He argued that "the only way to finish terrorism is to undermine its social power, that is, to keep in the legal ground those people whom the terrorists manage to attract. The thing to do is not pressure, provocation, or discrimination, but a faster integration of these people into society. . . . [This law] was *born* out of a search for ways of separating the people from the terrorists and garnering the support of people against terrorism" (Law No. 5562). He finished by saying that Law No. 5233 improved the confidence of Kurdish people in the state and became a diplomatic success in the view of the international public that called for public policies for the Kurds that were harmed (Law No. 5562). For the AKP's Naci Aslan, the law also served as a tool of counterpropaganda against the terrorists who told the villagers that "the state does not regard you as a first class citizen" (Law No. 5562).

In its struggle for national power, the CHP, as well, responded to the AKP's politics of social assistance with novel social policy propositions. Against the observation that the AKP had strengthened its electoral base with extensive social assistance provision, the CHP developed a full-scale social policy program proposition that marked the 2011 election campaign and afterwards. The "Family Insurance Program" was presented by the CHP as the most important element of the CHP's elections campaign. The CHP proposed to give an average of US\$350 to poor families as part of the Family Insurance Program. The CHP program harshly criticized the social assistance policies of the AKP for being "humiliating, voluntary, conditional, occasional, paternalistic and ambiguous" (CHP 2011, 14). Instead, the Family Insurance Program that the CHP offered was to be a citizenship right—the CHP referred to it as an unconditional citizenship stipend. Yet the details of the program prospectus showed that the CHP would stipulate conditions for the Family Insurance Program. These conditions included some typical means tests and health/education-based cash transfer conditions. They also included some conditions related to the penal system. For instance, if children of the family committed a crime, the insurance would be terminated.

The third biggest political party, the Nationalist Movement Party (MHP), which is an extreme right-wing Turkish nationalist party, did not remain outside of the social assistance policy competition between the

AKP and the CHP in the 2011 election. Through a program called the "Hilal Card," the MHP offered to give regular income transfers to 13 million poor people in the country. Also, the poor would receive regular rent aid and heating aid under the MHP program. The "Hilal Card" program of the MHP did not differ much from what was already set up by the AKP. Yet, in its 40-year-old history, this was the first time the party had developed a social policy program proposition. This showed the extent to which social assistance policies gained significance in Turkish politics.

In sum, there is a movement from the "too many too weak" party competition of the 1990s to a two-party competition between the AKP and the CHP in the 2000s. The lone holdout among the other parties is the Kurdish party, which has been able to consistently hold on to a large share of Kurdish voters. The competition can be seen in class or ethnic terms. In ethnic terms, the AKP and the CHP are competing for ethnic Turkish voters, while the AKP and the Kurdish party are competing for ethnic Kurdish voters. In class terms, the AKP and the CHP are competing for better-off voters, while the AKP and the Kurdish voters are competing for less well-off voters. The AKP and the CHP do not, in fact, really compete for the same voters, as most of the CHP voters are secularists who will not vote for the AKP and most of the AKP voters are hostile to the CHP. There is very little shifting of allegiance between the backers of these parties. It is the Kurdish section of the informal proletariat that is most at play. Muslim and Kurdish parties have been competing for the allegiance of these people in different ways since the 1990s.

Conclusion

Recent Turkish political history has shown that political factors have significantly shaped the evolution of the Turkish welfare system. Political parties pursue partisan interests, wage struggles against each other, and respond to grassroots mobilizations. Structural factors lead to welfare policy outcomes insofar as they are translated into political threats and opportunities for the major political actors.

This analysis of the transformation of the Turkish welfare system warrants several general observations. First, the direction and extent of the welfare system changes depend on the level and form of political party competition. All major waves of declines in employment-based benefits occurred in single-party government periods of the 1980s and 2000s—including the military junta rule in the early 1980s. During the 1990s, the political arena was characterized by intense competition among a number of weak parties. This multiparty competition was accompanied by an overall expansion of employment-based benefits. The neoliberal reforms that entailed cutbacks in employment-based benefits were implemented mostly during the powerful single-party governments (e.g., ANAP rule from 1983 to 1987). Therefore, one can conclude that coalition governments do not perform well for neoliberal purposes—this most certainly explains the heavy anticoalition and pro-single-party rhetoric of neoliberal circles. These single-party governments, once they garnered extensive political popular support through various ideological positions, managed to implement neoliberal policies with minimum risk of losing the government to another competing party. More recently, the AKP was involved in a dual-party competition with the CHP for national power, which has indeed turned into a struggle over the political regime, and welfare provision has been a key element in garnering political support among the poorer sections in the urban slums and rural areas.

During the 1990s, center-right, center-left, and Islamist political parties were engaged in an intense political competition that led to a series of unstable coalition governments. These governments hesitated to implement policies targeting the rights of formal sector workers because they needed the political support of wider sectors of the population. As opposed to the exigencies of a neoliberal economy, these governments expanded employment-based welfare benefits during the 1990s as overt concessions to the formal working class. Moreover, the expanding informal proletariat benefited from the political competition as well. A good example here is the Green Card program, the free health care provision for the poor, which was established by the DYP-SHP government in 1992.

Second, political instability and social unrest have also led governments to reorganize welfare provision in ways that would maximize the efforts to contain threats to the system. For instance, the rapid expansion of employment-based benefits during the early 1990s was a direct response to waves of labor strikes between 1989 and 1991, the so-called Spring Actions. Moreover, the Green Card program was initiated in this period when the PKK also mobilized the Kurdish poor in the east in a widespread insurrection against the Turkish state. As such, Turkish social welfare policy legislation has been shaped to a significant extent by grassroots mobilization, which presented direct challenges to the ruling governments or offered support for opposition political parties. The considerable expansion of employment-based benefits during the neoliberal period has been an unexpected response to grassroots mobilization by a declining formal proletariat. No matter how weak the formal proletariat is, government policies have always been responsive to the power of the formal proletariat. In contrast, income-based social assistance policies have been responses to the political activism of the informal proletariat, which has become the main grassroots political threat for governments, as illustrated in chapter 3. Governments have chosen which segment of the informal proletariat toward which social assistance is directed. Their choice depends on which part of the informal proletariat is more threatening at the time. In the 1990s, social assistance offered by municipalities ruled by the Islamist party was used to mobilize the poor toward radical Islamism. In the 2000s, the Islamists became the governing power and pursued policies to contain the Kurdish informal proletariat. Thus, welfare provision was used by the Islamists in both periods.

This chapter shows that various political factors, which cannot be reduced to structural processes, have been shaping the trajectory of changes to the Turkish welfare system. Political parties are self-serving organizations; they pursue political interests and wage struggles against each other. These political concerns can convert existing structural dynamics into grassroots political threats or support. Structural factors lead to welfare policy outcomes insofar as they are translated into political threats or opportunities for governments. Government strategies to respond to the shift in grassroots politics have been a key force driving the transformation of the Turkish welfare system as the whole. Turkish governments have used welfare provision as a political means of containing grassroots political instability and mobilizing popular support in the competition for national power. There were periods of fluctuations in this macro strategy corresponding to political contentions that occurred in different decades. These factors include international hegemonic policy recommendations, economic development strategies, the nature of political party competition, and forms of grassroots politics.

Parliamentary discussions show a separation between contesting political parties when referring to structural and political factors. It has usually been the case that governing parties referred to structural factors in policy discussions, while opposition parties referred to political factors. Governing parties never mention a transformation of the welfare system from employment-based social security policies to income-based social assistance policies. Opposition parties make this point, however, identifying a change in policies from "social welfare state to social assistance state" (and sometimes to a charity state). For the government, there are two separate processes: first, regulatory changes in employment-based benefits, which involved rising retirement ages, decreasing wages and pensions, rising flexibility and declining job security, and processes necessitated by structural constraints. Second, there is an expansion of social assistance programs as a response to growing poverty. These two processes put together indicate a transformation from employment-based social security policies to income-based social-assistance policies. For laws reducing employment-based policies, there are a wide set of structural factors mentioned by governing parties, including informalization, increasing dependency ratios, and budget deficits. These factors have also been at the center of academic explanations. As such, structural factors appear to be the main justification of these welfare policy changes.

When it comes to laws that expand income-based policies, we see both structural and political factors. Affecting the structural factors, rising poverty, rapid urbanization, and declining informal assistance networks are most often mentioned. However, political factors are mentioned (even by government parties) as well, especially concerning the issue of social unrest. The issue of social assistance programs being used as mechanisms to contain social unrest has been frequently brought up by political parties. Here, the main political foci were the Kurdish unrest and the threat coming from the slums due to rapidly increasing poverty. Income-based social assistance programs have been expanded by the parliament, which often takes into account the social turbulence in urban slums and by the Kurds. For politicians, social welfare became an issue mostly when public order or political interests were at stake. Governments have expanded social assistance not when the people become poor—but when the poor become politicized.

Considering welfare politics, the main demarcation line between political parties is whether or not a party is in government or in the opposition. Whether or not a party is a center-left or center-right or Islamic party, parties lean toward reducing employment-based policies and expanding income-based ones when in the governing position, while opposition parties object to the reduction in employment-based policies and support income-based benefits. Opposition parties, even right-wing parties, embrace rule-based regular cash transfers.

Political competition among the parties and efforts to mobilize popular support have not been the only political forces driving Turkish welfare policies. Political instability and unrest have also led governments to reorganize welfare provision in ways that would maximize the efforts to contain these threats. For instance, the rapid expansion of employment-based benefits during the early 1990s was a direct response to waves of labor strikes during the period between 1989 and 1991, the so-called Spring Actions. It was also of importance that the Green Card program was initiated in this period, when the Kurdish poor in the southeastern and eastern regions were involved in widespread insurrections against the Turkish state. It was telling that the law regarding the Green Card included a clause that stated that the Green Card program would start in the mostly Kurdish southeast and eastern regions (Law No. 3816).

On the other hand, during the 1990s, a good number of center-right, center-left, and Islamist political parties were engaged in a harsh political competition to win government office. This competition and the inability of each political party to present convincing claims to a vast majority of the electorate resulted in equivalent levels of votes for parties in elections and in a series of coalition governments. These governments hesitated to implement policies that would reduce the rights of formal sector workers because they needed the political support of wide sectors of the population. As opposed to the exigencies of a neoliberal globalizing economy, these governments expanded employment-based welfare benefits during the 1990s as overt concessions to the formal working class.

Moreover, the concessions were not limited to the formal proletariat. The expanding informal proletariat benefited from the political competition as well. Examples here are the free health care provision for the poor, the Green Card program, and the Social Assistance and Solidarity Fund that was founded by the ANAP in 1986. The division between the state and government is critical to understanding the politics of welfare transformation. While government represents political mobilization, the state represents political containment. Often governments assume both positions, but, many other times, they are accused of prioritizing the political mobilization concern. This has been considered an opportunistic attitude by the opposition. This dichotomy crystallized in the 2000s during the

CHP-AKP competition. The CHP, backed by the military and the civil bureaucracy, represented the state while the AKP positioned itself against the state and assumed the position of the government of the people. This has been deeply reflected upon during social policy discussions. The CHP has called for rule-based, regular cash transfers, which would make it possible to contain the turbulent informal proletariat, without the partisan mobilization of the AKP. The AKP did its best to defer the institutionalization and rationalization of the social assistance system, which would minimize discretion, ambiguity, and political clientelism. Thus, the AKP has tried to combine political containment and mobilization: the strategy is to contain social unrest by mobilizing the support of the poor for the AKP. The CHP has tried to politically attach the poor to the state by creating legitimacy for the state apparatus through rule-based programs. So far, it seems like the AKP is the most successful in obtaining its objectives.

In its struggles with rivals from different ideological positions, the AKP garnered popular legitimacy and power mainly from the activism and massive support of the urban and rural poor (Öniş 2013; Yörük 2012b). Erdoğan managed to survive the Gezi Protests, the 17–25 December corruption operations, and the coup attempt. Although the party's national power seems to be eroding since 2016, the AKP has still managed to win all elections with wide support from the poor, except for the defeat in the June 2015 election and the 2019 municipal elections (Yörük and Comin 2020). In this political setting, the party increased the level of pro-poor social assistance programs and used an anti-elite populist discourse (Yörük and Yüksel 2014). The AKP expanded social assistance programs as the most important platform for providing social inclusion for the vast informal and rural sectors that never had access to welfare benefits enjoyed by workers in the formal sector and by the middle class up until then. The mobilization of popular support among the poor in a national power struggle against the Kemalists and the containment of poor Kurds have driven the expansion of the welfare state. This has been achieved partly by means of reforming the existing welfare system and partly through the creation of new policies specifically targeting poor families, informal workers, small farmers, and the Kurds.

The separation between state and government has been an ongoing debate between governing and opposition parties since the 1980s. Opposition parties have also been conscious of the political threat to the regime, stemming out of the overlap between growing poverty and ethnic conflict, and they have also tried using social assistance to quell this threat.

Yet the common approach of opposition parties was to create legitimacy for the "state," rather than the "governing party," by depersonalizing and rationalizing the social assistance system. Governing parties, sharing similar concerns about the political threat of *ethnic cum class*–based unrest, have sought to attain double objectives by resorting to discretionary social policy mechanisms as much as possible: first, to quell the social threat, and second, to attract the socially threatening populations toward the political umbrella of the governing party.

CHAPTER 5

Welfare Policies and the Kurdish Conflict

The Turkish welfare system transformation during the neoliberal period
has been largely shaped by the Kurdish conflict as a result of government
efforts to use social policies as tools of counterinsurgency. In this chapter,
I will use quantitative and qualitative data to show the strong relationship
between welfare provision and the Kurdish conflict. Since the early 1980s,
the Kurdistan Workers' Party, or PKK, has led a Kurdish uprising against
the Turkish state. During the 1990s, under the Emergency State Rule, the
Turkish military forces evacuated and burned more than 3,000 villages in
Kurdish regions and initiated a policy of internal displacement to block
the growing Kurdish popular support for the PKK. Millions of displaced
Kurdish peasants fled to big cities and crowded the slum areas in the western cities of the country such as Istanbul, Izmir, and Mersin, as well as in
the Kurdish east (Ayata and Yükseker 2005; HUNEE 2006; White 2000;
Yegen 2011).

Since the 1980s, the Turkish economy has shifted from import-
substitutionist developmentalism to export-oriented growth and has been
shaped by neoliberal policies of privatization, flexibilization, informalization, and deregulation (Keyman 2007; Cizre-Sakallioglu and Yeldan 2000).
The combined social effect of these processes has been the creation of a
large, poor, and informal proletariat. The globally competitive sectors of
the Turkish economy—textiles and apparels, construction, shipbuilding,
and electrical equipment production—depend largely on subcontracting
chains based in the informal economy and an informal proletariat, which
crowded the slum areas of big cities starting in the 1990s (Keyder 2005;
Tugal 2009; Yörük 2009).

Displaced Kurds have become a major part of the emerging informal proletariat, by constituting a cheap labor force, lacking professional qualifications, and being ready to work in any job they can find (Yükseker and Kurban 2009). In other words, internal displacement, rapid urbanization and proletarianization of the Kurds, and the growth of the informal proletariat have resulted in two converging processes: the war has changed the ethnic composition of the working class in Turkey by proletarianizing the Kurdish population and Kurdicizing the expanding informal proletariat (Yükseker and Kurban 2009; Yörük 2009).

The informal proletariat of the slums, and particularly the Kurdish poor, have become the center of grassroots politics in Turkey, providing both potential threats as well as potential bases of popular support for elite groups. Thirty years of Kurdish armed struggle, migration, urbanization, proletarianization, and impoverishment have expanded the Kurdish political movement into the slum areas of big cities. The urban Kurds have increasingly radicalized and carried out massive uprisings during the 1990s in the Kurdish region, as well as in the metropolises in the western parts of Turkey. This ethnic threat to the regime has also been translated into electoral competition. Many Kurdish parties have been founded, each succeeding another because all of them have been outlawed by Turkey's Supreme Court. The latest of the Kurdish political parties is the People's Democratic Party (Halkların Demokratik Partisi, HDP), founded in 2012. During the 2000s, the governing Justice and Development Party (AKP) has been competing intensively with Kurdish parties in the entire Kurdish region of Turkey, as well as in the slum areas of metropolises. A survey done by KONDA, one of the leading public opinion research institutes in Turkey, showed that the AKP has managed to win broad support among the poor, while the secularist opposition has mobilized the middle classes (KONDA 2015). The survey also shows that the AKP and the Kurdish movement largely compete for the support of the lower classes. Over the course of the 2000s, Kurdish party votes increased from 6% to 13%.

As shown in chapter 3, the Kurdish conflict strongly escalated after the 1990s and transformed structural pressures into social policies unevenly, ultimately leading to an ethnic disparity in social assistance provision—there is a strong statistical association between free health-care card-holding status and Kurdish ethnic identity. As I will show using quantitative methods in the next section, this program is directed disproportionately at the Kurdish minority, to the Kurdish region of Turkey, and especially to the internally displaced Kurds in urban and metropolitan areas. This disparity cannot be explained only by higher levels of poverty among the Kurds. Rather, the impact of the Kurdish conflict in Turkey explains the striking ethnic disparity in social assistance provision. The Turkish government uses social assistance to contain the ongoing Kurdish unrest, which has become highly threatening with the participation of the poor Kurds in urban slums. After I show this relationship between ethnic identity and social assistance provision using quantitative methods in the following section, I will illustrate how this relationship materializes in daily, political, and bureaucratic encounters among poor people, state actors, and political activists. I will do this by analyzing a wide array of qualitative data from interviews, field observations, and documents. The combination of these quantitative and qualitative analyses will illuminate the use of social assistance as a tool of counterinsurgency.

Kurdish Ethnic Identity and Social Assistance Provision

Over the 2000s, the shares of the Kurdish southeastern and eastern regions in total social assistance expenditures have largely increased, while all other non-Kurdish regions' shares have consistently decreased. By 2007, the share of Kurdish regions (South Eastern Anatolia and Eastern Anatolia) in total Social Assistance and Solidarity Foundation expenditures has increased to 43.9%, education conditional cash transfers to 62.36%, and health conditional cash transfers to 77.21%, while only 17.31% of the total population lives in these regions. The channeling of social assistance to the Kurdish regions, however, cannot be explained by disparities in regional poverty rates.

Table 3 and table 4 show the high shares of the Kurdish regions in conditional cash transfers and free health care cards. There is a very large discrepancy between the coverage rates of free health care card and conditional cash transfers in the Kurdish Northeast Anatolia, Central East Anatolia, and Southeast Anatolia regions, on the one hand, and the non-Kurdish West Black Sea or Central Anatolia regions, on the other (Manafy 2005; White 2000). Yet the difference in poverty rates in the Kurdish and non-Kurdish regions cannot explain the uneven distribution of social assistance rates. Rather, social assistance rates seem to be correlated with the density of Kurds in each region. Furthermore, in conditional cash transfer applications, Kurd-

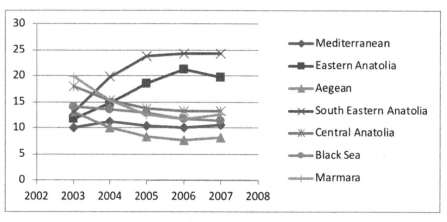

Fig. 25. Changes in Social Aid and Solidarity Foundation expenditures as a percentage of total expenditures by region (in the eastern and southeastern regions, the Kurds are the majority)

ish regions have a lower (25.84%) rejection ratio than the country average (53.26%) (Keyder and Üstündağ 2006). This implies that either unqualified Kurds apply for social assistance less than unqualified non-Kurds or that social assistance is more accessible in the Kurdish regions.

The relationship between social assistance and Kurdish ethnic identity is revealed by the results of logistic regression analyses of a dataset generated by a stratified, random, nationally representative sampling survey of 10,386 people carried out by KONDA.[1] Free health care card (Green Card) holding status is the dependent variable estimated in this analysis. Information with respect to holding a free health care card is quite accurate in KONDA data, in which the share of Green Card holders is 11.69%. The variable Green Card is an individual-level dichotomous variable, and it indicates whether or not the person holds a Green Card.

There are 10 independent variables used in eight models and all of them are dichotomous individual-level variables. Two of the independent vari-

---

1. KONDA used the government's Address-Based Population System to select the informants from the entire national population (KONDA 2011). Then, 55,000 neighborhoods and villages were clustered into categories of town, city, metropolis, or countryside in order to ensure that each subregion of the country was represented. The 874 neighborhoods and villages to visit were selected randomly by computer. Then 12 houses from each neighborhood and village were again selected randomly, and quotas for age and gender were applied. The selected informants were older than the age of 18.

TABLE 3. Distribution of Conditional Cash Transfers and Free Health Cards across Administrative Regions in 2007

| Region | Population (millions) | Number of families receiving conditional cash transfer | | | | Green Card holders | |
| | | Health | | Education | | | |
		Total	%*	Total	%*	Total	%*
Aegean/Marmara	31.50	139,997	0.44	50,750	0.16	1,461,000	4.6
Mediterranean	9.75	120,987	1.24	54,845	0.56	1,390,000	14.2
Central Anatolia	12.00	114,562	0.95	51,269	0.42	971,000	8.1
Black Sea	7.50	144,809	1.93	76,530	1.02	932,000	12.4
Eastern/ Southeastern	12.72	710,897	5.58	498,302	3.91	4,633,000	37.7
Total	73.47	1,231,252	1.67	731,696	0.99	9,555,000	13.2

Source: Author's calculations using State Planning Institution (2007) and Social Security Institution (2009).

TABLE 4. Regional Rates of Green Card, Poverty, and Kurdish Population, KONDA Dataset

Regions	Poverty rate (%)	Green Card holders (%)	Kurds in total population (%)
Istanbul	10.3	2.92	14.57
West Marmara	18.3	5.2	2.23
Aegean	27.9	4.16	5.03
East Marmara	20.8	2.16	2.47
West Anatolia	24.1	3.13	6.76
Mediterranean	31.4	13.23	8.69
Central Anatolia	37.2	11.33	2.16
West Black Sea	47.4	12.04	2.35
East Black Sea	29.5	13.75	0
Northeast Anatolia	50.2	44.8	27.6
Central East Anatolia	47.9	45.3	61.49
Southeast Anatolia	68.6	37.87	67.98

Source: Author's calculations. Regional poverty rates from State Planning Organization (2009), and the other two columns from the KONDA 2011 Barometer surveys.

ables are explanatory and eight are control variables. The key independent variable is "Kurd," which indicates whether the informant self-identified as Kurdish. There is an individual-level dummy variable "IDP" (internally displaced people), which indicates whether the respondent is one of those internally displaced people.[2] Among the individual-level dummy control

2. The survey asks whether the respondent has been harmed because of the Kurdish conflict. The respondents could choose more than one answer. I codified the dummy variable IDP as

variables, income, household size, age, and education levels have been presented for each corresponding segment. Dummy variables for house types have been ordered by an increasing economic value, from squatter house to villa. Employment status has been divided into employed and unemployed. The analysis has included one dummy variable for each geographical region of Turkey. Finally, a dummy variable is used to depict support for the governing AKP. This variable "AKP" indicates whether or not the informant would vote for the governing AKP if there were elections (it excludes the no opinions).

Income, household size, education, house type, employment status, age, and geographical region are significant factors predicting one's chances of holding a free health care card because they are basic indicators of socioeconomic status and poverty. They show whether the explanatory variable for ethnic identity is significant after controlling for socioeconomic status.

The descriptive statistics show that Green Card possession is much higher among Kurds (36%) than non-Kurds (7%), higher for AKP supporters (15%) than other party supporters (9%), much higher for the Kurdish regions (40%) than for the non-Kurdish regions (7%), and higher among the internally displaced (29%) than among those who are not internally displaced (10%). In addition, 45% of Green Card holders are Kurdish, while 10% of Green Card nonholders are Kurdish; 43% of Green Card holders live in the Kurdish regions, while 8% of Green Card nonholders live in non-Kurdish regions; 48% of Green Card holders support the AKP, while 36% of Green Card nonholders support the AKP; and 12% of Green Card holders have been internally displaced, while 3% of Green Card nonholders have been internally displaced. In total, 23% of Kurds have been internally displaced. The descriptive statistics suggest a strong relationship between Green Card–holding status and Kurdish ethnic identity, internal displacement, and support for the AKP. The subsequent multivariate analyses are conducted in order to determine to what extent these correlations are simply a product of Kurds being disproportionately poor.

The following is the empirical model of the estimation:

$$G_i = \alpha + \beta \, (\text{Kurd}_i) + \Phi X_i + N_i + \varepsilon \tag{1}$$

"1," if a respondent chooses either or both of these two answers: (a) "I was forced to leave the place [where] I lived because I was threatened to do so/my village was burned." (b) "I have migrated because of the conflict." As expected, the correlation between these two answers was high (0.409).

TABLE 5. Descriptive Statistics

	Total	Free health care card	No free health care card	Support for the AKP	Support for other parties	Kurds	Non-Kurds	Kurdish regions	Non-Kurdish regions	Internally displaced	Not internally displaced
Free Health card holding											
	0.11	1.0	0.0	.15	.09	.36	.07	.40	.07	.29	.10
	(.32)	(0.0)	(0.0)	(.36)	(.39)	(.48)	(.26)	(.49)	(.26)	(.45)	(.31)
Kurdish ethnicity											
	0.14	.45	.10	.15	.14	1.0	0.0	.65	.07	.71	.11
	(0.35)	(.49)	(.30)	(.35)	(0.35)	(0.0)	(0.0)	(.47)	(.26)	(.45)	(.32)
Support for the AKP											
	.37	.48	.36	1.0	0.0	.38	.37	.45	.36	.25	.38
	(.48)	(.50)	(.48)	(0.0)	(0.0)	(.48)	(.48)	(.49)	(.48)	(.43)	(.48)
Kurdish region											
	.12	.43	.08	.15	.10	.55	.05	1.0	0.0	.33	.11
	(.33)	(.49)	(.27)	(.36)	(.31)	(.49)	(.21)	(0.0)	(0.0)	(.47)	(.47)
Internally displaced											
	.04	.12	.03	.03	.05	.23	.01	.12	.03	1.0	0.0
	(.21)	(.32)	(.19)	(.17)	(.23)	(.42)	(.12)	(.33)	(.18)	(0.0)	(0.0)

where, subscript i refers to the household (or individual). In equation (1), G is a binary indicator of whether the informant has a Green Card or not; "Kurd" represents whether the household is a Kurdish household or not; X is a set of family-level dichotomous controls, which are binary household size, household income, education, house type, age, and employment status; N is a vector of neighborhood dummies and ε is the idiosyncratic error term.

The objective of the regression analysis is to see whether there is a relationship between the likelihood that a person holds a Green Card and the ethnic characteristics of the person. The coefficient for the variable Kurd is positive at the beginning and remains positive after controlling for possibly intervening socioeconomic factors such as household size, family income, and employment status. Education and age indicators further control for family-level unobserved heterogeneity that may affect Green Card acquisition.

Additionally, neighborhood fixed-effects methodology is used to account for neighborhood and regional level determinants of Green Card eligibility and acquisition. For instance, people who live in areas with higher poverty levels are more likely to receive a Green Card than those in areas with lower poverty levels. Similarly, the distance to the "Green Card office" or the attitudes of regional government officers may influence the probability of Green Card acquisition. Controlling for neighborhood fixed effects accounts for these and any other neighborhood-specific factors affecting the likelihood of receiving a Green Card. Because there are only 12 households per neighborhood interviewed in the KONDA survey, neighborhood dummies strongly control for the common characteristics of each neighborhood. It is worth mentioning that a neighborhood (or, in Turkish, *mahalle*) refers to a quite small residential area; that is, a *mahalle* is very comparable to a census block or census block groups that exist in the United States. Hence, neighborhood fixed effects strongly account for neighborhood-level unobserved heterogeneity.[3]

In Model 1, the probability of holding a Green Card is estimated for being Kurdish with no other control variables. The coefficient 0.287 for the variable Kurd means that the probability of holding a Green Card

---

3. The command "dprobit" is used, because all the variables are dichotomous. "Dprobit" yields the estimates of marginal effects. In all models, the results represent the marginal effects. From Models 1 to 8, the pseudo-R^2 increases, indicating the increasing explanatory capacities of the models.

TABLE 6. Logistic Regression Estimates for Green Card Holding Status
Models (1) to (5)

VARIABLES	Model 1 (Kurds Only)	Model 2 (Regions Only)	Model 3 (Kurds + Controls)	Model 4 (Regions + Controls)	Model 5 (Kurds + Regions + Controls)
Ethnicity (reference: non-Kurds)					
Kurd %	0.287***		0.115***		0.0678***
	(0.0126)		(0.0105)		(0.0100)
Party support (reference: other parties)					
AKP %			0.0226***	0.0103**	0.0138***
			(0.00474)	(0.00427)	(0.00429)
Income (reference: <300)					
300–700			−0.0536***	−0.0440***	−0.0418***
			(0.00544)	(0.00505)	(0.00500)
700–1,200			−0.0902***	−0.0759***	−0.0733***
			(0.00625)	(0.00582)	(0.00576)
1,200–2,000			−0.0926***	−0.0796***	−0.0765***
			(0.00488)	(0.00481)	(0.00473)
2,000–3,000			−0.0652***	−0.0555***	−0.0537***
			(0.00342)	(0.00329)	(0.00321)
>3,000			−0.0565***	−0.0475***	−0.0457***
			(0.00366)	(0.00365)	(0.00360)
Household size (reference: < 3)					
3–5			0.0253***	0.0222***	0.0195***
			(0.00714)	(0.00659)	(0.00648)
5–8			0.0942***	0.0791***	0.0655***
			(0.0145)	(0.0134)	(0.0124)
>9			0.162***	0.136***	0.107***
			(0.0260)	(0.0241)	(0.0217)
Education level (reference: illiterate)					
literate			−0.0244***	−0.0185***	−0.0192***
			(0.00750)	(0.00706)	(0.00682)
Primary school			−0.0433***	−0.0385***	−0.0329***
			(0.00671)	(0.00609)	(0.00603)
Secondary school			−0.0371***	−0.0370***	−0.0335***
			(0.00574)	(0.00484)	(0.00496)
High school			−0.0614***	−0.0595***	−0.0544***
			(0.00606)	(0.00550)	(0.00547)
University			−0.0646***	−0.0602***	−0.0566***
			(0.00450)	(0.00394)	(0.00395)
House type (reference: squatter house)					
traditional			−0.000604	−0.00773	−0.00392
			(0.00851)	(0.00799)	(0.00796)
Naked-wall building			−0.0194	−0.0129	−0.0106
			(0.0121)	(0.0117)	(0.0120)
Building			−0.0487***	−0.0263***	−0.0239***
			(0.00785)	(0.00789)	(0.00788)

TABLE 6—Continued

VARIABLES	Model 1 (Kurds Only)	Model 2 (Regions Only)	Model 3 (Kurds + Controls)	Model 4 (Regions + Controls)	Model 5 (Kurds + Regions + Controls)
Gated building			−0.0334***	−0.0284***	−0.0267***
complex			(0.00821)	(0.00782)	(0.00792)
Villa			−0.0214**	−0.0212***	−0.0208***
			(0.00850)	(0.00754)	(0.00736)
Employment status (reference: employed)					
unemployed			0.0278**	0.0196*	0.0209**
			(0.0112)	(0.0103)	(0.0103)
Age (reference < 29)					
29–43			0.00859	0.00348	0.00568
			(0.00592)	(0.00527)	(0.00525)
>43			−0.0253***	−0.0287***	−0.0242***
			(0.00574)	(0.00515)	(0.00511)
Regions (reference: East Black Sea)					
Istanbul		−0.0846***		−0.0532***	−0.0570***
		(0.00738)		(0.00551)	(0.00511)
West Marmara		−0.0565***		−0.0343***	−0.0341***
		(0.00859)		(0.00593)	(0.00557)
Aegean		−0.0696***		−0.0513***	−0.0510***
		(0.00774)		(0.00468)	(0.00446)
East Marmara		−0.0819***		−0.0526***	−0.0518***
		(0.00565)		(0.00390)	(0.00374)
West Anatolia		−0.0743***		−0.0491***	−0.0492***
		(0.00653)		(0.00432)	(0.00406)
Mediterranean		−0.00357		−0.0189**	−0.0224***
		(0.0137)		(0.00773)	(0.00699)
Central Anatolia		−0.0163		−0.0322***	−0.0313***
		(0.0140)		(0.00581)	(0.00561)
West Black Sea		−0.0116		−0.0239***	−0.0239***
		(0.0141)		(0.00718)	(0.00683)
Northeast An.		0.244***		0.0974***	0.0713***
		(0.0397)		(0.0274)	(0.0240)
Central East An.		0.244***		0.0590***	0.0142
		(0.0357)		(0.0205)	(0.0142)
South East An.		0.176***		0.0119	−0.0176**
		(0.0287)		(0.0122)	(0.00790)
Observations	10,386	10,386	10,386	10,386	10,386
Pseudo-R^2	0.1051	0.1928	0.2957	0.3336	0.3443

Note: Robust standard errors in parentheses.
*** $p < 0.01$, ** $p < 0.05$, * $p < 0.1$

TABLE 7. Logistic Regression Estimates for Green Card Holding Status
Controlling for Neighborhood-Level Fixed Effects; Models (6) to (9)

VARIABLES	Model 6	Model 7 (non-Kurdish Regions)	Model 8 (Metropolitan Areas)	Model 9 (Urban and Metropolitan Areas)
Ethnicity (reference: non-Kurds)				
Kurd %	0.143***	0.173***	0.0815**	0.105***
	(0.0292)	(0.0424)	(0.0318)	(0.0293)
Internally displaced				
IDP (%)				0.109***
				(0.0388)
Party support (reference: other parties)				
AKP %	0.0445***	0.0414***	0.0394**	0.0324**
	(0.0152)	(0.0143)	(0.0184)	(0.0160)
Income (reference: <300)				
300–700	−0.113***	−0.107***	−0.0759***	−0.102***
	(0.0201)	(0.0180)	(0.0255)	(0.0235)
700–1,200	−0.225***	−0.183***	−0.123***	−0.187***
	(0.0168)	(0.0162)	(0.0245)	(0.0208)
1,200–2,000	−0.240***	−0.170***	−0.109***	−0.203***
	(0.0115)	(0.0113)	(0.0175)	(0.0145)
2,000–3,000	−0.196***	−0.131***	−0.0794***	−0.152***
	(0.00828)	(0.00751)	(0.00974)	(0.00843)
>3,000	−0.163***	−0.115***	−0.0723***	−0.129***
	(0.0171)	(0.0109)	(0.0121)	(0.0138)
Household size (reference: < 3)				
3–5	0.0463*	0.0258	0.0368	0.0342
	(0.0239)	(0.0195)	(0.0277)	(0.0256)
5–8	0.114***	0.0911***	0.141**	0.110***
	(0.0307)	(0.0299)	(0.0573)	(0.0363)
>9	0.154***	0.128**	0.227**	0.200***
	(0.0441)	(0.0573)	(0.101)	(0.0583)
Education level (Reference: illiterate)				
Literate	−0.0580**	−0.0332	0.00998	−0.0370
	(0.0266)	(0.0297)	(0.0404)	(0.0295)
Primary school	−0.0922***	−0.0620***	−0.0712***	−0.0851***
	(0.0210)	(0.0224)	(0.0235)	(0.0219)
Secondary school	−0.124***	−0.0706***	−0.0693***	−0.105***
	(0.0190)	(0.0197)	(0.0153)	(0.0181)
High school	−0.179***	−0.128***	−0.106***	−0.173***
	(0.0176)	(0.0172)	(0.0163)	(0.0170)
University	−0.191***	−0.135***	−0.102***	−0.156***
	(0.0124)	(0.0102)	(0.0109)	(0.0118)
House type (reference: squatter house)				
traditional	0.00993	0.00653	−0.0480**	−0.0172
	(0.0248)	(0.0223)	(0.0238)	(0.0257)
Naked-wall building	0.00382	0.0111	−0.0293	0.00857
	(0.0534)	(0.0517)	(0.0409)	(0.0543)

TABLE 7.—*Continued*

VARIABLES	Model 6	Model 7 (non-Kurdish Regions)	Model 8 (Metropolitan Areas)	Model 9 (Urban and Metropolitan Areas)
Building	−0.0217	0.000314	−0.0278	−0.0273
	(0.0306)	(0.0284)	(0.0281)	(0.0282)
Gated building	−0.137***	−0.0985***	−0.0847***	−0.0956***
complex	(0.0365)	(0.0279)	(0.0102)	(0.0317)
Employment status (reference: employed)				
unemployed	0.0927***	0.126***	0.0227	0.135***
	(0.0316)	(0.0375)	(0.0363)	(0.0382)
Age (reference < 29)				
29–43	0.0323*	0.0189	−0.0327*	0.0126
	(0.0175)	(0.0165)	(0.0167)	(0.0178)
>43	−0.0716***	−0.0527***	−0.0842***	−0.0814***
	(0.0179)	(0.0169)	(0.0165)	(0.0177)
Observations	4,395	2,990	1,135	2,883
Pseudo-R^2	0.3128	0.2737	0.3357	0.3160

Note: Robust standard errors in parentheses.
*** $p < 0.01$, ** $p < 0.05$, * $p < 0.1$

increases by 28.7 percentage points for the Kurds. Since the incidence of holding Green Cards is only 11.6%, this means being Kurdish increases the likelihood of holding a green card by 246% (calculated as 28.7/11.6). Yet analyses of variance show that Kurds do have lower household incomes. For that reason, it is necessary to answer whether Kurds are more likely to have a Green Card because of their lower socioeconomic status.

Model 3 controls for income, household size, education, house type, employment status, and age in addition to the variable Kurd. As expected, Green Card acquisition decreases with increasing income, education, and house type levels, and increases along with increasing household size and unemployment. Green Card acquisition is higher for people aged 29–43 and lower for those older than 43. This is probably because the elderly are less capable of handling the application procedures. The variable Kurd remains statistically significant with a highly positive coefficient, 0.115. In comparison to the average Green Card holding rate (11.69%), being Kurdish is associated with a 99% higher chance of receiving a Green Card after controlling for the poverty related factors listed above. Being Kurdish has a highly positive effect on Green Card holding beyond one's socioeconomic status. Poor Kurds are more likely to hold Green Card than poor non-Kurds.

Model 2 examines the effect of one's region of residence on Green Card holding status. Here, the non-Kurdish East Black Sea region was omitted as the reference category. While all other non-Kurdish regions are less likely to receive Green Card services, the Kurdish regions are more likely to do so. Analysis of variance also shows that Kurdish regions are poorer than non-Kurdish regions. Model 4 includes the effect of poverty by controlling for variables of socioeconomic status. Kurdish regions are still more likely to have greater rates of Green Card holding with statistical significance in comparison to other regions, after controlling for socioeconomic status.

Model 5 introduces the variable Kurd in order to understand the effect of ethnicity in this regional disparity. The result is that the significance of Kurdish regions vanishes. The Kurdish South Eastern Anatolia's coefficient even turns negative. This indicates that strikingly higher Green Card holding in the Kurdish regions can be explained not only by higher levels of poverty in these regions but also by the fact that a huge majority of the population in these regions are Kurdish.

Models 6 to 9 control for neighborhood-level fixed effects. This controls for the unobserved heterogeneity at the neighborhood level. Model 6 shows that the variable Kurd has a coefficient of 0.14. After controlling for all socioeconomic factors and neighborhood-level fixed effects, being Kurdish increases the likelihood of receiving Green Card by 120%, which is a very high effect. Importantly, the coefficient of the variable AKP is 0.0445, indicating that voting for the governing AKP is associated with a 38.2% increase in the likelihood of holding a Green Card in comparison to the average Green Card level. Among the poor, those who support the AKP are more likely to hold a Green Card.

Model 7 makes the same estimation for non-Kurdish regions of the country. Kurds outside of the Kurdish region are also much more likely to receive social assistance than non-Kurds. Model 8 looks at the effect of the same variables in metropolitan areas. This shows that being Kurdish significantly increases the likelihood of receiving a Green Card in the metropolitan areas, once again after controlling for socioeconomic status and neighborhood-level fixed effects. Finally, Model 9 controls for the variable IDP (internally displaced people) for metropolitan and urban areas. In comparison to the average Green Card holding rate, internal displacement is associated with a high (93.9%) increase in Green Card receiving status at the neighborhood level, after controlling for ethnicity, party support, and socioeconomic status. Being both Kurdish and internally displaced greatly increases the likelihood of Green Card holding in urban and metropolitan areas.

These regression models indicate that there is a strong association between free health care card-holding status and Kurdish ethnic identity. This association is even stronger for the internally displaced Kurds in urban and metropolitan areas. Living in Kurdish regions of Turkey also greatly increases one's chances of holding a free health care card due to the ethnic characteristics of these regions, in addition to their poverty. Yet the Kurds in non-Kurdish regions also receive higher social assistance. The models also show that there is a strong association between voting for the AKP and Green Card acquisition. These findings hold true after controlling for socioeconomic factors. The strongest aspect of the analysis is that the neighborhood-level fixed effects are controlled for, which shows that Kurds are much more likely to hold a Green Card than non-Kurds even in the small vicinity of a neighborhood or village.

These statistical analyses show that social assistance programs in Turkey are directed at the Kurdish minority and the Kurdish region in a disproportionate manner. This is not limited to the Kurds in the Kurdish region. Thus, ethnic disparity in social assistance provision in Turkey is not only because of the concentration of social assistance programs in the Kurdish region. There is an ethnic targeting of social assistance toward the Kurdish minority. Kurds across the country are more likely to be qualified for social assistance not because of their poverty but rather due to their ethnicity. This is the case for the Kurds in the metropolitan regions and especially for the internally displaced Kurds, who are most likely to receive social assistance. The models have controlled for possibly intervening socioeconomic factors and neighborhood-level fixed effects. Thus, the analysis rules out the possibility that the Kurds, the Kurdish region, and the internally displaced Kurds receive more social assistance simply because they are poorer.

The Political Motivations of Social Assistance: Welfare as Counterinsurgency

If Kurds receive more social assistance on the basis of their ethnic identity, what would explain this disproportionate targeting? In this section, I will make use of descriptive quantitative and mostly qualitative data and analyses in order to account for potentially political targeting. The governing AKP uses social assistance provisions to quell Kurdish unrest, which has become highly threatening with the massive popular support of poor Kurds. This is especially true for the Kurds in the metropolitan areas and the internally displaced Kurds in the urban and metropolitan areas. The high level of political radicalization among these displaced Kurds is a possible explanation for their outsized inclusion in social assistance provisions.

Kurdish political radicalization take place through the mobilization of the Kurdish political movement, whose legal component, that is, Kurdish political parties, have been close competitors of the AKP in all national and municipal elections. Examination of the electoral data from recent elections reveals the scope of the electoral competition among the AKP, CHP, and Kurdish parties. This data demonstrates that the AKP and Kurdish parties have been competing for the votes of the informal Kurdish proletariat. The CHP is largely kept out of this competition and the party gains votes mainly from the middle classes. In the 2002 national elections, the AKP won 34.28% of the votes, the CHP won 19.39%, and the Kurdish party of the time, the Democratic People's Party, won 6.14%. In the general elections in June 2015, the distribution of votes was as follows: AKP, 40.87%, CHP, 24.95%, and Kurdish party HDP, 13.12%. In the 2018 general elections, the AKP gained 42.56% of the votes, the CHP 22.64%, and the HDP 11.7%.

A KONDA survey conducted in December 2019, which was designed by the author, illustrates what percentage of each social class voted for the AKP, CHP, and HDP in the 2018 general elections (table 8) and the class composition of AKP, CHP, and HDP voters (table 9). The AKP and the HDP have largely competed over the lower classes, while the CHP has largely depended on the middle classes. Another study by KONDA conducted after the 2015 June elections illustrates that the largest portion of swing votes between the 2011 and 2015 elections occurred between the AKP and HDP voters. The competition between the AKP and the CHP is not basically to win the support of the same social classes. Instead, the AKP tries to keep its electoral support among the lower classes in order to counter CHP support among the middle classes. On the contrary, the competition between the AKP and HDP is over the same social base, the mostly Kurdish informal proletariat.

During the 2000s, the AKP managed to sharply increase its votes in

TABLE 8. Voting Preferences of Class Groups in 2018 Elections

	AKP	CHP	HDP	Other	*Total*
Capitalist	21.67	26.67	3.33	48.33	100
Executive	15.38	38.46	3.85	42.31	100
Professionals	23.48	34.09	3.79	38.64	100
Petty bourgeoisie	40.65	21.02	2.77	35.56	100
Formal nonmanual proletariat	30.95	22.92	2.08	44.05	100
Formal manual proletariat	43.39	19.03	4.19	33.39	100
Informal proletariat	38.13	13.23	12.84	35.8	100
Peasant	47.73	18.18	6.36	27.73	100
Retired	42.89	23.51	0.62	32.98	100

TABLE 9. Class Composition of AKP, CHP, and HDP in 2018 Elections

	AKP	CHP	HDP
Capitalist	1.04	1.87	2.02
Executive	0.63	3.75	1.01
Professionals	3.13	8.43	5.05
Petty bourgeoisie	17.24	16.1	11.11
Formal nonmanual proletariat	9.82	13.86	7.07
Formal manual proletariat	27.17	21.72	24.24
Informal proletariat	9.4	6.18	32.32
Peasant	10.97	7.49	14.14
Retired	20.6	20.6	3.03
Total	100	100	100

the Kurdish region in general and in its largest city, Diyarbakir. Winning the elections in Diyarbakir has always been a critical issue between the AKP and Kurdish parties in establishing hegemony over the entire Kurdish region and people. Prior to the 2009 municipal elections, Prime Minister Tayyip Erdoğan said that gaining the office of the mayor in Diyarbakir was one of their most important aims in the elections. In reply, the Kurdish party of the time (the Democratic Society Party) declared that Diyarbakir was their "fortress" and that they would do everything not to lose Diyarbakir to the AKP.

During interviews in Istanbul and Diyarbakir in 2011, Kurdish party representatives indicated that the social assistance policies that the AKP implemented helped shift part of their mass base to the AKP during the 2000s. They said that most of their activists as well as their mass base were composed of people who had temporary jobs, low income jobs, or were unemployed, and that many of these people received social assistance. However, the local head of the Kurdish party in Beyoğlu, the central district of Istanbul, added during the interview that

> many of our people keep supporting us although they receive social assistance. Also, many times if a person supports us actively, he cannot get social assistance easily. They have to go through a legal procedure to get a Green Card. This procedure includes a check at the police center. If, say, a person participated in an illegal event, or got arrested in the past, then he cannot get social assistance easily.

The AKP's social assistance strategy attempts to address both the class and ethnic dimensions of the Kurdish question. With regard to its class aspects, the AKP uses populism by combining the provision of services with a heavy antielitist rhetoric against the secularist bourgeoisie. As for the ethnic dimensions of the Kurdish question, the AKP offers inclusion on the basis of "Islamic solidarity" by distributing economic rent through diffuse clientelistic networks. Up until the mid-2010s, a growing economy created the conditions for this strategy. If there was growing support for the AKP then, it is not because Kurds were increasingly conservative or Islamist at the expense of their Kurdish identity. On the contrary, many Kurds felt that they could comfortably experience their Kurdish ethnicity under Islamic solidarity while their class position was strengthened through the material networks of the AKP (Yörük and Günay 2019). Poverty-alleviation programs for the Kurds are on the rise even though such programs are not a focal point of the state's explicit discourse on the Kurdish conflict. Indeed, the AKP clandestinely channels social assistance programs to Kurds without officially instituting a positive discrimination policy.

While Kurdish parties have doubled their electoral support during the last decade, the AKP's response to rising Kurdish power has been fluctuating and ambivalent. The AKP gained significant consent and support from Kurds by occasionally using discourses and policies that were described as the "Kurdish Overture" and the "Peace Process." This included public television broadcasting in Kurdish and legalizing the teaching of the Kurdish language. Nevertheless, the AKP had already launched a period of repression in the mid-2000s, including police operations targeting the Kurdish parties. Despite the cease-fire with the PKK in the decade after September 11, 2001, Turkey prosecuted a third of all terrorism convictions in the world by 2011 with a figure of 12,897 convictions (Independent Evaluation Group 2011). With regard to the provision of public services, the AKP also uses the withdrawal of social assistance to punish the radical oppositional political activism of Kurds. After the 2009 municipal elections, it was reported that in many Kurdish provinces, including Mus, Diyarbakir, Tunceli, and Van, the government took away the free health care cards of poor people who supported the Kurdish party. In Van Province, the police administration gave negative reports for the social assistance applications of many Kurdish families who voted for the Democratic Society Party. In 2008, the government of Adana, a big city where thousands of internally displaced Kurds live in slums, declared that it would withdraw social assistance benefits and free health care services for families whose children took part in street protests (Radikal 2008). Therefore, social assistance has also become an instrument of political sanction against the Kurds who support the Kurdish political movement.

In the context of these fluctuations, Kurdish popular support for pro-Kurdish parties continued to expand over the 2000s. This is due in part to the Kurdish movement's countermove in the field of social policy: establishing heterodox social assistance programs. This not only combats the AKP's paternalist regulating of the Kurdish poor through social assistance policies, it also mitigates the effects of the AKP's targeted withdrawal of these benefits as a form of punishment. Consequently, social assistance provisions have transformed into another battleground for the political struggle between the Turkish state and the Kurdish movement. The HDP governs about 100 municipalities in the Kurdish region. They became the epicenter of reaching out to the Kurdish poor. This strategy included the formation of NGOs that deliver services and benefits. For example, the HDP-run municipality of Diyarbakır, the largest city in the Kurdish regions, worked with Kurdish civil society organizations to establish the Sarmaşık Association, a local NGO that provides poor Kurds with, among other things, food, cash, and clothing.

The Turkish state attempts to make invisible the ethno-political aspects of Kurdish poverty by forcing poor Kurds to choose being poor over being Kurdish in order to be eligible for social assistance. Conversely, the HDP emphasizes the Kurdishness of poverty by pointing to the intersections of class and ethnicity in the deliberate impoverishment of Kurdistan. In a personal interview, the director of Sarmaşık pointed out that the association presents an alternative to the existing systems of social assistance in

Turkey by activating the political agency of the Kurdish poor rather than pacifying it:

> We designed this project in order to satisfy basic needs of the people without humiliating them, as opposed to those existing poor relief systems of the government that pacify the people, make them dependent and disconnected from the economy. We told the people that we are not philanthropists (*hayırsever*). Their poverty stems from the insufficiency of the institutions and organizations of the [Kurdish] region. I see that families have adopted our perspective. They started seeing what they get as a right. Some of them even wanted to stop receiving social assistance when they were better off.

During interviews in 2010, Kurdish party leaders acknowledged that the AKP's social assistance programs worked well to gain support from the Kurds. For Kurdish activists, it was no longer true that Kurds would keep supporting the Kurdish party even though they received social assistance. Activists of the Kurdish party of the time (Peace and Democracy Party, BDP) in Diyarbakir stated that the Sarmaşık was a political defense against the AKP's effort to gain support of the Kurdish poor with social assistance, and it has contributed largely to the electoral successes that the Peace and Democracy Party gained in 2009 and 2011. Sarmaşık officially presented its mission with regard to the surrounding social political context as follows:

> We are not a philanthropic association. We work with other mass organizations in order to mobilize social forces capable of fighting against the poverty of our people. We think that poverty in the Kurdish region has a peculiar content and underlying structure. Poverty is a common phenomenon in Turkey, but it is very different in Diyarbakir. A significant amount of resources is allocated for investment and job creation in every region of the country, but in Diyarbakir, everything possible has been done in order to impoverish the city. There is deliberate action aimed at destroying the historical texture of the city. (http://www.sarmasik.org)

Similarly, other Kurdish municipalities established "education support houses." They provide educational activities for poor Kurdish children and prepare them for competitive national exams for placement in Turkish universities. The AKP responded to this countermove with a familiar mix of cultivating consent while imposing coercion. The double-edged strategy of the AKP has not only increased the level of government-led social programs but has also criminalized and outlawed Kurdish-led programs.

The escalation of armed conflicts between the PKK and the Turkish state has revealed the use of social assistance as a counterinsurgency strategy. In July 2012, for example, the PKK, following an intense guerrilla warfare effort, gained de facto control over the countryside of Hakkari Province, located between Iran and Iraq. This happened for the first time in Turkish history and created a huge public outcry. When the PKK also called for another popular revolt among the Kurdish people, the Turkish public became worried about a possible Kurdish Spring following the roots of the Arab Spring. A journalist asked Prime Minister Erdoğan in a live TV show: "It is a reality that in eastern regions Kurdish people support the PKK. This is what makes the PKK survive. How do you think this support can be cut?" The prime minister answered: "During the Ramadan month, six ministers and many deputies are in the region. They are searching the entire region. This is the month to help the poor. We have distributed 350 thousand packets of food aid across the whole country" (interview published at www.ntvmsnbc.com, 5 August 2012). Social assistance was presented by the Turkish prime minister as a central method to delink the PKK from Kurdish support—a tradition that the AKP has carried over from the Welfare Party of the 1990s. The mayor of Ankara, Melih Gökçek, one of the founders of the Welfare Party and one of the popular figures of political Islam, said in 2010 that "if there is no social explosion in Ankara today, the effect of social assistance programs on this is very important" (Gazete Vatan, 29 March 2010).

The Perspectives of High-Ranking and Low-Ranking Social Policy Officials

Welfare bureaucrats and caseworkers provide enlightening insights into the ethnic politics of social assistance provision in Turkey. According to the general director of the General Directorate of Social Assistance whom I interviewed, the first and the only objective of social assistance programs was to help poor people stay out of poverty. If this effort of the Turkish state, as a welfare state, happened to diminish terrorist activities, this would only be an unintended and positive consequence. He also thought that "it was not necessarily true that the poor would fight against the state, only some of them did this," adding that the "Green Card might help in this sense." For him, a plausible answer to the question of why Kurds are disproportionally targeted might be that Kurds were more willing to apply for a Green Card than non-Kurds—a claim that is discredited by statistical analysis. He believed that in many places in the western parts of the country, poverty was higher than in the eastern and southeastern regions, but people in these regions found it humiliating to apply for a Green Card. Yet, in the eastern regions, he said, "the poor were told by some people that [the] Green Card was their right." By "some people," he obviously meant the Kurdish political movement. For him, rather than an oversupply of social assistance toward the Kurds, the reason might be that the Kurdish political organization encouraged the Kurdish poor to demand a Green Card, as the interview reveals.

Nevertheless, for lower level officials and experts, this answer should be sought for in the supply side: since 2003, that is, during AKP rule, the budgets allocated for the eastern and southeastern (Kurdish) regions have been 50% higher than the level they should have been, which is normally calculated according to the total population and average income level in a region. This seems to explain much of why there is disproportionate targeting of Kurds, at least in Kurdish areas. According to another expert, the European Union sometimes demanded programs that would favor ethnic minorities, especially the Kurds. Also, Green Cards were granted much more easily in this region compared to other regions. Many times gendarme and police forces were involved in means-test investigations as primary agents. The expert argued that security forces often invited people to security centers, rather than making house visits, putting heavy pressure on applicants politically. But at the same time, since security forces did not know how to conduct investigations, they tended to grant a Green Card to people more easily.

According to a high-ranking bureaucrat from the Ministry of Development, the disproportional allocation of Green Cards to Kurds might occur because Green Card allocation procedures might be more subjective than other social assistance procedures: "Depending on the attitude of the local office administration, you can observe two cities or cases with the same level of poverty but with different easiness at which the Green Card is granted. There is more subjectivity here. It depends on the attitude of the applicants, too." Another expert, who works under this bureaucrat and joined the interview, intervened at this point and said that "it is easier to get [a] Green Card in the eastern regions." He then asked if "it is really easier to get Green Card in eastern regions," and the high-ranking bureaucrat replied hesitantly, "well, yes, this is the case."

For one of the experts at the Social Assistance and Solidarity Fund, in the 2000s, two parallel political developments gave rise to a concern with poverty and social assistance, First, the changing economic dynamics led to grievances among the poor and some incentives were needed to convince people of the benefits of the new economic system. Second, implying a possible reason for the rise of the AKP, the expert referred to a center-periphery dualism, an analogy that has remained quite popular among conservative intellectual circles in Turkey.

> I am not claiming that there is a trade for the votes in social assistance. But people reward public services. The center-periphery hierarchy has recently changed. The old establishment has lost its power and the periphery, i.e., those previously excluded, has gained power. The people, the periphery gained consciousness, and now it is not easy to lead people. Migration, rise of squatter houses . . . The slum people, especially second and third generations, have started to raise demands. Earlier generations of slum dwellers used to compare their life [living] standards with those of villagers. Plus, they were still receiving money, food, etc. from the village. The new slum dwellers compare themselves with the rich people of the cities. And this increases grievances, and social policy helps out at this point. There is one more thing: the government put social assistance on an ever-growing agenda and this has also boosted the demand for social assistance. Sometimes people criticize us that if there is such a big increase in the number of people receiving social assistance, this would mean that there were higher number of poor people. But this is not true. There used to be not much demand from the people for social assistance.

In a similar vein, an expert from the Ministry of Development interpreted the expansion of social assistance programs by referring to social and political transformations that had occurred since the 1980s. She mentioned the rapid rural-to-urban migration, the rise of the informal economy, and the increase in slums. Yet she connected these developments to waves of social unrest in slum areas.

> Poverty leads to social explosions (*sosyal patlama*), and the government intervention occurs at this point. Until the 1980s, people used to have their own networks of solidarity, which have now weakened largely. Economic crises have always become critical points that led governments to create big social assistance programs, because people really suffer and then take to [the] streets during crises. In each crisis, the government looks at the ever worsening conditions and takes further measures. This first happened with Özal, and, after the 2001 crisis, with the AK Party.

The experts and officials from central social policy institutions in Ankara implied that social unrest has become an issue in social policymaking. Yet how social policy can diminish the threat of social unrest can only be understood by analyzing the grassroots operations of social assistance institutions, which have been reflected by the interviews and observations from local social assistance offices in Istanbul.

The Micro Politics of Social Assistance Offices

Social assistance becomes a productive political tool for Turkish government actors through micro-political encounters in which social assistance and public security are intertwined, and social assistance brings dependency and subordination. Micro politics here refers to the daily interactions of power between citizens and local welfare officials, the caseworkers of social assistance.

The Social Assistance and Solidarity Fund operates a number of means-tested social assistance programs: cash aid, food aid, medical material aid, aid for education purposes, disaster aid, conditional cash transfers, and aid for the disabled. Yet the rules of means tests for both social assistance and a free health care card seem rather ambiguous. For instance, households having a per capita income lower than one-third of the minimum wage and no formal employment are eligible for social assistance and a free health care card. However, it is impossible to officially determine the income because the applicants are required not to have formal jobs. In these cases, local authorities resort to indirect ways of income determination.

To determine if the family is a deserving poor family, caseworkers visit the house to interview the applicant, and if they do not trust what the applicant says, they talk to neighbors, shopkeepers, and to the elected local administrator (*muhtar*) of the neighborhood. Caseworkers ask detailed questions about employment, income, marital status, what the spouse does, whether (s)he receives alimony, what the children do for a living, and generally pry into all monetary transactions of the household. Oftentimes, police officers join the visits: "People are often scared of the police and they tell the truth," says one Social Assistance and Solidarity Foundations (SYDV) caseworker. Often applicants are also required to visit police departments to go through investigations. Following house visits, officials fill out an evaluation report. The following are two inspection reports (one positive and one negative) that SYDV officials prepared after house visits and that were shared with me during my fieldwork:

Inspection Report 2 (Positive):

Thought and judgment: After the inspection made for H (29) who has applied for cash transfer, I have come up with these following conclusions: She lives in G neighborhood with her husband and their three children. She pays a rent of 450 Liras. She does home-based textiles work in putting-out system and she sews accessories to garments. Her husband B (26) works as a casual worker at constructions as far as he can find a job. For two months he has not been able to work because he had an orthopedic problem at his back. Their oldest child M (7) goes to elementary school and the others M (6) and K (1) are below school age. They have applied for the basic needs of their household. Upon inspection, it is found that their economic conditions are poor. It will be appropriate to give them social assistance.

Inspection Report 3 (Negative):

Upon inspection, I have seen that the applicant P (47) lives with her son who is married, his wife and child, and her two daughters and another son in a rental apartment with the rent of 700 Liras in K neighborhood. She is a housewife. Her husband passed away in 1998. Her son C (25) works as a motor-delivery employee at a restaurant with a salary of 800 TL [Turkish lira] and he has social security. C's wife works as a cleaning worker at F hospital with a salary of 600 TL and social security. Her daughter B (23) works at a call-center for 500 TL without social security. Her other daughter Y (19) does not work or study. Her other youngest son C (13) goes to elementary school. She has a granddaughter, A (3). The applicant benefits from the social security of her son. Her children are working adults, and the household has a total income of 1200 TL. The house looks in normal conditions. Upon inspection, I have come to conclusion that it will not be appropriate to give her social assistance because P can meet her basic needs with the help of her children.

SYDV caseworkers have extensive and detailed knowledge about the residents of neighborhoods. They remember the names and social/economic characteristics of most applicants. They ask very detailed and personal questions, including whether someone had a good relationship with family members in order to see whether they could support each other. The following conversation that I witnessed between a SYDV caseworker and a social assistance applicant in the SYDV office reveals the domination as well as the intimacy between the two:

OFFICIAL1: What do you sell?
APPLICANT: I don't sell anything.
o1: Don't lie! I saw you selling something last month.
A: Brother, on my oath I am not lying, I don't sell anything.
o1: What does your husband do?
A: He's just came from the military service.
o1: Do you have a Green Card?
A: No.
o1: Perhaps we can get you a compensatory aid every two-three months. But we cannot get you a regular transfer. I remember your previous husband passed away, when?
A: Long time ago, I don't remember. Will you get me money?
o1: They will decide in the board meeting, I don't know.
A: Will you get me money?
o1: I will check it out. Did you ever get the coal aid?

A: No, we've spent the winter freezing to death. Now, where shall I go next?

ol: Go home, where else?

A: I don't have any money!

ol: Nothing can happen before the board meets.

A: Where shall I get the letter of poverty?

ol: (getting angry) You keep asking me all the same questions! I will also be happy if you get this money!

A: I've kept running all around for this money since yesterday, bro! I don't know what to do. My mom is sick too!

ol: Hope she will get better soon. You should keep on selling these things.

A: Which one?

ol: Selling flowers.

A: Bro, I don't sell anything, you kept telling me keep on, keep on.

ol: You should make it. It is also a good job. Do you have permission from the municipality?

A: I don't sell anything!

ol: I am telling this for your good!

This reveals an ongoing negotiation between the applicant and the caseworker, where the caseworker has authority over the applicant. Yoltar (2009) claims that the eligibility criteria for social assistance, as well as disenrollment procedures, are always ambiguous and leave "ample room for discretion" and power for local public authorities to include and exclude certain ethnically or politically stigmatized groups. The requirements of means tests for the Green Card and social assistance come within "a terrain full of uncertainties" in the process of verification of poverty (Yoltar 2009, 773). Uncertainty, complexity, illegibility, and the individualizing effects of the rules serve to enhance state power over poor citizens as they are constantly forced to interact with the state (Yoltar 2009, 776). This implicit state power comes along with an explicit government intention for electoral manipulation by the use of social assistance.

A caseworker indicated that in February 2011, only four months before the elections, the amount of cash transfers available for a family was increased from 100 TL to 300 TL, and the total budget that was available for the local SYDV branch also increased from 25,700 to 104,000 Turkish liras. For the caseworker M from the SYDV, "the government might make the increase because of the elections." The uncertainty and ambiguity in social assistance procedures are fed by deep suspicion against the applicants. During the interviews, both the police and the SYDV caseworkers kept complaining about the "self-interested," "dirty," and "dangerous" residents of these neighborhoods. When the caseworkers talked about the social assistance applications and applicants, they used a specific discourse, much of which shared the language of the security forces. They often uttered phrases such as "interrogation" or "reporting," which implicitly revealed an underlying assumption that there was something suspicious about the applicants and the caseworkers needed to reveal the truth behind what the applicants said. Thus, applicants needed to prove not only that they were poor but also that they were proper citizens, politically, legally, and morally.

House visits also show how well social security and state security are integrated. The neighborhoods where police accompany the caseworkers on house visits are "dangerous" ones where residents are mostly of Kurdish and Gypsy (Roma) origins. Yet they clearly differentiate Kurdish and Gypsy responses to social assistance activities, as the Kurds represent a political threat while the Gypsies seem to be considered merely as criminals. One of the police officers said "when we go to K neighborhood with a single car, the Gypsies attack us because they want more money. But the Kurds attack us for political reasons because the PKK influences them." A security guard (*bekci*) who joined the house visits identified social assistance as a cause of tension between oppositional groups and the state: "In M neighborhood, terrorists are powerful. I try not to pass through their places when I go to house visits. I feel uncomfortable if they see me around. Why? Because they do not like us, they try to create hostility between the state and the citizens. They try to stop the state from serving the people. Because the people move from terrorists to the state as they receive social assistance." That is why, he believes, the caseworkers cannot enter these neighborhoods without special terror unit police forces.

There is a significant difference in attitude between those applying to SYDV and free health care card offices. The people applying to the SYDV office usually claimed an extreme degree of suffering. SYDV applicants often tried hard to convince the caseworkers that they suffered even more than the caseworkers would think, for example, that they were poorer than they might be thought of, they had serious health problems, or their landlords were cruel. However, although the eligibility criteria were the same as in SYDV applications, the free health care card applicants—they were usually the same people as the SYDV applicants—made their applications in a much more tranquil setting, submitted their documents, and asked some questions without trying to further prove their destitution. The difference in attitudes of the applicants at each office can be attributed to the difference in the degree of flexibility at which the benefits were distributed at each office. SYDV offices offer a number of different social assistance programs and most of the time applicants might be eligible for many of them. The process was said to be rule based, yet, in each specific point of evaluation and assessment, the personal discretion of the caseworkers came to dominate the decision of how much of a certain benefit one would obtain. Therefore, the application process was structured in such a way that would allow the "degree of suffering" that an applicant performed to determine the amount of social assistance that would be granted: the amount of benefit is deemed to be proportional to the degree of suffering, that is, it was a linear function of suffering. This is because SYDV caseworkers had ambiguous attitudes toward the applicants, fluctuating between rebuffing and helping. When applicants first came to the office desk, caseworkers started behaving distantly and then antagonistically. However, as applicants increasingly performed the suffering role, caseworkers became more helpful and tolerant—suffering performances were effective.

On the other hand, in the free health care card office, the free health care card was the only benefit available regardless of the degree one suffered. Thus, once applicants "proved" a minimum degree of their monetary and medical need, that is, once they passed the required threshold of need, an excessive amount of suffering performance would be unnecessary. This created the main difference of attitude in each office. Whether the government supplies higher social assistance or whether people demand more assistance, the point is that social assistance has become a mechanism that attaches poor people to the state by creating a symbolic and material exchange economy. These exchanges have created a relationship of intimacy between the state and poor citizens, who would have otherwise been left more easily to the influence of radical groups.

Conclusion

As the Kurds have been rapidly urbanized through internal displacement, have become a growing part of the informal proletariat, and finally have become politically more radical, they have become a growing source of political threat in Turkey. Thus, the Turkish government seems to give social assistance not simply where the people become poor, but where the poor become politicized. These findings indeed support Fox Piven and Cloward's (1971) thesis that social assistance is driven by social unrest, rather than by social need. The highly positive statistical effect of being Kurdish on Green Card holding status cannot be merely attributed to the socioeconomic characteristics of Kurds. Rather, Kurdish ethnic identity seems to be the main factor explaining the disproportional access of Kurds to the Green Card program. Against the backdrop of the recent history of political conflicts in Turkey, the strong statistical associations from the analysis, the interviews with welfare officials, experts, and caseworkers, and trends in social assistance provision indicate that political motivations are very likely to have shaped the expansion and ethnically uneven distribution of social assistance in Turkey.

There is an intense political competition between the governing AKP and the Kurdish parties over the slum-dwelling informal proletariat. The AKP also tries to garner the support of the slums and the Kurds in order to compete with the main opposition party, CHP, for national power. These rivalries for power have created competition in social assistance programs in which all parties have started to provide forms of social assistance. This is especially critical in the Kurdish region. Interviews with high-ranking social assistance officials in Ankara and Istanbul about the motivations for providing social assistance clearly illustrate that the creation and effectiveness of social assistance programs is an instrument of politics.

The AKP has increased social assistance in an effort, first, to mobilize the popular support of lower classes in Turkey in its competition with the CHP and, second, to contain the Kurdish parties and co-opt their supporters, the Kurdish poor informal proletariat. Social assistance provision is one of the bases of popular support of the increasingly entrenched and globally influential Islamic government in Turkey because the poor make up a significant part of AKP supporters. This strategy can explain the rapid and uneven expansion of social assistance in Turkey. In response, the CHP and the Kurdish movement have been involved in social policy as well, in order to better compete with the AKP.

Moreover, these conclusions do not mean that the directing of social welfare to Kurds has been the main government strategy for the Kurdish issue. Rather, all recent Turkish governments have utilized parallel and fluctuating repressive and conciliatory strategies to deal with the long-lasting Kurdish unrest. The period between 2007 and 2009 was marked by the so-called Kurdish Opening of the AKP, promising the Kurds constitutional recognition of identity rights. This period has, however, been succeeded by another wave of heavy repression, which, as yet, has not sufficed to pacify the Kurds, either (Gusten 2012; Economist 2012). Scholars of security politics have already shown that poverty among the Kurds has been one of the structural causes for the durability of this Kurdish radicalism, which suggests that, in addition to repression, "increased investment in social welfare can result in reduced terrorism," echoing the emerging international literature on welfare and counterterrorism (Akyüz and Armstrong 2011; Burgoon 2006; Feridun and Sezgin 2008; Krieger and Meierrieks 2010). It appears that the AKP government has embraced this proposed strategy very enthusiastically. Whether or not social assistance is successful in ultimately quelling the Kurds depends on the effectiveness of the programs in political targeting and the political mobilization of the Kurdish political movement in resisting these state efforts.

Conclusion

This book is about the politics of the welfare state in Turkey. I provided a politics-based explanation for the neoliberal transformation of the Turkish welfare system. While the Turkish welfare state in general has expanded, the relative weight of social assistance policies has increased compared to employment-based social security. As such, I explained the causes of a sweeping shift in the nature of public welfare provision in Turkey during recent decades that extends far beyond Turkey, as this transformation has been part of a global trend. Most scholarship about Turkey, as about similar countries, has explained this shift toward social assistance as a response to demographic and structural changes including aging populations, the decline in the economic weight of industry, and the informalization of labor, while ignoring the effect of grassroots politics. In order to overcome these theoretical shortcomings in the literature, I revisited the concepts of political containment and political mobilization from the earlier literature on the development of the mid-twentieth-century welfare state and incorporated the effects of grassroots politics in order to understand the recent welfare system shift as it materialized in Turkey, where a new matrix of political dynamics has produced new large-scale social assistance programs. I argued that a global political economy, in which the poor have gained political predominance as the main grassroots source of political threat to and political support for governments, has pushed Turkey to provide extensive and decommodifying forms of social assistance as a central element of a new welfare system in a strategy to contain and mobilize the political power of the poor. While structural changes underlie these changing welfare policies, I investigated the political causes of the transformation, which have mediated structural pressures, shaped specific policies, determined the timing of their enactment, and influenced the way benefits are distributed. In short, I have shown that Turkish governments have been acting primarily on political concerns in their welfare policy-making.

In order to explain why and how the Turkish welfare state has expanded during neoliberalism and why social policies have shifted from social security to social assistance, I focused on the rivalries among mainstream parties and the impact of grassroots politics, as well as the political mechanisms that mediate and transform structural pressures into policies. My analysis has shown that political efforts to contain the political radicalization of the informal proletariat and to mobilize its electoral support have driven the expansion of social assistance policies during the post-1980 neoliberal period. Turkish state authorities now see the informal proletariat as a more significant political threat and source of support than the formal proletariat, whose dynamism drove the expansion of the welfare state during the postwar developmentalist period. I provided a historical analysis of the interaction between parliamentary processes and social movements in order to account for the transformation of welfare provision in Turkey. I engaged in the long-standing debates between advocates of structural and political explanations for welfare policies by advancing a politics-based argument. The extent to which state authorities expand or contract welfare provisions depends on the extent to which grassroots groups become politicized. Structural changes and new social needs do not automatically lead to welfare system changes. Rather, welfare changes occur when new grassroots groups and their social needs are politicized by contending political actors. Structural factors are effective in shaping welfare policies to the extent that they create and are translated into political contentions.

I have shown, as opposed to the common belief among scholars and the public, that grassroots politics in Turkey has continued to strongly influence state policies in the neoliberal era. The level of grassroots political activism in the neoliberal era has been comparable to the 1970s, the heyday of grassroots political activism in Turkey. In fact, except for the late 1970s, when the country was on the verge of civil war, the level of activism in the 1990s and 2000s is even higher than that in the 1970s. The main change in grassroots politics is not attenuation, but a shift: over the last four decades, the center of grassroots politics has shifted from the formal proletariat to the informal proletariat as well as from the ethnic Turks to the ethnic Kurds. Despite fluctuations, while the grassroots political activism of the formal proletariat and ethnic Turks has decreased, that of the informal proletariat and Kurds has increased. The containment of the political radicalization of the informal proletariat, especially of Kurdish origin, and the mobilization of its popular support are key factors that explain the rise of income-based social assistance programs and its ethnically uneven distribution.

In the 1970s, the socialists were the most powerful grassroots organizers and they radicalized the formal proletariat. In the 1980s all political movements were repressed. During the 1990s, it was the Islamists who most successfully mobilized anti-neoliberal grievances. In the 2000s, because of the deradicalization of the Islamist movement that enabled the imposition of neoliberal hegemony in Turkey, it was the radicalization of the Kurdish movement that became the main force resisting this hegemonic establishment. That is, the leftwing Kurdish movement has replaced Islamists as the main center of anti-neoliberal mobilization targeting the informal proletariat. There is also an increase in grassroots political activities in rural areas, while there is a declining trend in city centers (except for the informal proletarian activism). Although the rural population has significantly shrunken in the neoliberal era, rural grassroots activities sharply increased because of the popular mobilization and warfare of the PKK. The Turkish state carried out the internal displacement of Kurds to contain this rural threat. This has led to a rapid proletarianization of Kurds and a parallel Kurdification of the informal proletariat. The growing informal proletariat has also become the main source of political power for competing mainstream political parties and this has also contributed to the expansion of social assistance programs.

In sum, the informal proletariat has grown as the main source of political support and threat. The Kurds have become the most radical faction of the informal proletariat and this has led to the disproportionate number of Kurds on social assistance programs, providing more support for my political containment argument. At the same time, the fluctuations in social security system changes corresponded, and indeed, responded to the grassroots activism of formal proletarians as well as to political party concerns to garner their popular support. Fluctuations mainly occurred because governments gave concessions to the formal proletariat as soon as these workers became politicized. Parliamentary discussions show that the direction and extent of the welfare system changes also depend on the level and form of political party competition. Insofar as there is competition between numerous, weakened political parties, neoliberal retrenchment of employment-based policies stops. Retrenchment is possible only with strong single-party governments that bring "political stability." This shows that structural factors do not dictate policy changes, but rather present a range of possible policy choices, within which political actors seek the most efficient ways of containing and mobilizing grassroots forces. In other words, political factors drive the actual policy decisions, given the structural constraints.

My analysis has illustrated that social assistance is mainly directed toward Kurds who are politically the most active faction of the informal proletariat, to Kurdish areas where grassroots activities have expanded, and to rural and slum areas where grassroots activities are most extensive and the government receives higher votes. The Turkish government does not expand social assistance where people become poor, but where the poor become politicized. A key function of social assistance is its political effect, which creates political allegiance for governments independently of its actual capacity to reduce poverty. In that sense, low-cost social assistance programs are economically efficient instruments of political containment and mobilization of the informal proletariat. This instrumentalization occurs through macro state policies and micro interactions between welfare officials and the informal proletariat.

All of my findings suggest that political factors that operate independently of structural dynamics have changed the trajectory of the welfare system in contingent directions. Political parties, actors, and organizations have pursued political interests and struggled against each other, and these competing political concerns have mobilized existing social forces into either a grassroots political threat or support. The extent to which state authorities expand or contract welfare provision depends on the extent to which grassroots groups become politicized by mainstream and radical political groups.

Consider Prime Minister Turgut Özal, who decided to hold a referendum in 1987 to remove the political ban on older generation party leaders. He took a political risk because he aimed to eliminate possible political rivals with the use of public voting. However, he lost the referendum and other leaders began to lead political parties again. This initiated a decade-long political competition between numerous, weakened political parties, resulting in the expansion of populism and discontinuation of the neoliberal transformation. Özal's decision cannot be explained by structural forces because it was a decision by an interest-seeking politician. Yet this decision has altered the entire history of neoliberalism and welfare state transformation in Turkey. Thus, the history of neoliberalism and neoliberal welfare reform is not structurally determined.

The Kurdish struggle against the Turkish state has shaped the trajectory of the Turkish welfare system transformation into directions different than what structural forces would entail. The Kurdish political movement has mobilized and radicalized the informal proletariat, and the state has subsequently expanded social assistance and directed it to Kurds in order to contain the Kurdish unrest. This means that neither the rapid expansion of social assistance nor its ethnic targeting is the only historical alternative. Likewise, take the example of real wages in Turkey: they followed the level of labor productivity until 1980, yet, after the 1980s, a significant wedge formed between real wage labor and productivity. This wedge was closed only in certain periods, such as the early 1990s. After the 1980s, wages followed the productivity level only insofar as there were strikes, as in the case of the early 1990s. At times without strikes, the capitalists have managed to push wages down significantly. When Demirel promised and executed wage increases and started the free health care card in the early 1990s, his main concern was to contain the workers and the Kurds. Demirel's government delivered concessions to the formal proletariat and social assistance benefits to the Kurdish informal proletariat, in response to the double threat coming from these groups in the same period.

I acknowledge that structural factors are also effective in shaping welfare policies. It is a structural change that the financial burdens of the employment-based social security system have escalated. Yet this change has pushed the shift in welfare policies to the extent that it has become economically inefficient to contain or mobilize popular groups with the use of employment-based policies. Income-based social assistance policies were adopted because they made it possible to politically contain or mobilize the maximally politicized sectors of society with a minimal economic cost. Again, it is a structural change that led the informalization of labor to dominate the economy. Yet this structural change led to policy changes as it has made it impossible for the employment-based policies to exercise political functions. While there has been a decline in union and strike activities, there has been an increase in political activism in slum areas and by those groups who are not included in the formal economy. Structural changes are translated into policy outcomes as they have created hierarchies, suffering, and contradictions among grassroots groups and the elites. When combined with other forms of cleavages (ethnic, gender, or religious), this creates fertile ground for the mobilization of these groups by contending political actors. For a poor Kurdish woman who joined a rally organized by the Kurdish parties, a textile worker who threw stones at the police in Istanbul, or a young unemployed man from a poor slum of Diyarbakir who voted for the Islamic governing party, an old age pension would probably mean nothing because these people all are aware that they would never be eligible for a pension in a highly informal economy. However, free health care or social assistance programs are immediate opportunities for them and hence politically very functional for the government. As such, my political-structural explanation managed to account for the spatial and temporal puzzles in the Turkish welfare transformation that existing structural theories could not successfully address. My perspective explains the disproportionate targeting of Kurds and Kurdish areas for free health care provisions, the rapid expansion of social assistance programs in the 2000s despite declining rates of poverty, and the revival of employment-based policies in the 1990s despite no backward shift in structural factors.

I contend that the shift from employment-based social security to income-based social assistance policies has altered the mode of political negotiation between the working classes and the state. In the developmentalist system, a central object of negotiation between workers and the state was the welfare state itself. In the neoliberal system, the informal proletariat mostly does not struggle for social assistance, but rather for other economic, ethnic, or religious demands. Most importantly, the Kurds demand cultural rights but they are provided with free health care. In other words, Kurds are provided with social assistance while they are struggling for something else. Yet, it is important to note that, during the 1970s, the formal proletariat acquired maximum concessions when their struggle became radicalized under the mobilization of the socialist movement and when they became a political threat—that is, when they struggled for a radical social change, not for welfare provision. The argument follows that one result of the political struggles of radicalized grassroots groups against the state is the expansion of social welfare and that this is an unintended consequence. Most effects of social movements are unintended, rather than intended, consequences, including concessions and repression. I analyzed the effect of contentious politics on welfare policies in this broad sense, in which people receive social assistance benefits as a by-product of social reform for which they may or may not be struggling. Turkish governments deliver new welfare benefits not only because there are organized movements of the poor demanding these benefits, but also because there are "poor people's movements" radicalized on other political, ethnic, or religious grounds that need to be contained through violent or benevolent means, or both.

My book also contributed to the fledgling literature about the growing political influence of the poor in developing countries. As opposed to its public and academic image as the passive victim of neoliberalism, the informal proletariat is currently actively capable of shaping government policies as much as the formal proletariat used to be capable of shaping them in the past. This explains the basis of popular support of the increasingly entrenched and globally influential Islamic government in Turkey, the AKP that has used welfare provision for political purposes since the beginning of its rule. This book sheds light on the strategies that this unusual pro-globalization Islamist party has pursued vis-à-vis domestic political and social challenges, especially those regarding the informal proletariat and the Kurds, the current crux of grassroots politics.

Drawing on an earlier tradition of scholarship that emphasized the role of grassroots politics in welfare policy-making, this book examined the ethno-political aspects of welfare policy in Turkey in relation to the shifting dynamics of the Kurdish conflict since the 1980s. I have shown that alongside military measures, Turkish governments and policymakers have considered socioeconomic policies as the main means of containing the Kurdish unrest. While regional development policies have been the primary measure in the Turkish authorities' containment toolkit, changes in the Kurdish movement's political strategies and shifts in the geographical distribution of the Kurdish population pushed the state to incorporate new policies whose main target was that population. In other words, as the Kurdish movement evolved into a mass movement supporting democratization and political, cultural, and socioeconomic rights and became capable of mobilizing Kurds who have been dispersed across Turkey as a result of the state's counterinsurgency strategies, governments have increasingly considered social assistance as a means of containing the Kurdish unrest. With their invasive means-testing mechanisms that allow state officials to inquire about both economic and noneconomic aspects of applicants' and beneficiaries' lives, social assistance programs provided the state with an invaluable opportunity to collect otherwise obscure information about this potentially "unruly" population and render them more governable under the guise of state benevolence. Securitization of social assistance policies depends on an understanding that radical groups may transform poverty-related grievances into political activism and alleviating poverty might be seen as an "instrument," rather than an end in itself, to undermine the conditions of this radicalization.

The changes in the Turkish welfare system are not unique to Turkey. On the contrary, they are part of a global change that is taking place in many other countries as well. These political concerns, that is, containing and mobilizing the informal proletariat of the global slums, have been effective in shaping the macro-level changes in welfare systems. In this regard, Turkey should be compared with other emerging markets, including Brazil, China, India, and South Africa, which are undergoing similar transformations in their welfare systems, from employment-based to income-based policies and which have constituted a new welfare state regime, the populist welfare state regime. It is likely that political exigencies involving the growing social and political weight of the informal proletariat have led the governments of populist welfare state regime countries to develop such social assistance policies. The growing economic success of emerging markets has depended heavily on an abundance of cheap labor, mostly provided by the growing informal proletariat of the slums. Yet these slums have also become the new spatial and social epicenters of both popular threat to and support for these governments. The political reaction of the slums worldwide against rising poverty has increased government efforts to contain this threat. On the other hand, their numerical strength and their being "ideologically promiscuous in endorsement of populist saviors" may also make them the objects of political mobilization by the rulers (Davis 2006). It is likely that new social assistance programs have been driven by this political change.

In populist welfare state countries, political and politicized identities, such as voting behavior, protest participation, ethnicity, race or religion, are much more important in determining citizens' chances of benefiting from social assistance programs than their actual level of poverty, which is officially declared to be the sole determinant of program eligibility. Major programs are systematically and disproportionally directed to insurgent ethnic minorities, protestors, and unruly social movements that challenge populist regimes and to potential or actual voters who constitute the electoral base of the populists. Examples include the Prospera program being used against the Zapatistas in Mexico (Yörük, Öker, and Şarlak 2019); the National Rural Employment Guarantee Act against the Naxalite insurgency in India (Koyuncu, Yörük, and Gürel forthcoming); Dibao against rural protestors in China (Yörük et al. under review); Bolsa Familia against the Movimento dos Trabalhadores Rurais Sem Terra (or MST), the landless peasants' movement in Brazil (Yörük, Gürel, and Kına forthcoming); and the Child Support Grant against black riots in South Africa (Yörük and Gençer 2020).

It can be argued that, in many emerging markets, the rising poverty of the informal proletariat has also tended to interact with existing racial and ethnic grievances to generate domestic political disorder. It is probable that, in response, governments tend to direct social assistance programs to specific ethnic groups based on their ethnic identity. Scholars need to examine whether the use of social assistance programs has become a common strategy to cope with ethno-political problems in emerging economies. Therefore, this book calls for future work on other countries with populist welfare state regimes to examine similar political exigencies that may have fostered new welfare state programs. It is highly probable that Fox Piven and Cloward's thesis holds true at a global scale almost four decades after its formulation and that indeed global social assistance is driven by a global social unrest of the informal proletariat. A comparative political analysis of the welfare systems in emerging economies is required to examine this possibility fully. Thus, a broader research project must analyze political exigencies that drive welfare system changes in each of these countries and to test similar hypotheses in other similar countries and on a global scale.

References

Adaman, A., and Ç. Keyder. 2006. *Poverty and Social Exclusion in the Slum Areas of Large Cities in Turkey*. Report prepared for the European Commission and the Ministry of Labour and Social Security of Turkey.

Ağartan, T., Ç. Keyder, N. Üstündağ, and Ç. Yoltar. 2007. *Avrupa'da ve Türkiye'de Sağlık Politikaları* [Health care policies in Europe and Turkey]. Istanbul: Iletisim.

Agarwala, R. 2008. "Reshaping the Social Contract: Emerging Relations between the State and Informal Labor in India." *Theory and Society* 37: 375–408.

Agarwala, R. 2009. "An Economic Sociology of Informal Work: The Case of India." In *Economic Sociology of Work (Research in the Sociology of Work, Volume 18)*, edited by L. Keister, 315–42. Bingley, UK: Emerald Group.

Ahmad, F. 1993. *The Making of Modern Turkey*. London: Routledge.

Ahmed, F. 1994. "The Development of Working-Class Consciousness in Turkey." In *Workers and Working Classes in the Middle East: Struggles, Histories, Historiographies*, edited by Z. Lockman. Albany: State University of New York Press.

Aiddata. 2012. *Data Search Turkey*. http://www.aiddata.org/content/index/data-searc h#bef5f0e4e8395ba8e11056b2172de733

Aiyar, S.1998. "Lessons in Designing Safety Nets." *World Bank Notes*, no. 2, 1–4.

Akkaya, Y. 2000. "Devlet, Sendikalar ve Korporatist İlişkiler—II" [State, Trade Unions, and Corporatist Relations—II]. *İktisat Dergisi*, 404.

Akkaya, Y. 2006. 'İşçi Hareketinin ve Örgütlenmenin İhmal Edilen Alanı Veya Bir İmkân Olarak 'Enformel'Gruplar/Örgütler' ['Informal' groups/organizations as a neglected field of workers' movement and organization or an opportunity]. *İçinde: F Sazak (Der), Türkiye'de Sendikal Kriz ve Sendikal Arayışlar, Ankara: Epos Yayınları*, 209–36.

Akpinar, E., and E. Saatci. 2007. "Assessing Poverty and Related Factors in Turkey." *Croatian Medical Journal* 48 (5): 628–35.

Akyol, M. 2011. *Beni Çok Ararsınız: Pırlanta Kalpli Adam* [You Call Me A Lot: The Man With The Diamond Heart]. Ankara: Akçağ.

Akyuz, K., and T. Armstrong. 2011. "Understanding the Sociostructural Correlates of Terrorism in Turkey." *International Criminal Justice Review* 21 (2): 134–55.

Ali, A. 2011. "Assisting in Regional Reform to Maintain Development Gains." *The G20 Cannes Summit 2011: A New Way Forward.* G20 Research Group and News-desk Media Group.

Álvarez, S., and A. M. Guillén. 2001. "Globalization and the Southern Welfare States." In*Globalization and European Welfare States: Challenges and Change*, edited by R. Sykes, B. Palier, and P. Prior, 103–26. New York: Palgrave.

Amenta, E., C. Bonastia, and N. Caren. 2001. "US Social Policy in Comparative and Historical Perspective: Concepts, Images, Arguments, and Research Strategies." *Annual Review of Sociology* 27.

Ansell, B. 2014. "The Political Economy of Ownership: Housing Markets and the Welfare State." *American Political Science Review* 108 (2): 383–402. https://doi.org/10.1017/S0003055414000045

Anthony J. B., D. Mitlin, J. Mogaladi, M. Scurrah, and C. Bielich. 2010. "Decentring Poverty, Reworking Government: Social Movements and States in the Government of Poverty." *Journal of Development Studies* 46 (7): 1304–26. https://doi.org /10.1080/00220388.2010.487094

Arrighi, G. 1990. "Marxist Century, American Century: The Making and Remaking of the World Labour Movement." *New Left Review* 179 (1): 29–63.

Arrighi, G. 2009. "The Winding Paths of Capital: The Winding Paths of Capital (Interview by David Harvey)." *New Left Review*, no. 56 (April): 61–94.

Ashman, S., and N. Pons-Vignon. 2014. "NUMSA, the Working Class, and Socialist Politics in South Africa." *Socialist Register 2015:Transforming Classes* 51 (October 12). http://socialistregister.com/index.php/srv/article/view/22096

Auvinen, J., and E. Nafziger. 1999. "The Sources of Humanitarian Emergencies."*Journal of Conflict Resolution* 43:267–90.

Avcioğlu, D. 1969. "Soyut'tan Somut'a" [From Abstract to Concrete]. *Devrim*, no. 66 (19 January).

Ayata, B. 2008. "Searching for Alternative Approaches to Reconciliation: A Plea for Armenian-Kurdish Dialogue." *Armenian Weekly*, 26 April: 38–42.

Ayata B., and D. Yükseker. 2005. "A Belated Awakening: National and International Responses to the Internal Displacement of Kurds in Turkey." *New Perspectives on Turkey* 32: 5–42.

Aytaç, S. E., and Z. Öniş. 2014. "Varieties of Populism in a Changing Global Context: The Divergent Paths of Erdoğan and Kirchnerismo." *Comparative Politics* 47 (1): 41–59. https://doi.org/10.5129/001041514813623137

Backer, G., and U. Klammer. 2002. "The Dismantling of Welfare in Germany." In *Diminishing Welfare: A Cross-national Study of Social Provision*, edited by G. Goldberg and M. Rosenthal, 211–44. London: Auburn House.

Barr, N. 1995. *On the Design of Social Safety Nets.* Geneva: World Bank.

Barrientos A., and R. Holmes. 2007. *Social Assistance in Developing Countries Database Version 3.0.* Manchester, UK: Brooks World Poverty Institute.

Barrientos, A., and P. Lloyd-Sherlock. 2002. *Non-Contributory Pensions and Social Protection.* Geneva: International Labour Organization.

Barrilleaux, C. H., T. H. Holbrook, and L. Langer. 2002. "Party Balance, Electoral Competition, and Welfare in the American States." *American Journal of Political Science* 46: 415–27.

Barron, P., M. Humphreys, L. Paler, and J. Weinstein. 2009. "Community-Based Reintegration in Aceh: Assessing the Impacts of BRA-KDP." *Indonesian Social Development Paper* no. 12. Jakarta: World Bank.

Baulch, B. 2006. "Aid Distribution and the MDGs." *World Development* 34, no. 6: 933–50.

Belli, M. 1970. *Yazılar, 1965–1970.* [Essays, 1965–1970]. Ankara: Sol Yayinları.

Benabou, R. 1997. *Inequality and Growth.* Cambridge: National Bureau of Economics Research.

Beneria, L. 1989. "Subcontracting and Employment Dynamics in Mexico City." In *The Informal Economy: Studies in Advanced and Less Developed Countries,* edited by A. Portes, A. M. Castells, and L. A. Benton. Baltimore: Johns Hopkins University Press.

Bianchi, R. 1984. *Interest Groups and Political Development in Turkey.* Princeton: Princeton University Press.

Bora, A., I. Ceccacci, C. Delgado, and R. Townsend. 2010. *Food Security and Conflict.* World Bank, Agriculture and Rural Development Department, Washington, DC.

Boran, B. 1970. *Türkiye ve Sosyalizm Sorunları* [Turkey and the problems of socialism]. Istanbul: TekinYayinevi.

Boratav, K., E. Yeldan, and A. Köse. 2000. "Globalization, Distribution and Social Policy: Turkey, 1980–1998." *CEPA and the New School for Social Research, Working Paper Series* 20: 113–14.

Bosworth, B. 1980. "Reestablishing an Economic Consensus: An Impossible Agenda?" *Daedalus* (Summer): 59–70.

Brook, A. M., and E. R. Whitehouse. 2006. *The Turkish Pension System: Further Reforms to Help Solve the Informality Problem.* OECD Economics Department Working Papers. Paris: OECD.

Brooks, C., and J. Manza. 2006. "Why Do Welfare States Persist?" *Journal of Politics* 68 (4): 816–27.

Buğra, A. 2006. 'Türkiye'de Sağ ve Sosyal Politika' [The Right and social policy in Turkey]. *Toplum ve Bilim Dergisi* 106: 43–67.

Buğra, A. 2007. "Poverty and Citizenship: An Overview of the Social-Policy Environment in Republican Turkey." *International Journal of Middle East Studies* 39 (1): 33–52.

Buğra, A., and S. Adar. 2008. "Social Policy Change in Countries without Mature Welfare States: The Case of Turkey." *New Perspectives on Turkey* 38 (Spring): 83–106.

Buğra, A., and Ç. Keyder. 2003. *New Poverty and the Changing Welfare Regime of Turkey.* Ankara: United Nations Development Programme.

Buğra, A., and Ç. Keyder. 2006. "The Turkish Welfare Regime in Transformation." *Journal of European Social Policy* 16 (3): 211–28.

Burgoon, B. 2006. "On Welfare and Terror: Social Welfare Policies and Political-Economic Roots of Terrorism." *Journal of Conflict Resolution* 50 (2): 176–203.

Burstein, P. 1979. "Equal Employment Opportunity Legislation and the Income of Women and Nonwhites." *American Sociological Review* 44 (3): 367–91.

Burstein, P. 1985. *Discrimination, Jobs, and Politics.* Chicago: University of Chicago Press.

Burstein, P. 1998. "Bringing the Public Back In: Should Sociologists Consider the Impact of Public Opinion on Public Policy?" *Social Forces* 77: 27–62.

Burstein, P., and W. Freudenburg. 1978. "Changing Public Policy." *American Journal of Sociology* 84: 99–122.

Cam, S. 2002. "Neo-liberalism and Labour within the Context of an 'Emerging Market' Economy—Turkey." *Capital & Class* 26 (2): 89–114.

Carr, M., M. Chen, and J. Tate. 2000. "Globalization and Homebased Workers." *Feminist Economics* 6 (3): 123–42.

Castells, M. 2004. *Power of Identity*. Malden, MA: Blackwell.

Central Bank of the Republic of Turkey (Türkiye Cumhuriyet Merkez Bankası). 2002. *Para Politikasi Raporu*. Ankara: TCMB.

Central Bank of the Republic of Turkey (Türkiye Cumhuriyet Merkez Bankası). 2010. *Finansal İstikrar Raporu*. Ankara: TCMB.

Central Bank of the Republic of Turkey (Türkiye Cumhuriyet Merkez Bankası). 2011. *Finansal İstikrar Raporu*. Ankara: TCMB.

Chamlin, M. 1989. "A Macro Social Analysis of Change in Police Force Size, 1972–1982: Controlling for Static and Dynamic Influences." *Sociological Quarterly* 30 (4): 615–24.

Chen, D. 2003. "Economic Distress and Religious Intensity: Evidence from Islamic Resurgence during the Indonesian Financial Crisis." *PRPES Working Paper* no. 39. Boston: Harvard University.

Chen, J., and A. Barrientos. 2006. *Extending Social Assistance in China: Lessons from the Minimum Living Standard Scheme*. Chronic Poverty Research Centre Working Paper 67. Manchester, UK: Chronic Poverty Research Centre.

Chenoweth, E. 2007. *Government Capacity, Social Welfare, and Non-State Political Violence*. Conference paper presented at the Third International Student Conference "Empirical Models in Social Sciences," Izmir, Turkey, 13–14 April.

Chowdhury, S. 2003. "Old Classes and New Spaces: Urban Poverty, Unorganized Labour and New Unions." *Economic and Political Weekly* 37 (50): 5277–84.

CHP (Cumhuriyet Halk Partisi). 2011. "Aile Sigortası: Güclü Sosyal Devlet'edoğru." *CHP FYDP Studies*, 1 February.

Cizre, Ü. 1992. "Labour and State in Turkey: 1960–1980." *Middle Eastern Studies* 28 (4): 712–28.

Cizre-Sakalhoğlu, U., and E. Yeldan. 2000. "Politics, Society, and Financial Liberalization: Turkey in the 1990s." *Development and Change* 31 (2): 481–508. https://doi.org/10.1111/1467-7660.00163

Cnudde, C., and D. Mccrone. 1969. "Party Competition and Welfare Policies in the American States." *American Political Science Review* 63: 858–66.

Coşar, S., and M. Yeğenoglu. 2009. "The Neoliberal Restructuring of Turkey's Social Security System." *Monthly Review*, April.

Costain, A., and S. Majstorovic. 1994. "Congress, Social Movements and Public Opinion: Multiple Origins of Women's Rights Legislation." *Political Research Quarterly* 47: 111–35.

Cowgill, D. 1974. "The Aging of Populations and Societies." In *Aging, the Individual, and Society: Readings in Social Gerontology*, edited by J. Quadagno. New York: St. Martin's Press.

Cross, J. 1998. *Informal Politics: Street Vendors and the State in Mexico City.* Stanford: Stanford University Press.

Cutright, Ph. 1965. "Political Structure, Economic Development, and National Security Programs." *American Journal or Sociology* 70 (4): 537–50.

Davis, M. 2004. "Planet of Slums: Urban Involution and the Informal Proletariat." *New Left Review* 26 (March–April): 5–34.

Davis, M. 2006. *Planet of Slums.* London: Verso.

Dawson, R., and J. Robinson. 1963. "Inter-Party Competition, Economic Variables, and Welfare Policies in the American States." *Journal of Politics* 25: 265–89.

Deng, F. 1997. "Information Gaps and Unintended Outcomes of Social Movements: The 1989 Chinese Student Movement." *American Journal of Sociology* 102: 1085–1112.

Department of International Development (DFID). 2006. "Social Protection in Poor Countries." *Social Protection Briefing Note Series*, no. 1.

Dereli, T. 1968. *The Development of Turkish Trade Unionism.* Ithaca: Cornell University Press.

Díaz-Cayeros, A. 2008. "Electoral Risk and Redistributive Politics in Mexico and the United States." *Studies in Comparative International Development* 43 (2): 129–50.

Djebbari, H., and H. Mayrand. 2011. "Cash Transfers and Children's Living Arrangements in South Africa." *Universit´e Laval. Pas Publi´e.* https://www.semanticscholar.org/paper/Cash-transfers-and-children%27s-living-arrangements-Djebbari-Mayrand/3a518ddb227a7e2a10ca99174a19a2a745fa7169

Doğan, M. 2010. "When Neoliberalism Confronts the Moral Economy of Workers: The Final Spring of Turkish Labor Unions." *European Journal of Turkish Studies* 11: 1–17.

Dorlach, T. 2019. "Retrenchment of Social Policy by Other Means: A Comparison of Agricultural and Housing Policy in Turkey." *Journal of Comparative Policy Analysis* 21 (May): 270–86. https://doi.org/10.1080/13876988.2018.1466856

Eatwell, J. 1995. "The International Origins of Unemployment." In *Managing the Global Economy*, edited by J. Michie and J. Smith. Oxford: Oxford University Press.

Economist. 2012. "Rebellious Days: A Fresh Wave of Protests Shows How Far Turkey Is from Pacifying Its Kurds." 24 March.

Elveren, A. 2008. "Social Security Reform in Turkey: A Critical Perspective." *Review of Radical Political Economics* 40 (2): 212–32.

Ercan, H. 2007. *Youth Unemployment in Turkey.* Ankara: International Labour Office.

Erikson, R., M. MacKuen, and J. Stimson. 2002. "Public Opinion and Public Policy: Causal Flow in a Macro System Model." In *Navigating Public Opinion*, edited by J. Manza, F. Cook, and B. Page. Oxford: Oxford University Press.

Esping-Andersen, G. 1990. *The Three Worlds of Welfare Capitalism.* Princeton: Princeton University Press.

Esping-Andersen, G. 1996. *Welfare States in Transition: National Adaptations in Global Economies.* London: Sage.

Esping-Andersen, G. 1999. *Social Foundations of Postindustrial Economies.* Oxford University Press.

Estevez-Abe, M., T. Iversen, and D. Soskice. 1999. "Social Protection and the Formation of Skills: A Reinterpretation of the Welfare State." Paper presented at the Annual Meeting of the American Political Science Association, September 2–5, Atlanta. http://www.people.fas.harvard.edu/~iversen/PDFfiles/apsa992.pdf

Etöz, Z. 2002. *Sanduktan Sendikaya: Tekgida-İş'in Hikayesi* [From Imagination to Union: The Story of Tekgida-İş]. Izmir: Tekgida-İş Sendikası Eğitim Yayını.

Etxezarreta, M. 1995. *The Welfare State: Alternatives to Social Cuts and Deregulation.* Notes for discussion presented at the Workshop on Alternative Economic Policies for Europe: Approaches and Perspectives. Bremen: Arbeitsgruppe Alternative Wirtschaftspolitik.

European Commission. 1998. *Regular Report from the Commission on Turkey's Progress towards Accession.* Brussels: EC.

European Commission. 2004. *Issues Arising from Turkey's Membership Perspective. SEC (2004) 1202.* Brussels: EC.

Farnsworth, K., and Z. M. Irving, eds. 2011. *Social Policy in Challenging Times: Economic Crisis and Welfare Systems.* Bristol: Policy Press.

Fearon, J., and D. Laitin. 2003. "Ethnicity, Insurgency, and Civil War." *American Political Science Review* 97 (1) (February): 75–90.

Fenton, J. 1966. *Midwest Politics.* New York: Rinehart and Winston.

Feridun, M., and S. Sezgin. 2008. "Regional Underdevelopment and Terrorism: The Case of South Eastern Turkey." *Defence and Peace Economics* 19 (3): 225–33.

Ferrera, M., M. Matsaganis, and S. Sacchi. 2002. "Open Coordination against Poverty: The New European Social Inclusion Process." *Journal of European Social Policy* 12: 227.

Fiedler, E. 1975. *Measures of Credit Risk and Experience.* New York: National Bureau of Economic Research.

Flora, P., and J. Alber. 1981. "Modernization, Democratization, and the Development of Welfare States in Western Europe." In *The Development of Welfare States in Europe and America,* edited by P. Flora and A. Heidenheimer. New Brunswick, NJ: Transaction.

Flora, P., and A. Heidenheimer. 1981. *The Development of Welfare States in Europe and America.* New Brunswick, NJ: Transaction.

Fording, R. 1997. "The Conditional Effect of Violence as a Political Tactic: Mass Insurgency, Welfare Generosity, and Electoral Context in the American States."*American Journal of Political Science* 41: 1–29.

Form, W. 1979. "Comparative Industrial Sociology and the Convergence Hypothesis."*Annual Review of Sociology* 5: 1–25.

Fox Piven, F., and R. Cloward. 1971. *Regulating the Poor: The Functions of Public Welfare.* New York: Pantheon Books.

Franzoni, J. M., and K. Voorend. 2011. "Who Cares in Nicaragua? A Care Regime in an Exclusionary Social Policy Context." *Development and Change* 42 (4): 995–1022. https://doi.org/10.1111/j.1467-7660.2011.01719.x

Fretwell, D., J. Benus, and C. O'Leary. 1999. *Evaluating the Impact of Active Labor Programs: Results of Cross-Country Studies in Europe and Central Asia.* Washington, DC: World Bank.

G20. 2003. *Economic Reform in This Era of Globalization: 16 Country Cases.* Washington, DC: G20 Secretariat.

Gamson, W. 1990. *The Strategy of Social Protest*. Belmont, CA: Wadsworth.

Gao, Q. 2006. "The Social Benefit System in Urban China: Reforms and Trends from 1988 to 2002." *Journal of East Asian Studies* 6: 31–67.

Garraty, J. 1978. *Unemployment in History: Economic Thought and Public Policy*. New York: Harper and Row.

Gazete Vatan. 2010. "Gökçek'ten Büyük İtiraf" [A big confession from Gökçek]. https://www.gazetevatan.com/gundem/gokcekten-buyuk-itiraf-296765

Ginsburg, N. 2001. "Globalization and the Liberal Welfare States." In *Globalization and Welfare States in Europe: Challenges and Change*, edited by R. Sykes, B. Palier, P. Prior, and J. Campling. New York: Palgrave.

Giugni, M. 1994. "The Outcomes of Social Movements: A Review of the Literature." *Working Paper 197*. New York: Center for Studies of Social Change, New School for Social Research.

Giugni, M. 1998. "Was It Worth the Effort? The Outcomes and Consequences of Social Movements." *Annual Review of Sociology* 24.

Göbel, C., and L. H. Ong. 2012. "Social Unrest in China." London: Europe China Research and Advice Network (ECRAN). http://papers.ssrn.com/sol3/papers.cfm?abstract_id=2173073

Göçmen, I. 2014. "Religion, Politics, and Social Assistance in Turkey: The Rise of Religiously Motivated Associations." *Journal of European Social Policy* 24 (1): 92–103. https://doi.org/10.1177/0958928713511278

Goerres, A., and P. Vanhuysse. 2011. "Mapping the Field: Comparative Generational Politics and Policies in Ageing Democracies." SSRN Scholarly Paper ID 1799348. Rochester, NY: Social Science Research Network. https://papers.ssrn.com/abstract=1799348

Goldberg, G. S. 2002. "Introduction: Three Stages of Welfare Capitalism." In *Diminishing Welfare: A Cross-National Study of Social Provision*, edited by G. S. Goldberg and M. G. Rosenthal, 1–31, Westport, CT: Auburn House.

Goldberg, G., and M. Rosenthal. 2002. *Diminishing Welfare: A Cross-National Study of Social Provision*. Westport, CT: Auburn House.

Goldthorpe, J., D. Lockwood, F. Bechhofer, and J. Platt. 1969. *The Affluent Worker in the Class Structure*. Cambridge: Cambridge University Press.

Goode, J., and J. Maskovsky, eds. 2001. *New Poverty Studies: The Ethnography of Power, Politics, and Impoverished People in the United States*. New York: New York University Press.

Gough, I. 1996. "Social Assistance in Southern Europe." *South European Society and Politics* 1 (1): 1–23.

Gough, I. 2008. "European Welfare States: Explanations and Lessons for Developing Countries." In *Inclusive States: Social Policy and Structural Inequalities*, 39–72.

Gough, I., and G. Wood. 2004. *Insecurity and Welfare Regimes in Asia, Africa and Latin America: Social Policy in Development Contexts*. Cambridge: Cambridge University Press.

Grogan, C. M. 1994. "Political-Economic Factors Influencing State Medicaid Policy." *Political Research Quarterly* 47: 589–623.

Grutjen, D. 2008. "The Turkish Welfare Regime: An Example of the Southern European Model; The Role of State, Market and Family in Welfare Provision." *Turkish Policy Quarterly* 8.

Gümüşcü, Ş., and D. Sert. 2009. "The Power of the Devout Bourgeoisie: The Case of the Justice and Development Party in Turkey." *Middle Eastern Studies* 45 (6): 953–68.

Günal, A. 2008. "Health and Citizenship in Republican Turkey: An Analysis of the Socialization of Health Care Services in Republican Historical Context." PhD diss., Bogazici University.

Günay, O., and E. Yörük. 2019. "Governing Ethnic Unrest: Political Islam and the Kurdish Conflict in Turkey." *New Perspectives on Turkey* 61 (November): 9–43. https://doi.org/10.1017/npt.2019.17

Gürel, B. 2015. "Islamism: A Comparative-Historical Overview." In *The Neoliberal Landscape and the Rise of Islamist Capital in Turkey*, edited by Neşecan Balkan, Erol Balkan, and Ahmet Öncü. New York: Berghahn Books.

Gupta, S., M. Verhoeven, and E. Tiongson. 2001. *Public Spending on Health Care and the Poor*. IMF Working Paper WP/01/127. Washington, DC: International Monetary Fund.

Gurr, T. R. 1970. *Why Men Rebel*. Princeton: Princeton University Press.

Gusten, S. 2012. "Sensing a Siege, Kurds Hit Back in Turkey." *New York Times*, 21 March.

Güvercin, C. 2004. "Sosyal Güvenlik Kavramı ve Türkiye'de Sosyal Güvenliğin Tarihçesi."[Concept of Social Security and History of Social Security in Turkey]. *Ankara Üniversitesi Tıp Fakültesi Mecmuası* 57: 89–95.

Habermas, J. 1975. *Legitimation Crisis*. Boston: Beacon Press.

Haggard, S., and R. Kaufman. 2008. *Development, Democracy, and Welfare States: Latin America, East Asia, and Eastern Europe*. Cambridge: Cambridge University Press.

Hansen, B. 1991. *The Political Economy of Poverty, Equity and Growth: Egypt and Turkey*. New York: Oxford University Press for the World Bank.

Harvey, D. 2005. *Spaces of Neoliberalization: Towards a Theory of Uneven Geographical Development*. Stuttgart: Franz Steiner Verlag.

Haveman, R. H. 1978. "Unemployment in Western Europe and the United States: A Problem of Demand, Structure, or Measurement?" *American Economic Review* 68 (2): 44–50.

Heclo, H. 1974. *Modern Social Politics in Britain and Sweden*. New Haven: Yale University Press.

Heller, P. 1999. *The Labor of Development: Workers and the Transformation of Capitalism in Kerala, India*. Ithaca: Cornell University Press.

Hemerijck, A. 2012. *Changing Welfare States*. Oxford: Oxford University Press.

Hicks, A., and D. H. Swank. 1981. "Civil Disorder, Relief Mobilization, and AFDC Caseloads: A Reexamination of the Piven and Cloward Thesis." *American Journal of Political Science* 27: 695–716.

Hicks, A., and D. H. Swank. 1992. "Politics, Institutions, and Welfare Spending in Industrialized Democracies, 1960–1982." *American Political Science Review* 86: 658–74.

Hirose, K., and J. Angelini. 2004. *Extension of Social Security Coverage for the Informal Economy in Indonesia: Surveys in the Urban and Rural Informal Economy*. Working Paper 11, December. Manila: ILO.

Hirschman, A. 1980. "The Welfare State in Trouble: Systemic Crisis or Growing Pains?" *American Economic Review* 70 (2): 113–16.

Hong, L., and K. Kongshoj. 2014. "China's Welfare Reform: An Ambiguous Road Towards a Social Protection Floor." *Global Social Policy* 14 (3): 352–68. https://doi.org/10.1177/1468018113513914

Huber, E. 2005. "Globalization and Social Policy Developments in Latin America." In *Globalization and the Future of the Welfare State*, 75–105.

Huffschmid, J. 1997. "Economic Policy for Full Employment: Proposals for Germany." *Economic and Industrial Democracy* 18 (1): 67–86.

HUNEE. 2006. *Türkiye Göç ve Yerinden Olmuş Nüfus Araştırması.* Ankara: Hacettepe Üniversitesi Nüfus Etütleri Enstitüsü. https://kutuphane.fisek.org.tr/kitap.php?book_id=7399

Hunter, W., and T. Power. 2007. "Rewarding Lula: Executive Power, Social Policy, and the Brazilian Elections of 2006." *Latin American Politics and Society* 49 (1): 1–30.

Huntington, S. P. 2012. *The Third Wave: Democratization in the Late 20th Century.* Norman: University of Oklahoma Press.

Independent Evaluation Group. 2005. *Report No. 34783, Turkey: The World Bank in Turkey 1993–2004, Country Assistance Evaluation.* December 20. Washington, DC: World Bank.

Independent Evaluation Group. 2011. *Social Safety Nets: An Evaluation of World Bank Support, 2000–2010.* Washington, DC: Independent Evaluation Group, the World Bank Group.

ILO. 2010. *World of Work Report 2010: From One Crisis to the Next?* Geneva: International Labour Office.

ILO. 2011a. *World of Work Report 2011: Making Markets Work for Jobs.* Geneva: International Institute for Labour Studies.

ILO. 2012a. *Global Employment Trends 2012: Preventing a Deeper Jobs Crisis.* Geneva: International Labour Office.

ILO. 2012b. *World of Work Report 2012: Better Jobs for a Better Economy.* Geneva: International Labour Office.

ILO and IIL. 2009. *The Financial and Economic Crisis: A Decent Work Response.* Geneva: International Labour Organization.

ILO and IILS. 2011. *Building a Sustaining Job-Rich Recovery.* Geneva: International Labour Office.

İnce, S. 2010. *Sahi, Kürtler CHP 'dennasıl kovuldu?* 16 December. http://www.birgun.net/politics_index.php?news_code=1292490493&day=16&month=12&year=2010

Isaac, L., and W. Kelly. 1981. "Racial Insurgency, the State, and Welfare Expansion: Local and National Level Evidence from the Postwar United States." *American Journal of Sociology* 86: 1348–86.

Işik, O., and M. Pinarcioğlu. 2001. *Nöbetleşe Yoksulluk—Sultanbeyli Örneği.* Istanbul: İletişim.

Iversen, T. 2001. "The Dynamics of Welfare State Expansion: Trade Openness, De-Industrialization, and Partisan Politics." In *The New Politics of the Welfare State*, edited by P. Pierson, 45–79. Oxford: Oxford University Press.

Jackman, R. 1974. "Political Democracy and Social Equality: A Comparative Analysis." *American Sociological Review* 39: 29–45.

Jackman, R. 1975. *Politics and Social Equality: A Comparative Analysis.* New York: Wiley.

Jaime-Castillo, A. M. 2013. "Public Opinion and the Reform of the Pension Systems in Europe: The Influence of Solidarity Principles." *Journal of European Social Policy* 23 (4): 390–405. https://doi.org/10.1177/0958928713507468

Janowitz, M. 1977. *Social Control of the Welfare State.* New York: Elsevier.

Jawad, R. 2009. *Social Welfare and Religion in the Middle East: A Lebanese Perspective.* Bristol: Policy Press.

Jennings, A. 1979. "Competition, Constituencies, and Welfare Policies in American States." *American Political Science Review* 73: 414–29.

Jennings, E. 1983. "Racial Insurgency, the State, and Welfare Expansion: A Critical Comment and Reanalysis." *American Journal of Sociology* 88: 1220–37.

Jessop, B. 1994. "Post-Fordism and the State." In *Post-Fordism*, edited by Ash Amin, 251–79. Oxford: Blackwell. http://onlinelibrary.wiley.com/doi/10.1002/9780470712726.ch8/summary

Justino, P. 2003. *Social Security in Developing Countries: Myth of Necessity? Evidence from India.* Sussex, UK: University of Sussex Poverty Research Unit.

Katznelson, I. 1981. *City Trenches: Urban Politics and Patterning of Class in the US.* New York: Pantheon Books.

Kazemipur, A. 2000. "The Ecology of Deprivation: Spatial Concentration of Poverty in Canada." *Canadian Journal of Regional Science* 23 (3): 403–26.

Kersbergen, K. van, and B. Vis. 2013. *Comparative Welfare State Politics: Development, Opportunities, and Reform.* Cambridge: Cambridge University Press.

Keyder, Ç. 1987. *State and Class in Turkey: A Study in Capitalist Development.* London: Verso.

Keyder, Ç. 2004. "The Turkish Bell Jar." *New Left Review* 28 (July–August): 65–84.

Keyder, Ç. 2005. "Globalization and Social Exclusion in Turkey." *International Journal of Urban and Regional Research* 29:124–34.

Keyder, C., and N. Üstündag. 2006. *Doğuve Güneydoğu Anadolu'nun Kalkınmasında Sosyal Politikalar.* TESEV Doğuve Güneydoğu Anadolu'da Sosyalve Ekonomik Öncelikle Reporu, Bölüm IV, Boğaziçi Üniversitesi Sosyal Politika Forumu.

Keyder, Ç., and Z. Yenal. 2011. "Agrarian Change under Globalization: Markets and Insecurity in Turkish Agriculture." *Journal of Agrarian Change* 11: 60–86.

Keyman, E. F. 2007. "Modernity, Secularism and Islam: The Case of Turkey." *Theory, Culture & Society* 24 (2): 215–34.

Kiriş Çi, K. 2005. "Turkey: Political Dimension of Migration." In *Mediterranean Migration Report 2005*, edited by P. Fargues. Florence: Carim, European University Institute, Robert Schuman Centre for Advanced Studies.

Kitschelt, H. 2001. "Partisan Competition and Welfare State Retrenchment." In *The New Politics of the Welfare State*, edited by P. Pierson. Oxford: Oxford University Press.

Koç, I., A. Hancioglu, and A Çavlin. 2008. "Demographic Differentials and Demographic Integration of Turkish and Kurdish Populations in Turkey." *Population*

Research and Policy Review 27 (February): 447–57. https://doi.org/10.1007/s11113-008-9072-y

Koç, Y. 1999. *Workers and Trade Unions in Türkiye.* Ankara: Türk-İş.

Koç, Y. 2003. *Türkiye İşçi Sınıfı ve* Sendikacılık *Hareketi Tarihi.* Istanbul: Analyz BasımYayın.

KONDA. 2007. *Political Tendencies Survey Summary Report: 2007 General Elections Tendencies Survey.* Istanbul: KONDA.

KONDA. 2011. Dataset Acquired Directly from KONDA on Basis of Mutual Agreement. Istanbul: KONDA.

KONDA. 2015. "KONDA Barometer Survey." Istanbul: KONDA.

KONDA. 2019. "KONDA Barometer Survey Social Policy Module." Istanbul: KONDA.

Korpi, W., and J. Palme. 2003. "New Politics and Class Politics in the Context of Austerity and Globalization: Welfare State Regress in 18 Countries, 1975–95." *American Political Science Review* 97 (3): 425–46.

Koyuncu, M., E. Yörük, and B. Gürel. Forthcoming. "Social Assistance as Counter-Insurgency in India."

Krieger, S. 1991. *Social Science and the Self: Personal Essays on an Art Form.* New Brunswick, NJ: Rutgers University Press.

Krieger, T., and D. Meierrieks. 2009. *What Causes Terrorism?* http://ssrn.com/abstract=1148682 or http://dx.doi.org/10.2139/ssrn.1148682

Krieger, T., and D. Meierrieks. 2010. "Terrorism in the Worlds of Welfare Capitalism." *Journal of Conflict Resolution* 54 (6): 902–39.

Kus, B., and I. Özel. 2010. "United We Restrain, Divided We Rule: Neoliberal Reforms and Labor Unions in Turkey and Mexico." *European Journal of Turkish Studies* 11.

Lanjouw, P., M. Pradhan, F. Saadah, H. Sayed, and R. Sparrow. 2001. *Poverty, Education and Health in Indonesia: Who Benefits from Public Spending?* World Bank Policy Research Working Paper 2739. http://econ.worldbank.org/files/3184_wps2739.pdf

Lewis, J., and R. Surender. 2004. *Welfare State Change: Towards a Third Way?* Oxford: Oxford University Press.

Li, Q., and D. Schaub. 2004. "Economic Globalization and Transnational Terrorist Incidents: A Pooled Time-Series Cross-Sectional Analysis." *Journal of Conflict Resolution* 48 (2): 230–58.

Lindert, K. 2005. *Brazil: Bolsa Familia Program—Scaling-Up Cash Transfers for the Poor.* MfDR Principles in Action: Sourcebook on Emerging Good Practices. Washington, DC: World Bank.

Lipovsky, I. 1992. *The Socialist Movement in Turkey, 1960–1980.* Leiden: E. J. Brill.

Lipton, M., and S. Maxwell. 1992. *The New Poverty Agenda: An Overview.* IDS Discussion Paper no. 306. August. Brighton: Institute of Development Studies at the University of Sussex.

Lloyd, T. 2012. *The OSCE: Region of Change.* OSCE.

Lødemel, I., and H. Trickey. 2001. *"An Offer You Can't Refuse": Workfare in International Perspective.* Policy Press.

Lupu, N., and J. Pontusson. 2011. "The Structure of Inequality and the Politics of Redistribution." *American Political Science Review* 105 (2): 316–36.

Manafy, A. 2005. *The Kurdish Political Struggles in Iran, Iraq, and Turkey: A Critical Analysis*. Lanham, MD: University Press of America.

Margarita, E. A., I. Torben, and S. David. 1999. "Social Protection and the Formation of Skills: A Reinterpretation of the Welfare State." Paper presented at the Annual Meeting of the American Political Science Association, September 2–5, Atlanta.

Marsh, R. M. 2000. "Weber's Misunderstanding of Traditional Chinese Law." *American Journal of Sociology* 106 (2): 281–302.

Marshall, T. 1973. *Class, Citizenship, and Social Development*. Westport, CT: Greenwood Press.

Martin, J., ed. 2008. *The Poulantzas Reader: Marxism, Law, and the State*. London: Verso.

Marza, V. 2004. "On the Death Toll of the 1999 Izmit (Turkey) Major Earthquake." *ESC General Assembly Papers*. Potsdam: European Seismological Commission.

Marx, K. 1976. *Wage-Labour and Capital and Value, Price and Profit*. New York: International Publishers, 1976.

Matsaganis, M. 2012. "Social Policy in Hard Times: The Case of Greece." *Critical Social Policy* (June). https://doi.org/10.1177/0261018312444417

Maxwell, B. 2003. *Terrorism: A Documentary History*. Washington, DC: CQ Press.

McCracken, P., G. Carli, H. Giersch, et al. 1977. *Towards Full Employment and Price Stability: Summary of a Report to the OECD by a Group of Independent Experts*. Paris: OECD.

McNeill, W. H. 1982. *The Pursuit of Power: Technology, Armed Force, and Society since A.D. 1000*. Chicago: University of Chicago Press.

Mead, L. 1989. "Logic of Workfare: The Underclass and Work Policy." *Annals of the American Academy of Political and Social Sciences*: 156–69.

Mello, B. 2006. *Explaining Divergent Strategies in Turkish Labor History, 1960–1980*. Presented at the Annual Meeting of the Midwest Political Science Association.

Mello, B. 2007. "Political Process and the Development of Labor Insurgency in Turkey, 1945–80." *Social Movement Studies* 6 (3): 207–25.

Mello, B. 2010. "(Re)considering the Labor Movement in Turkey." *European Journal of Turkish Studies* 11. https://doi.org/10.4000/ejts.4305

Miliband, R. 1969. *The State in Capitalist Society*. New York: Basic Books.

Ministry of Home Affairs. 2008. "Ministry of Home Affairs Annual Report 2007–2008." New Delhi: Government of India.

Ministry of Rural Development. 2012. "MGNREGA Sameeksha: An Anthology of Research Studies on the Mahatma Gandhi National Rural Employment Guarantee Act, 2005, 2006–2012." New Delhi: Government of India.

Mishra, R. 1996. "The Welfare of Nations." In *States against Markets*, edited by R. Boyer and D. Drache. New York: Routledge.

Mitschein, T., H. Miranda, and M. Paraense. 1989. *Urbanização Selvagem e Proletarização Passiva /Savage Urbanization and Passive Proletarianization*. Belem: CEJUP–NAEA.

Mooney, G., J. Annetts, A. Law, and W. McNeish. 2009. "Exploring the Interrelationships between Social Welfare and Social Movements: Why This Matters for Social Policy." In *Social Policy Association Annual Conference: Learning from the Past.*

Moura, P. G. Martins de. 2007. "Bolsa Família: Projeto Social ou Marketing Político?"[Family Grant: Social Policy or Political Marketing?] *Revista Katálysis* 10 (1): 115–22.

Munk, A. 2006. "The Relationship between Access to Public Transport and Social Exclusion in London: A Case Study of London Underground." *DPU Working Paper* 134. Development Planning Unit, University College London.

Myers, Ramon H., and Yeh-Chien Wang. 2002. "Economic Developments, 1644–1800." In *The Cambridge History of China*, vol. 9, edited by Willard J. Peterson, 563–645. Cambridge: Cambridge University Press.

Myles, J. 1984. *Old Age in the Welfare State.* Boston: Little, Brown.

Nepal, M., A. K. Bohara, and K. Gawande. 2011. "More Inequality, More Killings: The Maoist Insurgency in Nepal." *American Journal of Political Science* 55 (4): 886–906. https://doi.org/10.1111/j.1540-5907.2011.00529.x

O'Connor, J. 1973. *The Fiscal Crisis of the State.* New York: St. Martin's.

OECD. 2011. *Pensionable Age and Life Expectancy, 1950–2050.* S.L.: Organisation for Economic Co-operation and Development.

OECD. 2019. *Social Expenditure Database.* http://stats.oecd.org/Index.aspx?datasetcode=SOCX_AGG

Offe, C. 1984. *Contradictions of the Welfare State.* Cambridge, MA: MIT Press.

O'Loughlin, J., and J. Friedrichs, eds. 1996. *Social Polarization in Post-Industrial Metropolises*, New York: Walter de Gruyter.

Olson, L. 1982. *The Political Economy of the Welfare State.* New York: Columbia University Press.

Öniş, Z. 2007. "Conservative Globalism versus Defensive Nationalism: Political Parties and Paradoxes of Europeanization in Turkey."*Journal of Southern Europe and the Balkans* 9 (3): 247–62.

Öniş, Z. 2013. "Sharing Power: Turkey's Democratization Challenge in the Age of the AKP Hegemony." SSRN Scholarly Paper ID 2254762. Rochester, NY: Social Science Research Network. http://papers.ssrn.com/abstract=2254762

Onuch, O. 2014a. *Mapping Mass Mobilizations: Understanding Revolutionary Moments in Ukraine and Argentina.* London: Palgrave MacMillan.

Onuch, O. 2014b. "The Puzzle of Mass Mobilization: Conducting Protest Research in Ukraine, 2004–2014." *Reviews & Critical Commentary: Council of Europe.*

Onuch, O. 2014c. "Who Were the Protesters?" *Journal of Democracy* 25 (3): 44–51. https://doi.org/10.1353/jod.2014.0045

Oyvat, C. 2010. "Globalization, Wage Shares and Income Distribution in Turkey." *Cambridge Journal of Regions, Economy and Society* 4 (1): 123.

Özbek, N. 2006. *Cumhuriyet Türkiyesi'nde Sosyal Güvenlik ve Sosyal Politikalar* [Social Security and Social Policies in Republican Turkey]. Istanbul: Emeklilik Gözetim Merkezive Tarih Vakfı.

Özbudun, E., and W. Hale. 2009. *Islamism, Democracy and Liberalism in Turkey: The Case of the AKP.* Abingdon: Routledge.

Özgür, B. 2014. "İşte Ak Parti'nin 'Sosyal Yardım' Gerçeği!" [Here is the JDP's "Social

Assistance" Fact]. 29 December, Online edition, sec. Politika. http://www.radikal.com.tr/politika/iste-ak-partinin-sosyal-yardim-gercegi-1260849/

Özler, I., and A. Sarkissian. 2009. "Negotiating Islam, Civil Society, and Secularism: The Justice and Development Party in Turkey." Paper presented at the American Political Science Association's 2009 Toronto meeting.

Page, B., and R. Y. Shapiro. 1983. "Effects of Public Opinion on Policy." *American Political Science Review* 77: 175–90.

Pampel, F., and J. Weiss. 1983. "Economic Development, Pension Policies, and the Labor Force Participation of Aged Males: A Cross-National, Longitudinal Approach." *American Journal of Sociology* 89: 350–72.

Pampel, F., and J. Williamson. 1985. "Age Structure, Politics, and Cross-National Patterns of Public Pension Expenditures." *American Sociological Review* 50 (6): 782–99.

Pankaj, A. 2015. "Employment Guarantee Scheme in India Social Inclusion and Poverty Reduction Through MGNREGS." Paper delivered for Expert and Inter-Agency Meeting on Implementation of the Second United Nations Decade for the Eradication of Poverty (2008–2017), May 27–29, Addis Ababa, Ethiopia. https://www.un.org/esa/socdev/egms/docs/2015/Pankaj.pdf

Parks, J. 2001. *Report No. PIN71: World Bank Board Discusses Turkey Country Assistance Strategy Progress Report*. Washington, DC: World Bank.

Parla, T., and A. Davidson. 2004. *Corporatist Ideology in Kemalist Turkey: Progress or Order?* Syracuse, NY: Syracuse University Press.

Paul, S., S. Mahler, and M. Schwartz. 1997. "Mass Action and Social Structure." *Political Power and Social Theory* 11: 45–99.

Paxson, Ch. 2002. "Comment on Alan Krueger and Jitka Maleckova, Education, Poverty, and Terrorism: Is There a Causal Connection?" *Working Papers 202*. Princeton University.

Pelham, L., E. Clay, and T. Braunholz. 2011. *Natural Disasters: What Is the Role for Social Safety Nets?* SP Discussion Paper no. 1102. Washington, DC: World Bank.

Perrin, G. 1969. "Reflections on Fifty Years of Social Security." *International Labor Review* 99: 249–89.

Petrol-İş. 1987. *'86 Petrol-İş Yıllığı* [1986 Yearbook of Petrol-İş]. İstanbul: Petrol-İş.

Petrol-İş. 1997. *'95–'96 Petrol-İş Yıllığı* [1995–96 Yearbook of Petrol-İş]. Istanbul: Petrol-İş.

Pflanze, O. 1990. *Bismarck and the Development of Germany*. Princeton: Princeton University Press.

Phillipson, C. 1983. "The State, the Economy and Retirement." In *Old Age and the Welfare State*, edited by Anne Marie Guillemard, 127–39. Beverly Hills, CA: Sage.

Pierson, P. 1994. *Dismantling the Welfare State? Reagan, Thatcher, and the Politics of Retrenchment*. New York: Cambridge University Press.

Pierson, P. 2001. *The New Politics of the Welfare State*. Oxford: Oxford University Press.

Piven, F. F., and L. C. Minnite. 2016. "Poor People's Politics." *The Oxford Handbook of the Social Science of Poverty*. https://doi.org/10.1093/oxfordhb/9780199914050.013.34

Portes, A., and K. Hoffman. 2003. "Latin American Class Structures: Their Composition and Change during the Neoliberal Era." *Latin American Research Review* 38 (1) (February): 41–82.

Poulantzas, N. 1978. *State, Power, Socialism.* London: New Left Books.

Powell, M., and E. Yörük. 2017. "Straddling Two Continents and beyond Three Worlds? The Case of Turkey's Welfare Regime." *New Perspectives on Turkey* 57 (November): 85–114. https://doi.org/10.1017/npt.2017.30

Quadagno, J. 1982. *Aging in Early Industrial Society: Work, Family, and Social Policy in Nineteenth-Century England.* New York: Academic Press.

Quadagno, J. 1984. "Welfare Capitalism and the Social Security Act of 1935." *American Sociological Review* 49: 632–47.

Quadagno, J. 1987. "Theories of the Welfare State." *Annual Review of Sociology* 13: 109–28.

Radikal. 2008. "'Açlıkla Terbiye' Kararına Tepki" [Reaction to the decision of "feeding with hunger"], October 30. http://www.radikal.com.tr/turkiye/aclikla_terbiye_kararina_tepki-905825/

Rawlings, B. 2003. "Columbia: Reforming the Social Safety Net." *World Bank en Breve,* No. 18, 1–4.

Rimlinger, G. V. 1971. *Welfare Policy and Industrialization in Europe, America, and Russia.* New York: John Wiley and Sons.

Rodrik, D. 1997. "Sense and Nonsense in the Globalization Debate." *Foreign Policy,* no. 107: 19–37. https://doi.org/10.2307/1149330

Room, G., R. Lawson, and F. Laczko. 1989. "'New Poverty' in the European Community." *Policy & Politics* 17 (2): 165–76.

Rucht, D. 1992. *Studying the Effects of Social Movements: Conceptualization and Problems.* Presented at European Commission for Political Research Joint Session, Limerick, Ireland.

Rustow, D. A. 1987. *Turkey: America's Forgotten Ally.* New York: Council on Foreign Relations Press.

Sanyal, B. 1991 "Organizing the Self-Employed: The Politics of the Urban Informal Sector." *International Labor Review* 39.

Saraceno, C. 2002. *Social Assistance Dynamics in Europe: National and Local Poverty Regimes.* Bristol: Policy Press.

Saracoğlu, C. 2009. "'Exclusive Recognition': The New Dimensions of the Question of Ethnicity and Nationalism in Turkey." *Ethnic and Racial Studies* 32 (4): 640–58.

Savran, S. 2010. "Turkey: The Working Class (Literally) Takes the Stages." *Bullet Socialist Project E-Bulletin* no. 299, 23 January.

Schram, S. F., and J. P. Turbett. 1983. "Civil Disorder and the Welfare Explosion: A Two-Step Process." *American Sociological Review* 48: 408–14.

Scruggs, L., and J. P. Allan. 2006. "The Material Consequences of Welfare States Benefit Generosity and Absolute Poverty in 16 OECD Countries." *Comparative Political Studies* 39 (7): 880–904. https://doi.org/10.1177/0010414005281935

Seekings, J. 2005. *Prospects for Basic Income in Developing Countries: A Comparative Analysis of Welfare Regimes in the South.* University of Cape Town. http://open.uct.ac.za/handle/11427/19413

Şener, M. 2010. "The World Bank's Risk Management Approach to Neoliberal Governmentality? The Case of the 'Social Risk Mitigation Project.'" PhD diss., University of Illinois.

Şenyuva, Ö. 2009. "Opposition for the Sake of Opposition? Polarized Pluralism in Turkish Politics."*Meria Journal* 13 (24): 51–55.

Shively, K. 2008. "Taming Islam: Studying Religion in Secular Turkey." *Anthropological Quarterly* 81 (3): 683–711. https://doi.org/10.1353/anq.0.0017

Sharma, A. N., and P. Antony. 2001. *Women Workers in the Unorganized Sector: The More the Merrier?* New Delhi: Institute for Human Development.

Shively, P. 2005. *The Craft of Political Research.* Upper Saddle River, NJ: Pearson Prentice-Hall.

Shonfield, A. 1965. *Modern Capitalism.* New York: Oxford University Press.

Silver, B. 2003. *Forces of Labor: Workers' Movements and Globalization since 1870.* Cambridge: Cambridge University Press.

Silver, B. 2004. "Labor, War and World Politics: Contemporary Dynamics in World-Historical Perspective." In *Labour and New Social Movements in a Globalizing World System,* edited by B. Unfried, M. Van der Linden, and C. Schindler. Leipzig: Akademische Verlagsanstalt.

Silver, B. 2006. "Donde el capital va, el conflicto capital-trabajo también irá" [Where the capital goes, the capital-labor conflict will also]. *Viento Sur,* no. 86.

Singer, A. 2014. "Rebellion in Brazil." *New Left Review,* no. 85 (February): 19–37.

Skocpol, T., and E. Amenta. 1986. "States and Social Policies." *Annual Review of Sociology* 12.

Social Security Institution (Sosyal Güvenlik Kurumu). 2009. *Work Life Survey 2009.* Ankara: SGK.

Social Security Institution (Sosyal Güvenlik Kurumu). 2010. *Work Life Survey 2010.* Ankara: SGK.

Social Security Institution (Sosyal Güvenlik Kurumu). 2010. *Aylik Istatistik Bilgileri 2010.* Ankara: SGK.

Social Security Institution (Sosyal Güvenlik Kurumu). 2011. *Aylık Sosyal Güvenlik Temel Göstergeleri.* Ankara: SGK.

Solana, J. 2003a. *A Secure Europe in a Better World: European Security Strategy.* Brussels: European Council.

Solana, J. 2003b. *Old and New Challenges of the Barcelona Process.* Brussels: European Council.

Soares, G. A. D., and L. T. Sonia. 2008. "Dois Lulas: a geografia eleitoral da reeleição (explorando conceitos, métodos e técnicas de análise geoespacial)" [Dois Lulas: The Electoral Geography of Reelection (Exploring Geospatial Analysis Concepts, Methods and Techniques)]. *Opinião Pública* 14 (2): 269–301. https://doi.org/10.1590/S0104-62762008000200001

Souza, A. P. 2006. *Fighting Long-Run Poverty in Brazil: Are Conditional Cash Transfer Programs Making a Difference?* S.L.: LAMES/LACEA.

Sridharan, E.. 2014. "Behind Modi's Victory." *Journal of Democracy* 25 (4): 20–33. https://doi.org/10.1353/jod.2014.0068

State Auditing Institution (Cumhubaşkanliği Devlet Denetleme Kurulu). 2009. *Araştır mavi inceleme raporu.* Ankara: DDK.

State Planning Organization (Devlet Planlama Teşkilatı). 2006. *2006 Yili Faaliyet Raporu*. Ankara: DPT.

State Planning Organization (Devlet Planlama Teşkilatı). 2009. *2009 Yili Faaliyet Raporu*. Ankara: DPT.

State Planning Organization (Devlet Planlama Teşkilatı). 2010. *Ekonomikve Sosyal Göstergeler (1950–2010)*. Ankara: DPT.

Stewart, F. 2002. *Horizontal Inequalities: A Neglected Dimension of Development*. QEH Working Paper No. 81. Oxford: Oxford University.

Stewart, F. 2010. *Horizontal Inequalities as a Cause of Conflict: A Review of CRISE Findings*. Washington, DC: World Bank.

Stimson, J., M. MacKuen, and R. Erikson. 1995. "Dynamic Representation." *American Political Science Review* 89 (3): 543–65.

Sugiyama, N. B. 2011. "The Diffusion of Conditional Cash Transfer Programs in the Americas." *Global Social Policy* 11 (2–3): 250–78. https://doi.org/10.1177/1468018111421295

Surender, J. 2004. *Welfare State Change: Towards a Third Way?* London: Oxford University Press.

Taş, H., and D. R. Lightfoot. 2005. "Gecekondu Settlements in Turkey: Rural-Urban Migration in the Developing European Periphery." *Journal of Geography* 104: 263–71.

Taydas, Z., and D. Peksen. 2012. "Can States Buy Peace? Social Welfare Spending and Civil Conflicts." *Journal of Peace Research* 49 (2): 273–87.

Tezcür, G. M. 2010. *Muslim Reformers in Iran and Turkey: The Paradox of Moderation*. Austin: University of Texas Press.

Tilly, C. 1988. *Coercion, Capital, and European States, AD 990–1990*. Cambridge, MA: Basil Blackwell.

Tilly, C. 1995. "Rights." *International Labor and Working-Class History* 47.

Trattner, W. 1984. *From Poor Law to Welfare State: A History of Social Welfare in America*. New York: Free Press.

Trempe, R. 1983. "The Struggles of French Miners for the Creation of Retirement Funds in the Nineteenth Century." In *Old Age and the Welfare State*, edited by Anne-Marie Guillemard, 101–15. Beverly Hills, CA: Sage.

Tuğal, C. 2006. "The Appeal of Islamic Politics: Ritual and Dialogue in a Poor District of Turkey." *Sociological Quarterly* 47: 245–73.

Tuğal, C. 2007. "NATO's Islamists." *New Left Review* 44.

Tuğal, C. 2009. *Passive Revolution: Absorbing the Islamic Challenge to Capitalism*. Stanford: Stanford University Press.

Turkish Parlimentary Proceedings Journal. Ankara.

Tüsiad. 1997. *Turk Sosyal Guvenlik Sisteminde Yeniden Yapilanma; Sorunlar, Reform Ihtiyaci, Arayislar, Cozum Onerileri* [Restructuring in Turkish Social Security System; Problems, Need for Reform, Searches, Solution Suggestions]. Ankara: TÜSİAD.

U.S. Mission to the OSCE. 2011. *Tolerance and Non-Discrimination*. Warsaw: OSCE.

Voyvoda, E., and E. Yeldan. 2005. "IMF Programs, Fiscal Policy and Growth: Investigation of Macroeconomic Alternatives in an OLG Model of Growth for Turkey." *Comparative Economic Studies* 47: 41–79.

Voyvoda, N. 2011. *Reconstruction of Workers' Mobilization in Turkey.* LAP LAMBERT Academic Publishing.

Wacquant, L. 2008. *Urban Outcasts: A Comparative Sociology of Advanced Marginality.* Cambridge: Polity Press.

Wacquant, L. 2009. *Punishing the Poor: The Neoliberal Government of Social Insecurity.* Durham: Duke University Press.

Wallerstein, I. 1976. "Semi-Peripheral Countries and the Contemporary World Crisis." *Theory and Society* 3 (4).

Walton, J., and D. Seddon. 1994. *Free Markets and Food Riots: The Politics of Global Adjustment.* Oxford: Blackwell.

Weiss, L. 1998. "Developmental States in Transition: Adapting, Dismantling, Innovating, Not 'Normalizing.'" *Pacific Review* 13 (1): 21–55.

Welch, S. 1975. "The Impact of Urban Riots on Urban Expenditures." *American Journal of Political Science* 19: 741–60.

White, P. J. 2000. *Primitive Rebels or Revolutionary Modernizers? The Kurdish National Movement in Turkey.* New York: Zed Books.

Wilensky, H. 1975. *The Welfare State and Equality.* Berkeley: University of California Press.

Williamson, J. B., and J. W. Weiss. 1979. "Egalitarian Political Movements, Social Welfare Effort and Convergence Theory: A Cross-National Analysis." *Comparative Studies in Sociology* 2: 289–302.

Winters, P., and B. Davis. 2009. "Designing a Programme to Support Smallholder Agriculture in Mexico: Lessons from PROCAMPO and Oportunidades." *Development Policy Review* 27: 617–42.

Wlezien, C. 1995. "The Public as Thermostat: Dynamics of Preferences for Spending." *American Journal of Political Science* 39 (4): 981–1000.

Wolfensohn, J. D. 2002. "Fight Terrorism by Ending Poverty." *New Perspectives Quarterly* 19 (2): 42–44.

World Bank. 1997. *Report No. 16992-TU: Republic of Turkey Country Assistance Strategy.* Washington, DC: World Bank.

World Bank. 2001a. *Turkey—Social Risk Mitigation Project: Report No. PID10515.* Washington, DC: World Bank.

World Bank. 2001b. *Report No. PID10515: Turkey—Social Risk Mitigation Project.* Washington, DC: World Bank.

World Bank. 2001c. *Report No. PID8315: Turkey—Social Development Project.* Washington, DC: World Bank.

World Bank, Human Development Unit. 2003a. *Turkey: Poverty and Coping after Crisis.* Vol. 1 of 2. S.L.: World Bank.

World Bank. 2003b. "Social Safety Nets in Transition Economies." *Social Safety Nets Primer Notes,* No. 2. Washington, DC: World Bank.

World Bank. 2004a. *Social Protection in ECA during Transition: An Unfinished Agenda.* Washington, DC: World Bank.

World Bank, Human Development Sector Unit. 2004b. *Report No. 31011-AL—Albania: Social Safety Net Review.* Washington, DC: World Bank.

World Bank, Human Development Unit. 2005a. *Turkey: Joint Poverty Assessment Report*, vol. 1 of 2. Washington, DC: World Bank and State Institute of Statistics.

World Bank, Human Development Unit. 2005b. *Turkey: Poverty Policy Recommendations*, vol. 2 of 2. Washington, DC: World Bank and State Institute of Statistics.

World Bank, Turkey Country Unit. 2005c. *Country Assistance Strategy Progress Report for the Republic of Turkey for the Period FY 2004–2007*. Washington, DC: World Bank.

World Bank. 2005d. *Report No. 29619-TU: Turkey Poverty Policy Recommendations Volume II*. Washington, DC: World Bank.

World Bank, Poverty Reduction and Economic Management Unit. 2010a. *Report No. 48523-TR: Turkey, Country Economic Memorandum, Informality: Causes, Consequences, Policies*. Washington, DC: World Bank.

World Bank. 2010b. *Report No. 5 1062-TR: Turkey: Restoring Equitable Growth and Employment Programmatic Development Policy Loan (REGE-DP)*. Washington, DC: World Bank.

World Bank. 2010c. *Analyzing the Effects of Policy Reforms on the Poor: An Evaluation of the Effectiveness of World Bank Support to Poverty and Social Impact Analyses*. Washington, DC: World Bank.

World Bank, Turkey Country Unit. 2010d. *Report No: ICR00001443, Implementation, Completion, and Results Report*. Washington, DC: World Bank.

World Bank, Central Asia Country Unit. 2010e. *Kyrgyz Republic Emergency Recovery Project*. Washington, DC: World Bank.

World Bank. 2011. *Report No. 59913-MD, Strengthening the Effectiveness of the Social Safety Net Project*. Washington, DC: World Bank.

World Bank. 2012. *Report No. 67189, Project Performance Assessment Report Republic of Djibouti*. Washington, DC: World Bank.

World Bank. 2015. *The State of Social Safety Nets 2015*. Washington, DC: World Bank. http://elibrary.worldbank.org/doi/book/10.1596/978-1-4648-0543-1

Wright, E. O. 2000. "Working-Class Power, Capitalist-Class Interests, and Class Compromise." *American Journal of Sociology* 105 (4) (January): 957–1002.

Xinzhen, L. 2011. "Redrawing the Poverty Line." *Beijing Review*, 10 January.

Yavuz, M. H. 1999. "Search for a New Social Contract in Turkey: Fethullah Gulen, the Virtue Party and the Kurds." *SAIS Review* 19 (1): 119.

Yeğen, M. 2011. *On Democratic Autonomy*. Working paper. http://www.hyd.org.tr/staticfiles/files/on_democratic_autonomy_-__mesut_yegen.pdf

Yeldan, E. 2006. "Neo-Liberal Global Remedies: From Speculative-Led Growth to IMF-Led Crisis in Turkey." *Review of Radical Political Economics* 38: 193–213.

Yilmaz, V. 2013. "Changing Origins of Inequalities in Access to Health Care Services in Turkey: From Occupational Status to Income." *New Perspectives on Turkey* 48: 55–77. https://doi.org/10.1017/S0896634600001886

Yilmaz, V. 2017. *The Politics of Healthcare Reform in Turkey*. Switzerland: Palgrave Macmillan.

Yoltar, Ç. 2009. "When the Poor Need Health Care: Ethnography of State and Citizenship in Turkey." *Middle Eastern Studies* 45 (5): 769–82.

Yoltar, Ç., and E. Yörük. 2021. "Contentious Welfare: The Kurdish Conflict and Social Policy as Counterinsurgency in Turkey." *Governance* 34 (2): 353–71. https://doi. org/10.1111/gove.12500

Yörük, E. 2009. "Labor Discipline in the Informal Economy: The Semi-formal Professional Code of Istanbul's Urban Apparel Factory." *Berkeley Journal of Sociology* 53 (January): 27–61.

Yörük, E. 2012. "Welfare Provision as Political Containment: The Politics of Social Assistance and the Kurdish Conflict in Turkey." *Politics & Society* 40 (4): 517–47. https://doi.org/10.1177/0032329212461130

Yörük, E. 2017. "The Radical Democracy of the People's Democratic Party: Transforming the Turkish State." In *From the Streets to the State: Changing the World by Taking Power*, edited by Paul Christopher Gray. Albany, NY: SUNY Press.

Yörük, E., and A. Comin. 2020. "Electoral Polarization, Class Politics and a New Welfare State in Brazil and Turkey." *European Review* 28 (3): 513–35.

Yörük, E., and A. Ş. Gençer. 2020. "The Politics of Social Assistance in South Africa: How Protests and Electoral Politics Shape the Child Support Grant." *Governance.* https://doi.org/10.1111/gove.12464

Yörük, E., B. Gürel, A. Bargu, and C. Göbel. Forthcoming. "Social Assistance as Political Containment in Contemporary China."

Yörük, E., B. Gürel, and F. Kina. Forthcoming. "Demobilization by Substitution: Containing Rural Unrest through the Bolsa Familia Program in Brazil."

Yörük, E., İ. Öker, and L. Şarlak. 2019. "Indigenous Unrest and the Contentious Politics of Social Assistance in Mexico." *World Development* 123 (November). https:// doi.org/10.1016/j.worlddev.2019.104618

Yörük, E., and H. Özsoy. 2013. "Shifting Forms of Turkish State Paternalism toward the Kurds: Social Assistance as 'Benevolent' Control." *Dialectical Anthropology* 37 (1): 153–58. https://doi.org/10.1007/s10624-013-9305-2

Yörük, E., and M. Yüksel. 2014. "Class and Politics in Turkey's Gezi Protests." *New Left Review* 89 (September–October). http://newleftreview.org/II/89/ erdem-yoruk-murat-yuksel-class-and-politics-in-turkey-s-gezi-protests

Yörük, E., İ. Öker, and G. Tafoya G. 2021. "The Four Global Worlds of Welfare Capitalism: Institutional, Neoliberal, Populist, and Residual Welfare State Regimes." *Journal of European Social Policy* (forthcoming).

Yükseker, D., and D. Kurban. 2009. *Permanent Solution to Internal Displacement? An Assessment of the Van Action Plan for IDPs.* Istanbul: TESEV Publications.

Yurtsever, H. 2002. *Süreklilik ve Kopuş İçinde Marksizm ve Türkiye Solu.* El Yayınevi.

Zolberg, A. R. 1995. "Response: Working-Class Dissolution." *International Labor and Working-Class History* 47:28–38.

Zucco, C. 2008. "The President's 'New' Constituency: Lula and the Pragmatic Vote in Brazil's 2006 Presidential Elections." *Journal of Latin American Studies* 40 (1): 29–49. https://doi.org/10.1017/S0022216X07003628

Index

public sector, 4, 42, 46, 52, 75, 78–80, 83, 84, 87, 119, 126–27, 132–33, 137, 138
public services, 123, 142, 171, 175

racial, 4, 5, 30, 35, 36, 192
radical, 4, 6, 12, 39, 40, 41, 51, 68, 69, 75–77, 79, 81, 85, 87, 90, 92, 95, 98, 100–102, 104–5, 107, 110, 112, 122, 143, 149, 171, 181, 182, 186, 187, 189, 191
radical left/leftists, 39, 75–77, 81, 85, 98, 101, 105
rank-and-file, 74, 80
rapid urbanization, 49, 74, 150, 155
Recep Tayyip Erdoğan, 1, 4, 95, 101, 103, 123
regression analysis, 10, 161
relief systems, 16, 30, 172
religion, 6, 124, 191
religious, 4, 12, 36, 39, 40, 68, 69, 92, 104, 114, 136, 142, 143, 189, 190
republican, 72
Republican People's Party, 13, 72, 82, 93, 107
retirement age, 47, 53, 55, 65, 113, 123, 125, 131, 137
revolution, 77, 83
right, 48, 51, 66, 68, 69, 73, 74, 79, 80, 82, 83, 91, 107, 112, 114, 117, 126–29, 131–34, 143, 144, 146, 151, 172, 174
rights, 16, 17, 21, 39, 44, 47, 48, 51, 74, 80, 85, 94, 95, 96, 102, 107, 108, 110, 113, 119, 123, 124, 126, 127, 132–35, 142, 143, 148, 151, 183, 189, 190
rural, 3, 4, 7, 8, 25, 26, 28, 31, 43, 64, 77, 88, 94, 96, 98, 111, 141, 148, 152, 176, 186, 187, 192
rural to urban migration, 4

sector, 4, 6–8, 26, 32, 47, 51–53, 56, 66, 72, 74, 84, 91, 126–27, 138
slum(s), 5, 7–8, 13–14, 30–33, 35–37, 69–70, 87, 90–92, 94, 98, 100–105, 120–21, 123, 129, 131, 145, 148, 150, 154–56, 171, 175, 176, 182, 187–89, 191

social assistance, 1–10, 12–14, 16, 22–27, 29, 30, 35, 36, 40–43, 45, 49, 50, 58–62, 64–67, 100, 108, 110, 112–16, 120, 121, 123–24, 128–29, 131, 138–47, 149–50, 152, 153, 155–57, 166–92
Social Assistance and Solidarity Fund, 10, 11, 60–62, 113, 115–16, 120–21, 129, 142, 151, 175, 176
social assistance offices, 10, 176
social assistance policies, 5, 6, 12, 16, 22, 23, 40–42, 45, 50, 59, 66, 110, 115, 140, 144, 146–47, 149, 169, 171, 184–85, 188–89, 191
social assistance programs, 1–3, 6–9, 12–14, 16, 23–25, 29, 30, 36, 42, 43, 58, 60, 62, 64–67, 108, 112, 115, 121, 138, 140, 143, 150, 152, 167, 170–73, 175–76, 182, 186–87, 189–92
social assistance schemes, 16, 23, 25
social democratic, 23, 79, 81, 129
social democrats, 81, 93, 101, 115, 119, 129
social expenditure, 23
social expenditures, 22, 40, 43, 110, 135
social explosions, 100, 126, 132, 176
social forces, 29, 36, 172, 187
social insurance, 20, 25, 38, 43, 49
Social Insurance Institution, 46, 47, 51, 56, 58
social movements, 12, 28, 29, 36, 37, 39, 68, 98, 100, 110, 185, 189, 191
social need(s), 7, 14, 29, 30, 41, 67, 182, 185
social peace, 81, 132, 144
social policies, 40, 66, 106, 138, 154, 155, 185
social policy program(s), 40, 66, 146, 147
social protection, 18, 42
social safety nets, 28, 38
social security coverage, 62
social security institution, 51, 62, 138
social security institutions, 48, 56, 57, 127, 145
social security policies, 6, 7, 12, 16, 17, 20, 21, 23, 42, 45, 46, 57, 59, 66, 107, 150